Making Love to GOD

The Path to Divine Sex

Ananda through
Tina Louise Spalding

Other Books by
Tina Louise Spalding

Great Minds Speak to You

Making Love to GOD

The Path to Divine Sex

Ananda through
Tina Louise Spalding

PO Box 3540
Flagstaff, AZ 86003
1-800-450-0985
1-928-526-1345
www.lighttechnology.com

I dedicate this book to my two sons who have loved me no matter what, and who have put up with a very unconventional mother. They are my constant friends, even when we are not in each other's presence. They have allowed me my quirky ways and impetuous choices with grace and constancy. They too have taught me how to love.

Contents

Editor's Note

When Ananda first delivered this guidance through Tina, the text was separated into three books. These separate texts have been combined and reorganized to give you the clearest, most concise guidance possible to help you reach the blissful heights you seek.

Preface

As I write this, the manuscript for this book has been finished just a few days ago by my hand, emanated from an intelligence that is wise, kind, and not of this world. The events that have led up to this unexpected and unique creative process are exceptional, and I would like to share them here to help clarify the amazing journey that I have been on.

I had just finished a two-year digital media design program, and a few days before my graduation I lay down to nap on the futon in my living room. It was midafternoon, and the day had been a normal one. I was enjoying freedom from the homework and design projects that had taken up so much of the past two years. As I lay there, beginning to relax into sleep, a strong sensation began to build at the base of my spine. It was not a pain at all, but a swelling and expanding feeling that was actually quite pleasant.

I had just finished reading two books on kundalini, the ancient Sanskrit name for sacred sexual energy, and I thought that perhaps this was what I was feeling. So I relaxed and began a breathing technique I had been practicing. The energy built and built, slowly rising up my spine. My body began to move of its own accord, and my back began to arch. Strong waves of energy rose up my back, bursting out of the back of my head in explosive bursts of ecstatic release. As I look back on it now, I am amazed that I wasn't afraid. I was completely calm. But I am a long-time student of the spiritual text *A Course in Miracles* and have a strong and well-established spiritual practice, so that must have prepared me for this experience in some way. The event lasted an hour and a half, with three rounds of the energy building and rising up my spine. All the

1

while, my body was not under my control. In fact, it seemed to be completely out of control, adjusting itself and flexing in what was the most
blissful and ecstatic experience of my life. I had never, in all my fifty-
three years, experienced anything like it. What was even more amazing
was that these events continued — one, two, or sometimes even three
times a day for the next three weeks. I was fascinated and, strangely, not
scared at all.

You see, the blissful and ecstatic events that I was experiencing
each day took me to a state of such heightened awareness and peace
that I was completely enamored. I had previously only read about such
experiences in spiritual texts about yogis and other dedicated spiritual
practitioners. To actually experience these things myself was, as you
might imagine, quite amazing. Many days I would walk down to the
beach, completely at peace — no thought for the future, no needs or
wants — and with a feeling of absolute openness, absolute love. "This
must be what they are talking about," I remember thinking. "This is
what it's like to be awake."

The energy sessions, as I began to call them, changed over that
three-week period. The movements of my body shifted and changed
as if different areas were being adjusted. The bursts of energy would
change their exit point from the back of my head to my heart, and then
to my throat. The events were powerfully blissful and the energy was
very sexual in nature. It was bewildering. I knew that something big
was going on spiritually; I just didn't know what. I began to feel as if
someone wanted to communicate with me. It was intuition, but it felt
right. Someone wanted to speak.

I am blessed with knowing a talented trance channel, whom I
emailed with the details of my experiences. Knowing she had gone
through her own spiritual awakening several years before, I knew she
would know what to do. It turned out she was running an automatic
writing workshop at the beginning of July, and she offered me a spot so
that I could perhaps get some answers and find out who, or what, was
having its way with me every day.

Over the three days of the workshop things did indeed clarify themselves. I began automatic writing almost immediately as we sat down
with our candles, pencils in hand. By the end of the first day I had ten
pages of "writing" that looked more like scribble at first. But as the

pages went along, it became clearer and clearer, and in the end one word stood out from all the others: *Ananda*.

That weekend I was informed in writing by Ananda — my new group of nonphysical teachers — that we would be writing a book together and that we had known each other before, as friends and seekers in the desert. I was told many things, but the topic of the book was a bit of a shocker: It would be about the connection between sexual energy and God. I was told the truth of this connection needed to be revealed to help teach everyone that this divine love was blessed and healing, that many of the problems we face today are because of the guilt and shame we have around sexuality and God.

What follows is that book. As you venture into these pages, you will sometimes see two streams of thought: the main text, which contains Ananda's teachings on the subject, and a second italic script, which shows you the personal guidance and comments they gave me each day. I have left those comments in for several reasons. One of those reasons is that many times when I read channeled texts I am annoyed when they mention that all personal references have been removed. I am always very curious what those comments might have been, and I would have loved to read them, so I won't deprive you of them. I also want you to see the beautiful words of encouragement and love that I received throughout this journey — pep talks when I needed them and gentle chastisement at other times. [Editor's Note: Much of this commentary is included in an appendix rather than interspersed throughout the teachings in an effort to avoid interrupting the flow of Ananda's guidance.]

Ananda has indeed become a dear presence in my life, coaxing, cajoling, and sometimes pushing me along this unusual path. Our energetic sessions have continued almost daily, and I have come to love and respect this group of teachers who have turned my life upside-down. They call me "dear one," and each separate section of dictation began with that address. I have left in some of these beginning and ending addresses so that you can see the loving and familiar relationship they have with me.

They have warned me that there will be many people who do not like the content of this book, who will call it blasphemous or evil. But I have decided to go ahead with the public sharing of this material because I believe with all my heart and all my experience that it is true.

We are in a mess in this Western culture, and something has to change or we will not survive ourselves. I believe Ananda has the answer for us all: love — passionate and spiritual, open and kind.

✳   ✳   ✳

Ananda began speaking through me just two weeks ago, and now they connect with me regularly to offer lectures on love, nature, world events, and of course my personal development and challenges as I travel with them along this path. Just three days ago they spoke to another person through me for the first time, chatting for an hour about health, spiritual growth, work, and lifestyle. During that event the energy I felt through my body was much larger, the expression through my voice much clearer than my solitary experiences, and they assure me that when they speak to a room full of people it will magnify even more. I am excited and nervous as this first public event rapidly approaches!

We are currently arranging Ananda's first public appearance on Sunday, October 21, 2012 on Salt Spring Island, where they have said they will begin their teaching and will eventually create a healing center. As you can imagine, this summer has been "out of this world" in the truest sense, and I look forward to sharing this amazing story sometime in the near future.

As I read over this book, I am taken by the clarity and beauty of Ananda's message. I am deeply honored to be given this experience and hope this book gives you hope for a better and more blissful future, full of passion and energy. I am as challenged as you, but I feel I have no choice but to try Ananda's recipe for heaven on earth. The alternative — to continue on as we are — is not acceptable.

So I offer you this text to read, hoping that it also inspires you to look at those areas of your life that are limiting and that block your ability to receive the joy and abundance that flows to us all day, every day. Their prescriptions are challenging, it's true, but so is the prospect of continuing struggle, impending sickness, and not reaching a state of happiness on this Earth journey we are all on.

So be brave, as I am being brave, and step out of what is normal into what is exceptional. Step out of the expected and into the unimaginable. I regret nothing on my journey into Spirit; nothing but positives

have come my way since I began studying and working with *A Course in Miracles* ten years ago. That text began this journey, and now Ananda holds the light that I am guided by. Each of you will follow your own instincts and teachers, but I hope Ananda forms a part of your developing wisdom and that you will share their message with those you love and care for.

— Tina Louise Spalding

And now Ananda writes ...

Introduction

The world is in a terrible state at the moment, which many of you will not deny. War, fear, and famine abound on this beautiful planet Earth, and none of this is necessary. The misteachings all of you are laboring under give power to the wrong places and people. Indeed, you are the most powerful people on the planet, and you do not realize this power in any way, shape, or form.

The rulers of the past fed off your fear, distress, and submission, but this need not continue. The power that resides in a mind connected to Source is limitless, and it is indeed this that past prophets tried to teach, but the message was lost over the years of fear and mistranslation. This message is the truth: Every thought you possess is the seed of fear or love, and love will create what you want while fear will create the mess you have. Follow love through all its lovely pathways to the Earth you wish to have. Fear has made the darkness you see, but at any point you may turn around and begin to walk toward the light.

We have called ourselves Ananda. The word means bliss, and that is indeed our mission: to show the world that power comes from love and not hate. We are here as teachers for you, the dear humans who are so lost in the mire of misinformation in your modern culture that claims to know so much. You are ignorant of the most important factor in your spiritual, physical, mental, and emotional well-being, and that is the connection between sexual energy and your spiritual nature. For centuries the words you have been taught and the principles that have guided the development of your cultures have been unadulterated lies, and this is the very reason you are in such dire straits at the moment in your planet's history.

The divine energy that is God is the passion in your life, and if you are separate from God and from passion, you will not manifest the love and sex life that you so desire. You see, those low-vibration elements of your life that are always nagging at you — failures of the past, broken love affairs, family resentments, and fears and prejudices that are woven throughout the matrix of your mind and life — are the blocks, and it is you who must remove them. That is why you were born in this time and place, to do this work, but no one has ever told you your part in this. The world in which you live teaches you many things, but those things are not the truth, and that is what this book is. It is the truth, and it is the pathway that will lead you clearly and inexorably to the future you dream of.

This material is controversial and will arouse many passions — and not just the good ones we are after. But these teachings hold the secret that the secret societies have always guarded: that you are indeed the owners of your own power. You just need to be told how to find this.

This will be a handbook for those of you wishing to achieve the heights of bliss that you are capable of. Through simple terms and simple explanations, we will happily supply you with a map to take you to the heights of sexual evolution, bringing along a desire for peace, joy, health, and well-being. It will be the catalyst to change your planet from the war zone of sickness and hatred that it now appears to be into a peaceful playground of happy, healthy, and compassionate humans, determined to love and help each other achieve their potential with amazing bliss and joyful offspring and families.

You are reading this because you are dissatisfied with the way your life and love life look, but we are here to tell you they are one and the same. This manual points toward the ideas in the Western mind that will trip you up the most on this path to transformation. This text is our treatise on the blocks in the Western mind to love's presence, a handbook to systematically and methodically analyze these blocks as they occur in your life. There are many fears, and there is no way around them. You must travel through them, and then they will lose their power.

Understand this going in, dear ones: This is a manual for the deconstruction of the barriers to love's awareness. Love is all. It is always flowing to you from the mind of God in which you are a beautiful thought, and every trial and every element of suffering you experience is where blocks to love's presence lie. So that is the path. Go to your tender places and your scary places, and indeed you will be healed. You have avoided these blocks long enough, and we are here to help. Our teachings, over time, will be the guide you need to clear the path and cleanse the body in which you are traveling for a time, and this clearing will open the channels for the divine to flow to and through you.

We are systematic in our approach, and those of you who were hoping for a sex manual only will be deeply disappointed, but we have to do it this way. The laws of the universe are as they are for a reason. It is only in the living of the wrong that you can truly understand the right. Once you have realized the right, you will then be moved to help others on their journey out of the darkness and into the light.

The "dear one," as we call her — Tina — is our dear messenger on the Earth plane, and we have offered her the opportunity to be our spokesperson for this information we are now teaching to the world. We are writing through her hands, as she has given us permission to use her physical presence to translate this information into text, word, and deed that will assist in this transformation. She has offered up this part of her life to this work, and we are grateful for this dedicated attitude and performance. Her part in this is a karmic agreement we have all made together at this time to bring the words of wisdom from ancient and faraway places to a culture that is in deep suffering, with no tangible way out, given the misinformation you have and are being told.

We are honored to be able to use and share her body on this journey. Her dedication to the sharing and production of this material with us is commendable, and she is becoming a clear and completely willing voice for us to use on this Earth-bound trip we are on. She has practiced the art of forgiveness and determination over many difficult years, some of which she barely survived, yet she carried on in the firm conviction that there had to be a better way. She was right, and we are firm believers in her journey and her story. She will be the way-shower for this walk we are asking of you.

We are here, speaking through our dear one, to help you understand why you are in such pain in your culture and your relationships, what can be done to change it, and how we can assist you on this journey. This is the beginning of a long and illustrious association, and we will be with her and you for some time, helping and shining a light on the path to bliss.

The peace you will find in this text will not be boring or empty, but full of life and passion. The love you will find will fill you in a way no food or drink can, and the sex you will have will be divine — no more mediocrity and boredom. This sex will send you through the day filled with a joy and connection that empowers and creates. It is not a lusting after, but a loving with, that will occur.

Many of you have suffered from a disconnection from your sexual energy, the true source of your power, and we ask with all our collective hearts that you begin the journey back home to love, sex, and healthy power beyond your imagination. This is indeed an act of faith, and all can see the pitfalls of the journey — the discipline and forgiveness, the ego's least favorite device. But do not let the ego win its battle against love. Collect your energies together, dear ones, and insist that war is over, inside and out, and that you will love each other deeply and surely into a future beyond imagination and beyond the darkness of the ego.

Perhaps that is a tall order, but we come with love in our hearts for those of you who are suffering, and with great authority from nonphysical realms, to spread the word of love and the teachings of sexual bliss and connection that will heal almost all the ills of your modern world. So please stay tuned and read the following pages with an open mind. We will challenge you, definitely; inspire you, hopefully; and tell the truth of the matters regarding love and sexual union from the sacred perspectives that have been hidden from you for so long.

So sit down, make a warm drink of a delicious and healthy sort, and start to read. We are sure you will sigh and roll your eyes at times, but you are here for a reason, and it is time to wake up. You know it; your body knows it. The dear Earth, your mother and manifested symbol of the creativity within you, needs you now to heal and manifest on this planet the love that you are all made of. Indeed, you will not be happy, fulfilled, and at peace until all the blocks are gone and you stand there, clear and whole, as the divine manifestation of realized love that you already are in our eyes.

We ask all who read this book to pass it along when they are done to those who they know will love it — but especially to those who will hate it. They are the ones who will throw it across the room, but they are the ones who need it the most. Indeed, it will be those who do not like it who will reap the most benefit from it. So read this book, and if you are loath to give it away, buy another, and give it to your enemy. That enemy will become a lover in the end, whether you believe it or not. Many lifetimes may have to pass for this to happen, but if you follow the recipe in here for love, you may well get it done in this life, and then the vistas that open up will be incredible indeed.

We are Ananda, the teachers of love and divine sexual union with God and you. With love in our hearts and joy in our expression, we are here to assist in whatever way we can to help bring peace, health, and abundance to your struggling society. We are here for you, with you, and beside you on this trip you are taking.

With love and
assistance always,
Ananda

I

How We Came
to Misunderstand
Sexual Energy

CHAPTER ONE

The Basic Problem

The basic problem within this Western culture's teachings, and therefore your experience within it, is that the very foundations of that which you have been told will bring you happiness will not. You have been taught that it is physical objects that you desire, the things you find in catalogs and on the Internet, that will bring you the passion, sexual fulfillment, happiness, and health that you desire. And this is indeed not true. The very basis of all your decisions — that monetary wealth is what will allow you to possess and achieve all that you think will make you happy — is, in fact, incorrect.

All the desires you possess within this culture are almost totally dictated to you by the companies that wish to sell you the products that you have been taught and convinced you need. The desires you feel seem real. The indoctrination is so complete that you cannot imagine that wealth and all the attendant possessions will not give you the peace and happiness you so desire with every fiber of your being. But the sad truth is you have been fed an incredibly expensive and pervasive lie that is bringing your culture, and indeed your health and happiness, to its knees in defeat.

You are innately energetic beings. All the feelings and emotions that bring you the greatest pleasure are not, in fact, caused by anything outside of you. Some would argue this point and insist that a car or house will bring them happiness, but have you truly looked at your life and the experience of lusting after something or someone? What truly happens when you achieve this most important goal? Either you are not as satisfied as you thought you would be, or you are, but very briefly —

and in both instances you are on to the next desire, the next thing that will *absolutely* make you happy. This is true for almost all of you, and if you honestly pose this question, you will see that you have been driven all your life by an endless stream of insatiable desires that, even when satisfied, leave no permanent release from the irritation of dissatisfaction and further desire.

What we are here to tell you is that there is a very good reason for this and that it can all be changed. The desire you feel is the dissatisfaction felt in a mind that is not at peace, and you, as Western consumers, have been told that this dissatisfaction is caused by your lack of material wealth and possessions. This is the second largest lie perpetrated on your confused minds. So here you are, seeking that which cannot be found in the place you have been told to look, and an endless stream of sadness and dissatisfaction results. We wish to tell you that all the dissatisfaction can be solved with the very simple — but not easy — path of this book.

Your Mind Is Not Your Brain

Your mind vibrates at the frequency of love. It was made by a loving Creator in the same frequency in which the Creator exists. Now, we will immediately mention that we said the *mind*, and not the body. This is an important distinction that must be mentioned early on in this discussion to keep things clear.

The mind is not contained within the body or brain as you believe it to be. It is an all-pervasive phenomenon that connects all living beings to one another and to their Creator. So the mind that you think is solely yours is *not* only yours. This is one of the reasons so many of you suffer from the same issues and problems. They come in many shapes and sizes — different forms, if you will — but they are all the same; feelings of grandiosity, feebleness, unworthiness, and fear are shared by all of you. Have you not wondered at the similarity of conversations that you have with friends both past and present? About the dissatisfaction with life, with your partners, with your families? This is because the mind is universal and connected, a most important piece of information in understanding and transforming the painful mental anguish in which many of you find yourselves.

There is a sweet and loving mind created in the likeness of Source energy. Some of you call this God, but that term is so divisive that we will instead use the terms Source energy, Universal Mind, and All That Is, as they are far less controversial and more likely to create a feeling of harmony in those who have had negative encounters with the Church and its teachings. This Universal Mind connects all living beings and is in tune with love, oneness, and kindness, calm and beautiful. There is also a mind we will call the ego mind, which is also connected — one mind — and it too shares traits throughout the minds of all humans who tap into its darkness and pain. It embodies fear, separation, hatred, judgment, and those most difficult of human feelings so many are tormented by.

We are saying there is a collective experience that you have not been taught about. You have been told that your thoughts and feelings are yours alone and do not affect anyone else unless they are acted on or spoken out loud, but this is not the case. All minds are connected in both ways, through the kind and loving transmissions of the love vibration, and through the fearful and separating dictates of the ego mind in which so many of you are immersed.

In understanding this basic structure of the mind and its manifestations, later explanations we make and prescriptions we suggest will make more sense and provide a reasoning that cannot be understood until this basic structure is comprehended. You see, when we suggest forgiveness or nonjudgment, the connections between this behavior and your own health and happiness become apparent. When you believe you are completely separate and that your thoughts are meaningless, you will keep them to yourself, unhealthy and unloving, believing that you do not affect anything at all. Indeed, you affect everything and everyone you think about very profoundly. This is the first — and perhaps most important — revelation we will share.

This is not a vague and "airy-fairy" idea of positive thinking or happy dreams, fantasized and having no true effect. The thoughts you have and keep to yourself shape the very world you walk in, the very people you meet, and the very experiences you have, down to the tiniest detail.

"And how does this happen?" you ask. Well, the world does not work as you have been told by the religions and old scientific ways that have been drummed into your confused, gullible minds. The truth of the matter is that you are responsible for every person, place, and thing you experience in your life, in no uncertain terms — good, bad, and indifferent. "No!" you shout, "this cannot be true! I am the unwitting victim of so much badness around me and people who hurt me when I am totally innocent." Yet we are here to tell you that is not the case. You are the most powerful creator, endowed with a force beyond your comprehension when you were conceived in the mind of Source, endowed with the same creative force that made you. This is a secret that has been kept from many of you for millennia.

The tides are now changing, and your growth and suffering are becoming so great — in potential for both good and bad — that this information must be brought to you time and again until you truly grasp the magnitude of that which you are. You are as gods, able to make worlds; you have just not been told the truth of this. Oh, you have heard small snippets in religious texts that allude to your greatness, but in the next line you will be told of your evil nature and your weakness. It's confusing, to say the least. But this has been by design, to keep the power and magnificence of your abilities out of your sight, to keep you passive and powerless. The time is over for this perpetration of untruths, and we will do our best to show you the path to limitless love and power that will help you heal the wounds you have suffered and the pains you endure without need.

We are here as teachers to tell you how to tap into this most sacred of energies so that you can create that which you wish to create. So many of you are creating that which you do not want without realizing your own part in this terrible misplacement of energies. You are creating in every waking moment you experience, and it is by your focus and thought that this occurs.

Sex as a Creative Force

Another principle that is not taught to your growing and confused culture is that sexual energy is spiritual and of God or Source. You have, for millennia, been told that it is "of the Devil" at worst, or at best just a dirty little thing you experience in private. This culture in its modern ways will dispute this, but have you looked at the arena in which sexuality is played out lately? The pornography industry promotes the most animalistic approaches to sexual union, and the means of selling products use sexualized images as the motivation for purchase. Within your families, many do not speak of sexuality at all, letting your youngsters find out from the Internet or ill-informed cohorts that the way to make love is through the sad and distorted forms they see on the computer screens you are all so attached to.

The truth of the matter is that sexual energy is the very foundation of the passions that create the energy in your life, and when that connection is broken, through subtle and not so subtle prohibitions, you are cut off from the most powerful energy you have access to. Our purpose is to tell you how your systems of creativity and energy work so that you can create that which you choose, so that you can experience the connection to Source and to each other that you are destined to create, giving you access to a beautiful and healthy existence full of passion, joy, physical health, and abundance.

God exists in all energy, all things. Sex is the most powerful creative force on Earth — and in the universe, for that matter. You can see its strength by what it drives people to do. They buy new cars and clothes and even risk life and limb, so it makes sense that this is where God is most forcefully expressed: in your most repressed, proscribed, and prohibited behaviors. What a horrible scene this sets up! The most beautiful energy in the universe, which contains so much of the Creator, is stopped, plugged, and misdirected into all sorts of strange and terrible manifestations.

We will help to explain the path to blissful union with the divine, although it will surely upset a lot of people and others will fear it terribly. It's a small wonder that the wars we see are the violence of souls disconnected from and fearful of the love most able to so gently guide them into a loving and fruitful life, the passions driven deep underground into darkness, where lies breed and fear is fed. Love is a thing of light that needs to be shown to the world and to each of you. Physical affection is good and lovely. There's no need to hide it or pretend it is not wanted.

Look at a cat or a dog and see how freely they ask for love and give it. You would be well served to pretend to be a cat or a dog when it comes to love. Indeed, they were sent to you to teach just that. But it seems to be missing the mark.

Sex is a thing of divine beauty, but fear and a lack of honesty pervert its expression, creating sexual deviations that hurt both the victims and the perpetrators. We ask that those reading these words see the

20

discomfort they feel as a sign that *what they believe* is wrong — not what is being written here.

God created all. God created sex as a pathway directly to him, her, or it. We assure you that no punishment or judgment is ever meted out to one who is loving and uses sex as a communication device with other humans, using his or her body to express the divine through the physical. It is only the scared mind of the misinformed that fears hellfire or damnation because of sexual experiences.

CHAPTER TWO

Misinformed Minds

When humans are conceived in the womb, there are many forces at play. You are not a brand-new being, as your scientists proclaim, but a multifaceted spiritual essence who chooses to create a body to experience things you have not understood in previous or simultaneous lifetimes. Sounds complicated, doesn't it? Well, in some ways the truth is far simpler and yet far more complex than you have been told. Those of you who believe in one life, and one life only, are way off the mark, and those of you who believe in reincarnation and a long and simple line of lifetime after lifetime, one leading into the other, are a little closer to the truth — but still way off the target that we are telling you about.

The truth is that your lifetimes are many and varied, and they occur simultaneously. They occur in many dimensions, all at the same time — patchworks in three dimensions that connect and affect each other all the time. Changes you make in this apparent life will affect those in the "past" and, indeed, those in the "future." This sounds fantastic within the context of the three-dimensional patterns that you believe are true, but this is the truth of the matter.

When you are conceived in the lifetime you think is your only existence, your higher self — what we will call your oversoul — is planning each and every birth, and there may be many, even hundreds, all going on at the same time. You see, the time and space model you believe in so strongly is only one small sliver of reality you have access to. We as spiritual teachers have a far wider rage of vision, so we can help you understand that which you do not comprehend, given the misinformation you have been fed.

You would not put a novice rider on an animal such as this, and neither should you put a novice in the path of kundalini awakening.

So that is it for warnings. You have been told, and now it is your choice whether to follow our prescriptions or not. It is up to you. We know you are curious. We know you are tired of the way you have been living and loving, but do take your time, dear ones. Know that we know more than you and that this is very important information to listen to.

There is a path to the heights of bliss that all humans can travel. It is part of your heritage, yet many of you only have tiny glimpses of that which is possible. For centuries you have been kept away from the truth of your magnificence, but it is now time to begin the exploration of these energetic pathways that were known by the ancient prophets who started many of your religions. They were ahead of their times, yet they came and offered you a chance — a taste of what was possible. But the information was lost, distorted, or both.

We come now to teach you the ancient ways, the paths to enlightenment through sacred union of male and female. It is time, and you are ready. Take heed of our warnings and you will fare well, but ignore them at your peril. It is powerful and heady stuff we will be sharing, and we hope you are strapped into your seats for the ride. We are not kidding when we say, "Hold on to your hats." You will be amazed, and at times afraid, but all is well, and if you keep within the bounds of the suggestions we make, you will enjoy the roller-coaster ride you are signing up for.

Meet the Ego Mind

This is the beginning of our discussion of sexual energy and how it works for the Western mind, taught so many incorrect ideas about this most amazing aspect of Universal Mind — or God, if you will. Sexual energy is divided into two different manifestations, and it is very easy to discern these two completely different avenues of its expression. We previously wrote of two shared experiences, that of the ego mind and that of the loving Universal Mind, so it is not surprising that each of these avenues of expression has its own version of sexuality and its playing out in the world of life as you see it.

The first is the one you are most familiar with, the ego mind. Its belief in physical survival and its need for continuing the physical expression of that which you call a body requires sexual reproduction, of course, to achieve its aims of survival. In this form, the sexual energy is felt as a desire to have babies, to form families, and to achieve a kind of physical transformation into minor gods. Being a parent gives this experience of something greater than the self, but if the ego is wielding too much power, the sexual expression of what we would call these lower concerns can get out of balance.

As the ego is concerned in the extreme with survival of the physical body, at times at the expense of others seen as outside the tribe you would call your family, it tends to be less than loving in its approach. It is generally motivated by fear and caution. Keeping safe and free from pain is its utmost goal, and in terms of sexual energy, this does not bode well for an ecstatic and otherworldly experience. The lower chakra centers that guide this aspect of sexuality are concerned with tribe, basic security, survival, and animal or physical aspects.

Because the spiritual connection to sexuality has been forbidden in this culture for many centuries, if not millennia, you have kept this energy firmly rooted in the lower chakras — the first three, to be exact. The heart chakra represents the area of the physical and spiritual bodies where transformation through love is achieved. It is only when sexual energies are raised from the lower three chakras through the heart and up into the higher realms that the transcendental aspect of sexual energy we are speaking about comes into play.

As your heart center opens through compassionate acts of forgiveness and unconditional love, the vibration of the body in which you function begins to change. When the ego mind is in play, you do not care for others as much as yourself, except perhaps for offspring. The concerns of the ego are more selfish and self-centered. It worries about its own protection first, its own gratification, and the avoidance of that which it fears. As the heart chakra is brought into play, through the practice of forgiveness, nonjudgment, and compassion — words you are indeed familiar with — the energies begin to transform and the sexual energies begin a shift to higher functioning.

Now, this process is not a quick one for many of you. There are deeply ingrained ego teachings in your culture that blatantly go against the grain of unconditional love and forgiveness, so there are barriers to the mind that wishes to experience the higher realms of sexual expression.

One of the first blocks to raising this energy is the belief in attack.

This is profoundly embedded in your culture's belief system. Every time you gossip, every time you argue, and every time you have hateful or judgmental thoughts, your belief in aggression is reinforced and grows. You are not at fault here; this is what you have been taught to do. You have been fed a steady diet of war and violence in your mainstream media, and in fact, many of you cannot imagine living without this violent food. Oh, it is disguised in tales of redemption and good winning over evil in your police shows and crime dramas, but it is all based on hatred and violence, and it is indeed contributing to the lack of love in your lives.

You see, the mind is a synthesizer of material, and what goes in and stays in through focus and repetition is created out in the physical world. Remember what we said about the mind and its manifestations? That which you focus on grows, and the love we are speaking about manifesting in the higher expressions of sexual energy through the activation of kundalini cannot coexist in the mire of attack and judgment in many of your minds.

The dire consequences of your culture's misteachings around violence are untold. And truly, we hope that when you realize just how detrimental this is and how you suffer from loss of connection and love through these incorrect teachings, you will become willing to address these issues.

The Sexual Energies of the Ego

The sexual energies many of you are experiencing are in the realm of the ego. It is the milieu in which you immerse yourselves, in which you create your experience. The sexual energies of the ego are unrefined — the purely physical mating of bodies striving for pleasure and, at times, dominance over each other. This does not paint a very pretty picture, we agree, but that is why we have come, for many of you experience the sexual energy of the ego and do not delight in it. Oh, you may have glimpses here and there of sex's potential, but there is much missing for many of you. You arrive with great expectations of what a new lover may bring you, but very shortly things begin to take a turn for the worse, and disillusionment sets in.

The ego is not a loving thing, and this is an important idea to understand. The higher realms of sexual expression are based on love, and the ego is not from or for love. It is made to take, to judge, to conflict, and to argue. It is its own worst enemy in many ways, and because you are not taught how to discern the difference between ego and Source energy, and because you live in a culture that feeds the ego the rich and repeated foods of hatred and judgment, you find yourselves lost in its mire and muck, unable to see the beauty and light that is your potential experience.

The sexual energies of the ego remain in your lower three chakras. For sure, some of you venture up into the love realms of the heart, and for that we are eternally grateful, or your world would not stand a chance at survival and evolution. But your misteachings around sexuality and God keep you from integrating the sexual energies and the God energies in any meaningful way, and so the path to heaven on earth through blissful sexual union eludes you to a great extent.

Another belief is that renouncing the physical on the spiritual journey means that you have to give up all things of joy, and this includes sex. But this is a misteaching that has occurred — that the sexual union between loving souls needs to be let go of somehow for them to be good and spiritual. This is not so. In fact, the divine sexual union of which we speak is one of the higher expressions of divine love. It is the opposite of what most of you have been taught — that in some way the lower self is at play in the bedroom.

The truth is that if the *ego* is in the bedroom, then yes, this indeed can be true. But when the ego is diffused through awareness and forgiveness, the pleasures of the body are enhanced. When the walls are gone and the need to protect is removed, a true connection can be made. The body must be used as a communication device only, speaking the language of love to your beloved partner with gentleness and defenselessness, opening the heart and the soul to the profound connection that shows the truth that you are all one and that loving yourself and others is not different at all; they are one and the same.

This understanding helps in the healing of the damage of past sexual events. Forgive the other and heal yourself, and then encounter your own sexual energies in private and with love, knowing that the love and tenderness you express with your own dear self will heal the wounds, and eventually, if you choose, bring you the love you desire to experience in the body of another. The journey will deepen and free up more layers of the human you are, feeling deeply the love of the world and others.

from your friends and family. You will begin to value peace, nature, healthy foods, and loving communications, and you will begin to value these things for a good reason.

As you start on this path you will begin to see the changes that are wrought very quickly. As you relinquish these things that are responsible for your suffering, you will begin to see a change in your relationships, your happiness, and your ability to be at peace. As you start to practice these principles and experience true peace for the very first time, you will understand the inestimable value of a peaceful mind. You will realize that so many things you have been told you need are not required. You will find satisfaction in the simplest of pleasures, and you will begin to find happiness.

We know you doubt us at this stage, but please, do stay tuned. We are going to continue teaching you the path to bliss and the deep and loving connections you truly wish to achieve in your lives instead of the shallow and unsatisfying relationships and activities that fill your time now, that leave you with a deep and abiding dissatisfaction with the lives you are living. We are talking about radical and profound change in your thoughts, words, and deeds that will bring a revolution to your life and rock the boat quite a bit.

We understand that those of you with elaborate lives delicately balanced on the activities you perform daily are getting a bit nervous. "What will I have to give up?" you ask. "All who depend on me must be okay." And we say this: All that is good and whole will remain. All that is undermining your true self-expression and joy will be retooled into a form that will help you achieve the love and peace you seek. Indeed, there will be changes, but if you follow the path of loving kindness and forgiveness, your life can only improve; it is the law. Love brings love, and hate brings hate. Just think about your actions. Are they all love-based, or are acts, desires, and jobs that are less than loving expressing themselves in your life? If they are, that is what is causing the suffering you are feeling.

Leave the Ego Behind

The sadness our dear one has experienced is profound, but this is what we are teaching: the suffering is not required, the mind is in need of discipline to achieve freedom, and the untrained mind is the most dangerous thing in the universe. It will destroy its owner if it is not taught the truth, which is that the energy of God is love and expressed through the body as sex and that is as it should be. This is the path to freedom, creativity, and joy, and the forces of love are always seeking to express themselves. If the mind is healed, healthy, and in touch with truth, the bliss of experience will outshine anything you can imagine. It is a force that desires the experience of love between humans in such a loving yet intense way that humans feel scared of it sometimes, as if they will be obliterated.

Indeed, the ego will be obliterated, and that is why the love approaching is a terrifying thing to the ego, why it always wants space between itself and others — because it knows, on some level, that its end will come if it allows love full reign in the world. So the ego is constantly trying to deceive you into battle and judgment, into separation and hatred. It will do what it can to teach the opposite of the truth that is love.

We are proponents of absolute honesty on this journey. Be honest with yourself first, and listen to your heart and emotions and what they want. Start to listen wholeheartedly and act on those desires. You will at first upset those around you who are used to you being sad, but once the first wave of discord passes, it will begin to change for the better, and you will begin to feel the life force enter back into your dear, closed-down heart. You will begin to take delight and eventually to soar to the height of heaven as you never imagined it.

These are the words of truth, and we are sure they are even a little intimidating at the moment. The idea of channeling this kind of energy scares the part of you that is used to being shut down and at the mercy of others. It feels as if its world will collapse. In some ways it will, but that world is not worth living in without God's passion in your heart and in your bed with you. That is the truth, and we will keep asking you to join on the journey home through loving yourself first, then sharing that amazing person and body with a like-minded soul who also loves itself.

These are the alliances that will heal the planet. Do follow your heart and our teachings to this path of awakening, and be free of the desperate measures you have been living under. These desperate measures are not for the likes of you. Take back the ability to love, and you will feed the souls of the planet and each other until you are full of light.

People imagine that peace is boring. As you are finding out, this is not so. The sensation of feeling at peace is so full of beauty and expressions of love that life becomes a beautiful expression of itself rather than a painful and turbulent expression of the ego — which will drive you mad and even drive you to kill yourself, one way or another. What do you think obsessions with food or alcohol are but the ego trying to kill you, slowly but surely? We see this and are aware that this is indeed an insane way to live, and it makes life such a burden, a pleasureless existence.

CHAPTER THREE

Your Body Is a Vehicle

Our subject here is the body and how the ego uses it in this world. It seems we say this with almost every subject we cover, but this one is very important in the human experience and on this spiritual journey.

At times the body feels like your enemy, and at times it feels like your best friend. It curses you with sickness, yet it blesses you with the physical experiences you seem to enjoy so much. We must unravel this enigma. It can also be called a paradox. Your body brings you to the edge of ecstasy, and it takes you to hell, so we will start with the hell end of things, as that is what we are seeking to remove from your existence here. Once hell is removed, you will find there is only a heaven of sorts left.

The hell that the ego creates of the body comes from the way it looks at it and, in turn, the vibration and thoughts that arise from the beliefs held about this confusing and beautiful contraption you seem to be stuck in. The ego loves the body and hates the body; it is its prison and its curse. You see, the body's death means the end of the ego's existence, so the ego knows on a deep primal level that its days are numbered and that is the fault of the body. So in its viciousness, the ego hates the body, judges it, feeds it the wrong foods, and stuffs it full of drugs and drink as if to say — we will use the phrase you know so well — "fuck you!"

The other side of this coin is the ego's worship of this very same thing. Because the ego only believes in the physical world and scoffs at talk of the spiritual, the body is the only place it can go for satisfaction and the meager joys of the physical world. So it worships the body, seeing it as the only thing in all the world that can give it what it wants.

You can see what a terrible dilemma this sets up in the mind. There are two diametrically opposed views, both believed in the same mind, and this is the insanity that you see around the body issues in this culture. There are not many of you out there with any spiritual beliefs that have been truly integrated into the mind. You may go to church, or you may do yoga, or you may believe in spirits of some kind, but that does not really affect your relationship to your body. You still believe in it as if it is real, and you treat it as a demon and a god all at the same time. It is these beliefs that you see played out in the yo-yo dieter, the anorexic, and the food addict. These extreme examples are often at one end of the spectrum or the other, but you are all in there somewhere, hating or worshiping the body to some degree. And that is why the insanity continues and causes so much distress.

It is the belief systems that you are adhering to that are causing the problem, not your dear bodies at all. The body has no desires as such. All the appetites you attribute to the body are in your mind. As we referred to in earlier writings, the body could eat one good food that would keep it alive and be very happy with that. It is you who layer all the meanings and blame the body for what you are actually doing. The body seems to drag you around by the short hairs, so to speak, yet it is not the body but the mind and all its conditioning and attachments that is dragging you around; the arena in which it plays out is the body.

So here you are, seeing the effect and calling it the cause. This is why the world seems so crazy to you at times: because it is. The rules of the ego are insane, and if you have lived on this plane for any amount of time, you know that this is the case. You all try to find some balance in the insanity, but it is a precarious and terrifying thing, and these imbalances in the mind make life exhausting and, at times, intolerable. Those who commit suicide have reached the last straw and cannot tolerate the mind anymore. It is an unfortunate event, because there is no escape in suicide; the mind will create another body to come back and repeat the lesson until it is learned. So if you are reading this and are at the end of your rope, reach out for help. Do not stay alone with an insane mind and contemplate this end. It will be of no avail. The moment you have killed the body, you will see that it was not the problem; the problem was indeed the mind, and it was all a terrible mistake.

Do Not Worship the Body

Now we will go back to the issue of the ego and the body. We have said that you will not find a sane escape from the body's apparent ball and chain of the ego. The ego hates the body or loves it, but the point is that the ego believes that the body is its prisoner and its salvation at the same time.

What the spirit does is see the body as a vehicle and communication device only. It does not attribute to it goals it cannot reach or decisions it cannot make. It sees it as the neutral object that it is. Indeed, what happens when you stop making all of these extreme judgments is that a peace arises in your mind because you are now seeing the truth. The body is not important, yet it is not hateful. It is the device you use to travel through this world for a short time — to experience what you need to experience, to see what you need to see — and it is valuable for that only.

You will see from all our later talk about food and nurturing the body that we wish for you to honor it, but honoring and worshipping are different things. When you honor something, you see the value it has but do not put it above or below you. You accept that it is of a certain use. Worship is setting an object or person high above you and giving it powers over you that you believe you do not have.

Now, there are many of you who will immediately say that the body does have power over you. It can die and get sick, and the experience you are having right now supports that view. But when you have spent some time cultivating the thoughts about the body that we have just suggested, its importance and the idea of its loss will fade into the background, and slowly you will not value it as much but will offer it more respect. This is part of the journey that you will need to take on faith at the beginning, but our dear one has had relief from almost-fatal body issues from this realm of study, which will be one of the stories that she will share on our journey together.

There are many of you caught in the hell of the body — be it sickness, dieting, or obesity — so this is an area that we will return to several times. We will reiterate the importance of this path as a source of relief from this hellish realm of thoughts and generated feelings. Many of you are tormented each day by these things that we have mentioned, and you cannot enjoy the experiences of this Earth plane because of the body issues at hand. We will leave this here for now, but we have just skimmed the surface. This is a lot to digest, pardon the pun, but we wish to make you smile in the sadness you may be feeling.

* * *

We are ready to go on the journey into the book one more time. So we are talking about the body, the way the ego uses it, and the way Spirit uses it. "But what does this look like in an ordinary life?" you may ask. Well, all of you of course are having the experience of being in a body, and that body feels incredibly real and solid. You have had a lifetime of conditioning telling you that this is indeed so, so what we are saying — that the body is not real, and that you are a spiritual being first and foremost — sounds like madness, does it not?

But what we are saying is the truth, dear ones, and as we mentioned, the guidance system you have in your experiences — this emotional body, these feelings — is giving you a clue about what you are thinking. The fact is, if you are suffering in your body in any way — hating it, worshipping it, or feeling ill — then there is a disconnect happening, and your guidance system is offering you some feedback. When you are on the mark and your thoughts are aligned with the God source — or love, if you will — you will be at peace and enjoy being in the moment. When you are identified with an untruth, you will suffer and have little or no peace around this subject.

So what we are asking you to do is acknowledge any suffering you are experiencing around this topic and accept that there is something wrong because of how you feel. The area of cause and effect again arises. You think you feel bad because of something that is wrong with your body — its shape, weight, or health — but the opposite is true: It is your vision of your body that is causing the issue, and you must trust us on this. As you start to tell a different story, that of the innocent body as a communication device and vehicle only, the profound and painful judgments you have around your body and its appearance will change.

This is the most basic change you can make in relation to this enigma, the physical self. You do not need to ignore it or despise it, but you do need to see it for what it is, and then it will assume the correct perspective. And you will be amazed by the results. Much of your emotional eating will subside — not all, we expect, but some of it. And you are likely to see improvements in health as you start to treat your body differently, giving it the correct fuel to run efficiently instead bombarding it with hatred and awful thoughts. Such thoughts are like a poison to the physical system, and all manner of things go wrong because of the constant barrage of thoughts against this neutral object that is your vehicle for a time.

Indeed, this leads us into the subject of death, and we will go there after a short break, dear one. This will be a good one, so stay tuned. We feel the body's need for movement, so we are giving you that for a few minutes.

CHAPTER FOUR

Death

On to this subject of death as it relates to the body. Many of you are now hearing of these near-death experiences — when a blissful example is felt while one is out of the body. This is indeed the truth of the matter. You will feel free when you die, and the body will fade away, especially if you have been doing this work for a few years before the event happens.

Indeed, much of the difficulty with the body and leaving it is the deep attachment to Earth and the experiences of the world, as if they were the only reality. This is the case if you only live in the ego's world, but if you venture into the spirit's world, as we are suggesting, the ties loosen and you will begin to leave your body at times during the blissful experiences we are urging you to pursue. Our dear one, Tina, has had many out-of-body experiences that have shown her, in no uncertain terms, what it is like when you die. And as much as she is not ready to go, she understands the deep sense of love and all-encompassing compassion that envelops you as you pass from this physical world. It is a sad story that you have been told about death, and it is told by the ego.

The ego does indeed fear this event. It loses all it values as this transition is undergone. As your spiritual life develops and you begin to experience a world of energetic and feeling experiences that are not attached to objects as such, you will begin to feel a loosening of the ties that bind. The fear of death will subside. There is always a moment of fear when the ego sees its demise. All except the truly enlightened will have a moment of fear, but it is not your true self that is dying. It is this thing called the ego that is associated with the physical animal you call the human being, and you are not just that, dear ones. You are spirits temporarily using these vehicles to explore some crazy ideas you had and thought seemed like good ideas at the time. When it is time to go — if you have woken up — the future in the spiritual realms will be an inviting adventure.

If, however, you have fed on and grown deeply attached to this Earth experience and you do not wish to move on to the higher realms and do not even believe in them, then death becomes a terrifying journey. You feel the loss of every earthly delight and are desperate to return, and you *will* return after a brief respite. For a lot of you, the return is so quick because of this deep need that you barely take a breath and are right back at it, so to speak. This can be a detriment, but as with all events, it is your choice, and the results depend on the focus you take. If the world is everything to you, then losing it is scary. If the spiritual path is a large part of your life, then death will intrigue rather than terrify you. But we mean the spiritual path that deals with the body as we have suggested — the gentle and slow reconditioning of the mind to see the truth of the setup, so to speak. Many of you will have further questions on this subject that we will deal with at another time, but for now that will suffice, and it is enough for many of you to think about at the moment.

CHAPTER FIVE

Faith in the Wrong Things

We are now going to talk about religious instruction and the many — no, the legion of — errors and mistakes that have taken place over the centuries. We are saddened by the terrible effects fear, lies, and human manipulations have had on people's views of God and spirituality. The Church has perpetrated the most heinous lies, and all have suffered from the promotion of guilt and punishment projected on a loving God by uneducated — no, miseducated — minds.

God is love. God is the most amazing and creative force in the universe, but he is portrayed as a human with anger and judgment at his core. This is absolutely the biggest fiction of all time and the reason sex is so maligned — because the humans who translated the scriptures and wrote their own version of the prophets' teachings were terrified of going to hell, of being punished by their culture. They wrote what would *not* get them crucified or banished from their families and countries. The religions of old need to be dismantled and replaced with loving practices that truly reflect the will of the Creator and the enlightenment that was experienced by Christ, Buddha, and all the other mystics who have received the wisdom of God directly.

Anyone who has felt the all-encompassing love of the Creator knows that only love, understanding, unconditional peace, and freedom exist in the mind of God. We are expressions of that divine light, and we are free to express that in any loving way we can. In fact, the religious leaders who ban sexual intimacy in whatever way they do will discover a harsh truth when their life lessons pass before their eyes. They will find that the things they taught are the very things that will come back to them so they can experience the losses they counseled others to follow. This is not a punishment, but all souls must experience, in the flesh, the mistakes they have perpetrated on others before they can truly renounce the wrong teachings, even if they were only doing what they were taught. Because of the intensity of the third-dimensional experience, this is the only way humans learn. The spirit already knows, but an aspect of the spirit has forgotten and come to Earth to play its own game and its own version of life, which is often really off the mark — nowhere near the truth of God's love and eternal patience with his or her dear children.

Reexamine Where You Place Your Faith

Many have a great deal of faith; it is just placed in the wrong things. This is the first issue that must be brought to the surface. You have faith in hard work; you have faith in the body; you have faith in your self-image. There are many places you place faith, yet these things are transient and impermanent, so you are always fearful. They can go at any time. We are asking you to start to develop a deep faith in Spirit — God, if you will — the unseen realms of energy that are the driving force behind creation. If you have faith in this, it will not let you down and will create what you wish to experience.

We are asking for many changes to cultivate the bliss energies, and you are taking a leap of faith in believing that what we are asking is indeed going to bring you to this place. There are many other tales of paths that lead you to particular destinations, but what is the destination, and is it worth the price you pay? Although the ego disagrees, we are not asking you to lose anything. We are only asking you to invest in the real source of your power, which is a powerful energy called kundalini or chi. It has many names around the world, but it is the God force that is created by thought, word, and deed. It is the power that is beyond all others.

The culture in which you live worships many idols, does it not? The body, the car, money, food — many things are set up on the altars to your gods, and you worship these things that cannot give you the support you want. So you are afraid. Some part of you knows that these things are not worthy of your devotion, yet this is what you have been taught to follow. So you suffer, not knowing why or how to break free from the tyranny of lies you have been fed.

This source of energy is love, and its desire is to create good and abundance. What so many of you do not realize is that the practices you have every day of thought, word, and deed are interfering with the flow of that energy, and you are powerless as a result. You still create, but it is a mess of inconsistent and often unwanted things that you have been thinking about and wishing for inadvertently.

Every time you think a thought, it joins with others of like vibration. And when there are enough to create a level of energy to bring something solid into manifestation, they will indeed do so. So if you are thinking all the time of sickness rather than health, you will manifest it. If you are always afraid and thinking fearful thoughts, images and events of that vibration will arise, perhaps in the form of accidents or robberies. These are not the rules you have been taught. Although the law of attraction is gaining followers, and this is a good thing, many are still under the impression that anything they think about is a story that is not going to manifest.

You will not receive a car if you are hating yourself; you will not become wealthy if you are hating your life and thinking about how you wish you were somewhere else. Theses are the subtleties of thought that need to be addressed, and it is your actions that will show you where your thoughts are. Attachment to safe routines indicates fear, gossip indicates a lack of focus on your own dream, and eating poorly reflects a lack of care for your body — and sometimes self-hatred. So what do you have faith in?

Place Your Faith Somewhere New

A set time of quiet prayer and perhaps meditation is a good place to start to set up a dialogue and begin a relationship with the creative energies of the universe. Begin to say mantras or loving phrases as you walk to work or lay in the bath. Say words of empowerment and love, such as "I am the perfect child of God, and all is well. All is coming to me that is in my highest good." You can have fun making up these mantras and using words that are comfortable for you — not the old prayers of school or a forgotten religion, but the words that ring true for you in the place you are, on this road to developing faith in the unseen realms of light and love.

Faith in the path we have set out is imperative. You must not only remove your faith from the world of objects, money, and food, and shift it to the path to bliss and the cultivation of the energies of which we speak. It is huge act of faith to make these changes without any guarantees in writing, so to speak, yet we again say that the guarantees of your current life are not solid — other than that you are guaranteed to get sick, age, and die in a difficult and frightening world. But you do not question it because the indoctrination is so solid. That is the beginning work, to change the indoctrination and begin to see a different future for you and your dear children.

Begin to see a life of unending health, prosperity, and sexual joy. This is now where faith must be placed — the visions held in the mind in place of the fears of loss and aging and sickness. Indeed, if you build faith on this path and practice the ideas and thoughts we have been sharing with you, the aging process will indeed change, and the future you have predicted based on your mistaken ideas will change into a future of gaining strength, joy, and beauty.

The human body is capable of so much that you are unaware of, and the longevity and joy that it can produce for the soul residing in its bounds are beyond your imagination. But it is in faith that this will manifest, so we are encouraging you to be brave and trade in the dire predictions of the current belief system and start to feed, literally and figuratively, the new paradigm of the eternal spirit, manifesting love and joy in a healthy future full of bliss. This is our vision for you, and we want it to be *your* vision for yourselves. We cannot do it for you; you must take the steps yourself on this road. And do not look too far ahead, except in the visioning process.

Take each day as it is, and love to the best of your ability in the moment. Each act of love, passion, and forgiveness will have huge repercussions in your future, and you will begin to feel the change in your minds manifesting as peace and a gentle joy that you are not familiar with. The changes will come quickly if you are faithful and disciplined in the healthy practices we speak of, and the help you ask for will be real and felt almost immediately. Pay attention to the energies in your body, the dreams you have at night, and any energetic events, and within a short time you will be given the evidence you need to add to the faith and grow the experiences until they pervade your whole life.

Celibacy Is Not Necessary

There are many who have been taught over the years that the sexual energies that run through the body are evil. In some ways, sexual energy ruled by the ego can be a demon. Examples such as rape, child abuse, and sexual violence of other kinds are examples of this energy, and this is the root of the belief in celibacy as the only holy path. Indeed, there are some arguments for this practice, as you can imagine. What are the sexual energies doing, and what are they creating in unevolved souls and the lives they live?

Many of you see the power of the sexual experience and the ego's constant search for this expression of the body. All the movies, books, songs, and clothes — all the things the Western mind seeks — are often sought with this goal of sexual experience. This is one of the reasons we are here giving these teachings to the Western mind. This energy must be harnessed to create the amazing and loving experiences the human soul really wants to have.

There are many of you who have lost interest in sex. You are not interested in its low-vibration manifestations as they occur in Western culture, and many women in particular feel the disrespect and hatred that is focused toward them through the ego's sexualization of their bodies and their lives. It is into this negative fear- and hate-driven soup of sexuality that we come to tell our story. Celibacy can indeed be a sound decision at the beginning of this path as the deeply rooted belief systems of hatred, fear, and sexual damage are rooted out and healed. For our dear one, this was the right path, and at the beginning of her journey into spiritual awakening she knew that the sex of her past experience was not what she wanted. Indeed, she led an isolated path toward study and spiritual cleansing. However, as she carried on with these practices, the sexual energies in her body began to reawaken with the vibration of love, and that is indeed what we hope for for those of you on this journey with us.

For each of you, the form will be very different on the outside, especially initially, when you are excavating the wounds and resentments in your heart that are blocking the flow of love in your life. Indeed, there will be marriages that dissolve and love affairs that begin. There is no right or wrong on this journey. You each come to this subject with your own needs, and if you are a focused student, you will receive specific guidance that only suits you. So once again, we reiterate that the use of sexual energies as you travel along this path with us will be very personal.

There will be young and undamaged ones who are openhearted and fearless as they explore the teachings, and there will be those reticent and scared individuals who will be celibate for some time. What we wish for you to know is that this energy of love is powerful and pure and holds no judgment. What it does do is require a certain vibration of mind, and when we suggest any changes in diet or of information going into the mind, it is purely vibrational and not at all moral in nature.

For example, the consumption of pornography is a dark and difficult energy that is creating an animalistic association with the energies of sex. It is a primal, not spiritual, approach to the subject. Those involved in this practice and consumption are driven wild at times by the primitive reactions it creates in the mind. High and fine energies will not flow in this environment, and this is why we condemn it, if you will — not because the pornography consumer is evil, but because such consumption will prevent any meaningful raising of the divine energies through the body. This is all.

We are expecting many areas of questioning and dispute around this subject. Sex is the most charged subject on the planet, and it is time for the doors to be opened on this discussion. It is time for the truth of the history, for the past lies and deceptions, misteachings and untruths to be unearthed. There are going to be heated discussions around this topic, but the truth remains, despite the fights and arguments that ensue. And the truth is this: Sexual energy is divine in nature, and it can be misused by the ego. But in the right hands, and with a spiritual base, it is the most powerful force on the planet. When this energy is harnessed, the body, mind, and demeanor of the practitioner are transformed into a powerful and loving being with only compassion and joy on its mind. The fears around sex are based on lies and the ego's manifestations, which have nothing to do with the teachings we are sharing with you.

Inherited Teachings

You inherit much of your teaching about sex from the past, so we want you to really look at this phenomenon. We are asking you to delete this past, much as we are asking you to delete other behaviors from your repertoire that have caused so many issues. We are asking you to delete this inheritance from the past in terms of lovemaking. There are those who will balk at this. Okay, all of you will balk at this. "I know what I like, and I know how to do it," we can hear you say, but how is that working, dear ones? Are you in a bliss-filled, ecstatic relationship filled with love, communion, and connection?

If that is the case, then you are right, and we wish you well. You are educated and awake, but it is not you we are speaking to. We are speaking to those of you who have developed a way of connecting physically that suits your limitations, fears, and, on some level, desire to keep the status quo going. What we want you to see is that there is another way of being, and this way of being, as challenging as it is, will bring you all that you desire.

Many of you learned to make love while in the backseat of a car, in front of a computer screen, or while inebriated in some way. And this we understand. We understand this is the damage caused by the secrets of sex no one taught you. No one told you how to make love, to connect to the divine energies, so you have created a fumbling and, at times, moderately pleasurable way of being with your partner. Yet here you are, reading this book. We are here to help, not to chastise. We are here to teach the way to the divine bliss we have been talking about, and we know you are scared — scared to lie naked caressing your lover with rapt attention and honor. We know you are scared to kiss and kiss and connect, to feel such deep connection and pleasure that the ego starts to get very nervous, sensing the threat to the well-guarded and limited access to your heart that it deems to be safe.

Dear ones, the ego does not keep you safe. It keeps you angry and alone. It keeps you poor and afraid, yet it says, "Follow me. This new teaching is bad. You will get hurt." We have never seen more hurt and lonely people anywhere than on this planet at the moment. You are all in such a state that we have come from far and wide, from different times and places, to teach you how to relieve the deep suffering you are in. And indeed, it is in the bedroom, in your relationship to yourself, your lover, and God that these hurts began.

There is a seeming disconnect in your mind from the bedroom and everywhere else, and this is your biggest error. The connections and deep love that you are able to access through the divine body, your own or another's, are the foundation for the rest of your life, and this is why your inheritance is so crippling. These are the conscious acts that connect you to God and your partner, that transform your awareness of oneness, that transform your awareness of your multidimensional nature, and that confirm your awareness that bliss and ecstasy are your real inheritance — not the fear-based paradigm that you have been sold.

We acknowledge that you will find this difficult. You will feel exposed, and what we say is this: We know that your feeling exposed means your heart is open and undefended, and that God energies can enter. Feeling scared means you are diffusing the ego's grip on your divine sex life, and that means that real love can enter. So please try the recommendations we have made and are making. These are the first real steps toward the divinity you have heard people talk about and you have seldom felt. This is the path to awakening the energies that power your creative life, the engine of your being, and your feelings of joy — those elusive things that the New Agers talk about but you are seldom aware of. Joy — we are teaching the path to joy.

Your inheritance is wrong and will not work, so be willing — at least a little — to access areas of your heart and mind that you have been scared to explore. Create a new inheritance — one that will bring you what you want.

CHAPTER SIX

Abundance

We would like to write about the idea of abundance and how it relates to our topic. It seems not to as you read it, but it plays a pivotal role in many aspects of the divine sexual relationship. You see, one of the ego's most profound beliefs is the belief in "not enough," and it is this belief that drives many of its behaviors, striving for more time, more money, more sex — more of everything. It always thinks there is not enough, so one of the things it does is project this into the future and scare those who believe it into panicking and grasping for what is there so it doesn't leave. These ego-believers are also never satisfied, believing that this — whatever "this" is — is not enough.

So let us explore this idea as it pertains to sexual relationships. When two people are involved in a sexual alliance such as we are describing, the belief in "not enough" will, in actual fact, tear it apart. This is because the ego, if allowed to run riot as it normally does, will be on constant alert for areas of your partner's behavior that it can criticize as not enough. The ego sees this lack of abundance in everything and will attack your partner without thought if it is allowed its full expression. What we want couples to do as they enter their relationship in awareness is accept at the very beginning that the other person is indeed enough and that they both have an abundance of love to give. What this does is set aside the ego's belief and allow some space and time for this abundance to express itself.

What normally happens is that any shortfall in the ego's vision is attacked and judged. What we are suggesting is that, with this idea of abundance kept in the forefront of the mind, any temporary shortfalls in the behavior wished for are seen only as a temporary state. It will fix itself if the other partner gives that very behavior themselves, proving he or she believes in the abundance. What this does is allow each person to fulfill his or her own needs if the other is temporarily unable to for some reason.

Let us give an example. Let us suppose that one partner feels there is not enough help in the domestic department and feels a lack of abundance coming from the other partner. What we are suggesting is that the upset partner does not look at it this way, but pours herself into this very activity, seeing an abundance of domestic help as she does so. This will indeed manifest it in her experience. What will happen if she focuses on the lack is that more of the lack will show up and resentment will be created, which will create further lack in other areas. The energy must always be expressed as if there is enough.

Now, many of you will disagree with this analysis and say that you have tried this and it hasn't worked. But what we guarantee is that you were not focused on the abundance of help as you were doing the work; you were focused on the lack, and that lack increased. Of course, as with all of our prescriptions, we cannot prove this. You must prove this yourselves. But it is the belief in abundance that will transform the situation.

This will happen with money, too, or with any other substance or behavior you feel is lacking. If your belief is in abundance, the outside condition will change. It may take a little while, but what will happen is not the increased lack and attack of the ego's way. This will feed your relationship rather than starve the connection. This is a challenging behavior, and it will be most difficult for those already together who have their routines and habits somewhat set, but we suggest you try it in those areas where your own strategy is not working to your satisfaction.

So the abundance of love that you visualize is one of the most powerful manifesting agents there is. When any situation arises in which the ego comes into play — and you will know this by how you feel, for it is always clear — employ the vision of abundant love as your solution. Envision you and your beloved happy and at peace, enjoying each other's company. If you do not feed the ego's demands for judgment, they will subside. But this is where the mental discipline comes in, and it does take work.

Most of you are so used to giving the ego what it wants that you bare-ly think about it at all. If you knew the consequences of the unguarded thoughts you have, you would be horrified. You would see that all of your creations — your thoughts and ideas, hatreds and resentments — grow like flowers from the seeds you plant with these nonphysical things called thoughts, and over time, it is your choice what will grow in your garden: hard and painful cactuses or beautiful and soft flowers. We know this is poetic, but we want you to understand the beauty you can create and the ugliness you can make. It is all up to you. Every decision you make is either one or the other; there is no other choice. This is what is meant by the phrase, "a man cannot serve two masters." You are either serving the ego or Spirit, walking to heaven or to hell.

That is the simple truth of it, yet it is all made so complicated, is it not? This is always the choice in every situation: abundance or scarcity. The good news is that love is all, and it is your natural state, under all the misteachings and the old wounds that will not be let go. So let go of the past and be very present in the now so that you can see the choices you have: to make it work or destroy it, bit by tiny bit. That is all.

CHAPTER SEVEN

Opinions and Arguments

I was in the process of reading a very wordy book on psychology that was difficult to understand.

We are with you again, dear one. It is interesting — is it not? — this reading of a book and witnessing the intellectual words that cloud the issue. We are attempting — and succeeding — in using very simple words in our books so that there is no misunderstanding of our communications. So do not think they are too simple. The principles are truth, and it is always simple.

On that note, this writing will be on opinions and arguments. This is a big area of disruption in the energetic field, and it causes many of the fights and arguments in your experience. What is an opinion, anyway, and what is wrong with having one? Well, the ego loves opinions and has many of them. It gets angry at those with differing ones and wishes for you to have the same ones it has. It is always probing and poking to find your opinion with the intention of engaging you in a "friendly" discussion that it will, given half the chance, turn into a fight. It is attached to forms and mental concepts that represent its concrete world, the world it believes in and values above all. Even if it hates something, it values this hate as real and of substance. So the ego's opinions are what it expresses in conversation, and its experiences, which it cites as proof of its rightness, are indeed true for it. What is interesting, though, if you think about, it is that another ego can have the opposite opinion and have just as many experiences to support its argument as the first ego.

So this is where we come in. The ego's opinion is not truth, although it will claim it is. The ego's opinion is a small and determined effort to make sense of a world it does not understand. It is frightened all the time, so it has an opinion about the evil out there that threatens it. It is never satisfied, so it has an opinion about the need for financial security and why it is so important. It has a reason for all of its behaviors as they relate to its opinions, and if you are in disagreement, it will fight — at times to the death — to prove that you are wrong. Indeed, this is a holy war and it is taking place all the time.

The ego's opinions are its gods on the altar it worships. Do not confront another ego, because that means you are in yours at that moment. There is a deep truth that sits quietly inside that does not need your loud and raucous voice to defend it. It is true whether or not you are there, whether or not you are even alive, so you can rest quietly in its presence, knowing that it does not need you to defend it or be a spokesperson.

There is no need to argue. If you find yourself in a situation in which an argument is beginning to boil, sit back for a minute and think about what it is for. If it is to defend your ego's opinion, you do not need to proceed, because as a student of divine bliss you do not want to strengthen your ego. So you will cease the pursuit. And if you are getting into an argument for truth's sake, do not bother; it does not need your defense, and it certainly does not want you to attack another for its sake. It is inviolate in its rightness. So that is the way to avoid these battles.

What also happens is you become afraid if you do not defend yourself when another is coming at you, so to speak, with a vociferous argument. You are, at that moment, not in touch with the truth. You are an eternal spiritual being with a validity that is beyond the need for anyone else's approval. You are totally and irrevocably approved of by the Divine, and you are an expression of that same divine energy. So you can relax and nod at a fellow who is creating the opportunity to battle. Again, sit back and remember these things, and ask, "Is there some common ground perhaps that we can share, and is there some way the communication can be gentled or stopped until there is a peace resounding in the room rather than an impending war?"

This is especially important in the creation of a loving, intimate relationship. There is no place for aggression, ever! And indeed, we mean *ever*. When the ego is aroused … let us say your partner has done something, again, that is annoying to you. Stop and go to your quiet room or out in nature. Realize that this annoyance is reflecting something in you that needs to be altered or healed. Are you too quick to judge? Are you insisting that your partner follow your schedule, which suits you but not him or her? Are you in some way impinging on your partner's freedom by insisting on your way? These are questions we want you to ask and to investigate.

The emotions of fear, anger, or frustration that are rising in you belong to you to deal with and to enlighten with your loving attention. Any attack in the deep and abiding love we are encouraging you to make will undermine your desire. You may feel that you need to change these emotions to be happy, but that is simply not the case. You need to change the way you are seeing these feelings to achieve peace, and that is the truth. The good thing is this is yours to control, and you understand your motivation if you can go inside and check out what is really going on. Let us give you an example of this to clarify what we are speaking about.

Perhaps your partner is often late and does not call. You are frustrated at this and do not like it. You tell him he is disrespectful and does not care for you. What you will see, if this situation is looked at, is that you are afraid of losing him. Perhaps you fear an accident — then you are believing in death and the big, bad world out there. If you are picturing infidelity, you are creating infidelity. You are responsible for the thoughts that are running through your head around this subject. You may still wish to discuss this with your partner, but do this analysis first and see more clearly why you are upset. It is more about the thoughts that are running through your head than the actual event. We assure you this is true. Your ego, however, will want to argue, so we rest our case here. The ego always wants to argue, does it not?

We are with you, dear one, feeling your little lostness and floundering. Do not worry. All is as it should be. Yes, you are feeling a little lonely, and as we have told you many times, it is time to relinquish the freedom for intimacy. And so it is done and will change soon.

CHAPTER EIGHT

Defenselessness

We will now write on this subject that you call defenselessness, and this will be no challenge for us, dear one. The wrong button was pushed and you deleted what we wrote, but we will write it again for you if you wish. This will give you a hint of our memory and skills, will it not?

This state we are calling defenselessness in your Western culture seems a foreign concept, and an extremely dangerous one. You have been raised in a time, and indeed a place, where to be open to love and experience is deemed very dangerous indeed. The minds with which you create this experience are conducting a war on the world and those people, places, and things around you. You are not aware of it. Indeed, you think it keeps you safe, yet it is this very phenomenon that is causing the fear and hidden desire to defend yourself from attack.

The process of creation, as we have said, is not what you think. The mind with which you make this all happen is not what you think. This world is a figment of your very vivid imagination, and you will balk at this statement. "It is solid," you say. "It is real." Yet the truth of this is you have dreamed all of this up to experience those things you believe in with all your hearts and minds. So there truly is nothing separate in the mind that you call the world. Just as you are not separate from the characters in your nighttime dreaming (they are all in your mind), so there is this other level of dreaming that you mistake for a reality that is absolute and not your creation.

So this is the dream you can change, but you first must understand that it is all your doing, that every thought you have is manifest in front of you. Many of the thoughts you are having — in particular, the judgmental and attacking thoughts — come back to you in the form of unconscious guilt and fear. You think something bad is going to happen, so you are not at peace. You feel an impending loss, an impending fear of the bad, and this is your creation, because you have mistaken cause for effect and do not access and accept your own creative power. You think that this is all happening to you, but it is not.

You defend against the effect that is caused by you. The enemy is within, and your defensiveness is pointless. All of the suffering, fear, and apparently outside events are your mind manifesting your beliefs in front of you to take a good look at. Are people always saying nasty things to you? Are you encountering betrayals and inconsistencies that are driving you mad and making you fearful? These are your ideas, and if you will take some time to look at your thoughts and what your mind is occupied with, you will see it manifested as experience in your world.

Many of you are so well defended that your experiences are distorted and difficult to truly feel. You are like a bomb disposal expert out in a minefield, afraid to move in case there is an explosion. You cannot love because you are too hidden in the layers you think are keeping you safe. You cannot be seen because you are so padded with fears, fat, and distractions that keep you from honest and deep connections.

There are many of you who do not think it is you we are describing, but spend some time in your minds. Spend a day watching what you judge or hate or avoid, and if you are honest, you will see some sad truths.

Those of you who are here because you wish to experience a deep and abiding love with your equal, a sexual relationship that will take you to the heights of bliss and delight, will have to remove your defenses to contact the deep and passionate energies inside you and your partner. There is no coming together in bliss while you are wearing that suit of armor, so to speak. You cannot feel your own desires and bodies, let alone anyone else's. So this is what we prescribe: Be willing to let go of all attack thoughts in your mind. It is these thoughts of judgment that are making the defensiveness you feel. You think it is the world that scares you, and in some ways it is. But it is these attack thoughts that are represented in your world as attack from without, and until you accept this deep connection to the world you see and experience, and your part in it, you will not understand any of this.

This is why we are not suggesting that you go out and hunt for the perfect sexual partner. You must first tame the mind that has been running wild, and you must understand the deep damage and stress you cause yourself when you attack anyone — and that includes you and your body. This is one of the most pervading forms of attack in your culture, the belief that the body betrays, that it is ugly or unacceptable. Even if we suggest you look at your body and give it an honest assessment, we are saying you should do it with love, for the love you wish to bring to your experiences.

This is how you cultivate the defenselessness you need to open your heart and connect in love to others in your world. You must become loving inside first, and you do not need to share this process with anyone. Indeed, we suggest you do not. This is a personal and internal process that is only your own business. Others will notice that something is up pretty soon, but you do not need to tell them what you are up to, unless you know that they will support and understand you. You see, this teaching goes against all the teachings of the Western world, and you will not get any support from those who still believe in its dictates. So do be aware of this, and only go to those on the same path. They will indeed understand and cheer you on.

That is all for now. The body is struggling and needs to move. We will write more later, and do save this, dear. Do save it.

CHAPTER NINE

Dissatisfaction

We are with you again, dear one, on yet another beautiful day. Is it not going on forever and ever, this summer of yours? It's leading you gently into the winter months that used to depress you so. Do you remember those days, dear one, when the thought of cold repulsed you and there was no joy? This is what we will be writing about now — the dissatisfaction with what is and how it dulls the bliss energies into depression and fear of the future.

There are many ways around these thoughts, the idea of disinterest or nonattachment. Yet in the West these ideas are very difficult to understand, as the culture wishes to control and manipulate, to achieve the ego's goals of material wealth. There are several reasons to look at this acceptance of what is. In some ways it is one of the largest barriers to the Western mind achieving success on the spiritual path. The acceptance of a situation seems weak and uninspired, in which case the ego will tell you of your failure and fears of nonachievement. There are indeed some deep issues to look at in this discussion.

The ego will not let go, so you must understand this deep split that is at play in your consciousness and side with spirit, at first in very small ways. As such, you may decide to take a day off from scheduled activities and just sit with the stories in your head of nonaccomplishment, guilt, or fear of some hidden reprisal from some god who cracks a whip to keep you running on the mill of doing.

There is a deeply ingrained belief, from centuries of teachings, that the Devil likes idle hands. What a curse this has become to the spirit who loves to sit and gaze or read for hours the wisdom texts of the past, which takes some time. We suggest this is where you start to become aware of even the smallest judgment of disliking what is.

The weather is a good example of a simple place to practice. Accept that each day is perfect for the plants and animals that live in the environment they are in. Tune in and accept both the rain and the sun. Many hate so much of the weather that other experiences fade into the background.

Then comes acceptance of the humans around you — these annoying creatures who do not do what you want and speak idiocy, at least from your ego's point of view. As you become aware of the small judgments you make about all the small things in your day, become aware of the constant judgment you make about the humans in your life. These judgments are more painful, however, as they feed the ego with more food that strengthens it. It creates a strength that becomes hard to deal with. The mind focuses on the faults, the heart becomes closed, and the spiritual connection is interrupted.

This is what causes the honeymoon period to end in marriages. The people involved think they are sculpting a person into the perfect partner, but the opposite is true. Every judgment creates a rift between the hearts, and it is here that the biggest changes need to be made on the path to bliss. All beings are doing the best they can in the moment, given what they have been taught, and they have been taught some terrible mistruths that cause awful behavior. When it comes to lovers or partners with whom you wish to engage your spirit in love, you are going to be more successful if you stop the tiny judgments, even if they are not spoken.

Dissatisfaction, Judgment, and Acceptance in Relationships

Even thoughts of judgment will create energy for the ego, and it will feed on this. It is imperative on this journey to stop all judgment, yet this seems impossible. This is why we suggest accepting the nonemotional first, and then objects and things of which you have simple expectations. This then leads to the more challenging area of relationships.

When you are in the company of one who is annoying you, understand that such people are mirrors for you to learn to grow, to see an aspect of yourself that is not well developed. So if you are feeling impatient with someone who is slow, stop and be willing to slow down. They will not make you so annoyed. If you are in the company of someone who is hateful, do not hate them; that means you are the same. Instead, step back, and even if it is just internally, feel compassion for the person living in a mind of such anger and hatred, and consciously send them love and peace.

These are the exercises that are needed to relieve the mind of its intense burden of judgment. You think it keeps you safe and makes you better, but all it does is make you tired and feed the ego, which in turn creates havoc and suffering in your own mind. These are indeed large changes in the Western mind, as judgment and individual achievements are the gods of your culture and will seem hard to relinquish to the peace of acceptance. These exercises will challenge you and cause confusion, at times quite deep. You will feel the loss of mental activity in the form of judgment and wonder what you will do with all that time. As a beginning, fill the space with education on the great truths of the world, but also allow creativity to surface. You may begin to write or paint, or for some it may even bring on a regular nap to feed the tired soul so bent on achievement. But as it is cleared, all the beliefs you have about stuff and achievement will arise for you to look at. This is the work that will allow you to see what you believe and what is driving you.

There are quiet summer fields to rest in if you choose, and the horizons will not be the futures of poverty that you expect. They will be of a fullness and peace that for now is a dream. This is the carrot we hold out to you: that there are dreams you have not yet dreamed, and there are joys you cannot yet imagine. Until the false beliefs you hold are let go of and replaced with the truth — that you are divine — the connection will be just a little weak because of the interference you have been allowing in your lives.

Those of you who are ruled by endless schedules: Begin to change one thing that is moveable, and then do ask us for help. We can see your path ahead, and we know your true nature and the possible future that awaits you. We will be able to plant seeds and ideas if you are able to quiet the mind and disempower the ego, even just a little. We will hint at a place, a person, or a thing to investigate, perhaps a book or a resting place that will help on the journey to your true self. So take our advice and replace shopping with rest, TV with education, and driving off aimlessly with a lovely hike on a hilltop. These are simple remedies that will save you money and suffering, and indeed you will thank us after the initial anxiety of change attacks the mind. So do not listen to these fears; they are the ego telling tales of starvation and failure. You cannot fail. You are a holy child of God, loved beyond your comprehension, and all will flow to you that you need to grow and achieve the peace along which bliss flows.

This seems a sad truth for those of you who only wish to have great sex added to the lives you have without relinquishing anything. But for many, the stress that exists is too great and disrupts the flow of bliss energy. This will be a decision you have to make. Does this busy and "successful" life make you happy? If so, keep on with it, buying your objects and cars. If it is starting to wear thin and you are beginning to get tired, stop and entertain the idea of this path. It cannot be forced but must be arrived at in your own time and in your own way. If you are not ready, that is okay; it will not go anywhere. But remember us at the end of a brutal week as you reach for your second drink: Is this what you want your life to look like? In the end, what will it matter? Will anyone care that you worked so hard and for so long? Will you look back and wish you had rested more and written that book? We think that yes, you will.

Again, we have challenged the beliefs in your mind. Those beliefs are causing your behavior, and it is there you must go to change the behavior. Go below the surface and check out the programming. Just as a computer runs by a program, until awareness arises, you too are run by the programming of your culture. The question is, is it what you want, or are you going down someone else's road?

Work and Lack

Why are so many struggling with poverty of the soul and of finances? It is because they are disconnected from the very source that creates it, and they are afraid to go there because of the spurious legends of hell and damnation that have been associated with sexual energy for centuries. The feel of the energy is not evil or mean, but loving and open. It's the fuel for life that so many lack and turn to in forms of food, drugs, alcohol, and television, living others' lives instead of their very own beautiful creations of the mind and soul.

The jobs people do are often a root cause of the problem. In environments of dark and electrical light, the body suffers after just a few hours. You can feel this if you are in an office environment for any period of time; even three hours is plenty for the body to start struggling.

We understand the modern world and how difficult it is to change one's livelihood and spend more time outside, but we think if humans truly understood the detrimental effects of these practices they would do their best to balance their lives more, take more time off, and buy fewer things. Their houses are full of objects that take their energy rather than give them fulfillment, and they are hooked up to televisions as their means of escape. They are poor.

There can be a real escape from this kind of poverty into the realms of spirit where real wealth lies, and ironically this leads to abundance on the Earth plane, if that is what you choose to create. The choice is yours, and the outcomes are yours to experience and judge for yourselves, but the overriding promise of joy and peace will surely lure even the most scared of you into the realms of divine sex to see — just see— if the carrot is as sweet as the one you are munching on right now. And we promise you it is sweeter than you can imagine.

Do What You Love

We are sure that the events of last night [when Tina spoke for Ananda for the first time] and the message this morning have woken up a place in you that is indeed excited about the coming events, and we are certain that this is indeed the lottery you wished for. There is no better way to live than by following your passion, and that is what we will write about now for our dear readers.

Dear ones, there is a terrible aspect to your culture that needs to be brought into the light and dealt with openly and honestly: the subject of your work and your life purpose. There are millions of you going to jobs you hate or are indifferent about, wondering why your love lives suck, as you say. Well, it is clear that you are spending most of your life disconnected from joy in an environment that is not good for the physical body. This is an area you must sincerely look at and be willing to change for the energies of passion to flow in your life. Your sex life and your existence cannot be separated from what you do all day long, every day, year after year. This must be made clear to you, dear ones.

You all have a passion for something, even if it is a damaged little remnant of what it once was. Gardening, cooking, painting, looking after children — there is no end to the areas where you can do work that you love. Indeed, our dear one was adamant about following her passions as an artist, a free being, and a writer. She has pursued her spiritual path with the same passion, and this is what has manifested this path with us. As we have said before, this will not happen to all of you; this is a particular service that Tina is doing for her soul's development and growth. But each of you has a future self who is engaged in a life doing what you love, and yes, for many this feels untrue, but time is not what you think. If you dream, see a future in which you are doing what you want in your mind. You can allow it to happen.

Notice that we said "allow" and not "force." All the manifestations you wish to make are a balance between inspired right action at the right time and surrender to the path of Spirit as it arises for you. This path will change and grow, and it is important to not be attached to any specific form of the outcome. Stay clear and at peace with a vision of your life at work as you wish it. And you will no longer call it "work" — that is too loaded a word in this culture; it puts the efforts to align with your soul in a box that is not big enough for the subject. So we would like to use the words "passion," "vocation," "dream," "fantasy," "future income" — anything that is vague and unlimited. Do not try to see specifics in your imagining, but see general feelings. Are you inside or outside? Creative or academic? Are you in a busy or calm place? These are all the qualities of what you will enjoy, and there is no lack of variety.

Some feel that if they did what they wanted the world would fall apart, but this is not so. The reason the world is falling apart is so many of you are disconnected from your passions and are dead for forty hours a week. Many of you lose half of Sunday because Monday is arriving, do you not? So this too is part of the path to bliss. You will become a partner and lover to yourself when you honor the deep desires of your soul. This is indeed loving behavior that will encourage the bliss energies to flow, and it will enhance your well-being beyond anything you can imagine.

All of you are able to connect with Spirit in a deep and powerful way. Do not think that our dear Tina's path is forbidden to you. You are able to engage the energies she has by following our prescriptions and living a life focused on manifesting love. Unfortunately, Western culture has split the human into sections, all of which are supposed to do a different thing. Mothers are to sacrifice; men are to be stoic and unfeeling. These are illusions that drive the truth of each being deep underground and prevent true nature from arising, which is one of love and deep communication with the self and others.

Notice we always say "self" first. This is where you will always start with any change you wish to make. Go inside and love your self, honor your self, and you will create that in your outside life. So many of you hate and abuse the self and wonder why you cannot find a good partner with whom to share your life. This is the reason, dear ones: You do not love yourselves. So if you want the best lover and most amazing sexual experience, think about this issue of passion for your work. We assure you that the energies that will begin to flow, even as you see this in your mind, will enhance the flow of the divine energies we wish to enhance, and they will assist you on this very journey.

It is a mutual flow of love and support. Love and support yourself, and the universe will give you the same energy back. Hate and abuse yourself, and the universe will give you the same energy back. There is no difference between the self and others, and many of you think that if you only help others, this will make you good. This is not so. If you help others out of a sense of sacrifice, you belittle yourself, not honoring your own journey. If a gift to another is given freely with love, then you will feel good doing it. It is not in the behavior, but in the love.

What is your motivating factor in the things you are doing? Many call this selfishness, but it is based on the old teachings of sacrifice as noble. This is not how the world of manifestation works. That was a story told by those who wished for control and compliance. We are not aiming for that. The world of divine bliss is empowered by love, and there is no room for weakness. The energies are powerful, and a strong sense of purpose and self must be brought to these exercises.

The self is not ego, however. You uncover the true self after forgiveness and peace are employed as a spiritual practice. For example, our dear one, Tina, was always very creative, yet there was a drain on her ability to reach her potential because of old wounds, fears, and resentments. As she released these systematically, the energy to create has risen and risen, so she is not different, and yet she is. There are no clouds across her vision. It is like a stormy sky versus a clear-blue sunny sky: Both are skies but not really the same.

This project can be undertaken while all the other efforts are under-way. Look at your work and see what arises. Perhaps you like the work but it is too restricted and you would like more time off. Then that is the project. Or perhaps you need to go back to school to learn the new thing you desire to do. There are many options. And to let you know in advance, the ego will tell you many reasons why you cannot do this — all those who will be upset, all the bills, all the fears, and so on. This is the way it will look, yet you must investigate this if you wish to be free and happy. That will be the challenge: not listening to the ego's voice, and asking the deeper you what it wants. If it does not know, keep ask-ing, and there eventually will be a part of you that responds. If you have repressed this information for years, it may be deeply buried, but we think many of you will know quite quickly what you would enjoy doing.

Passion is passion. You cannot lead a passionless day and have a passion-filled night; it will not happen. Be brave and venture into this analysis. Even the beginning steps will change your life. Even if they are little steps, take them. You have no idea where it will all lead.

CHAPTER TEN

The Power of Your Thoughts

Our dear one, Tina, as you can imagine, is facing many fears and indeed mastering them as we travel down this road to channeling together. From the very beginning of her journey to the self-realization that she is now very close to experiencing, there was a fearlessness to her, and she would often say that she had zero tolerance for suffering. This was true halfway through her life, but in the beginning and in her early twenties she had a tremendous ability to sit in suffering and to create more and more of it.

This is what we wish you to look at: All the suffering you are enduring is your own creation. This is not a lesson you are taught in the West, and sometimes that is a very difficult handicap to work with. You see, as long as you are looking at the cause and thinking it is the effect, you are stymied and there is no solution. So what we are telling you is that if you are suffering, it is your perception and your thinking about the subject that is wrong. The suffering lowers the vibration, and you get worse events coming your way.

At the beginning of this path to the energies of bliss and divine sex, we must make sure you are on the right track to manifesting the kind of energies you need for this journey. Remember what we said? Stop focusing on the solid objects of your world, and focus on the energy you are putting out and the energy you are ingesting. And on those levels, we mean ingesting information, food, company — all of those areas that put something into your mind. This is an important aspect of the world you are creating, and it cannot be too greatly emphasized. The world of suffering comes from judgment of what is, lack of acceptance, and the input of wrong information.

Look at Your Suffering

For example, if you are functioning under the misguided belief that sacrifice is noble, then you will not listen to the guidance system that was given to you, especially if it tells you to do something for yourself. It will seem selfish or evil, or any number of words may come to mind when you think of this thing that you would like to do. And so your suffering will increase. Not only will you not be doing what you want, but you will also feel guilty for even wanting to do so.

Many of you have these endless cycles of pain functioning in your lives, and at times it seems an impossible cycle to stop. Is it the chicken or the egg? You cannot quite see. So what we are proposing is that you first listen to your own desires and pretend that there are no other humans in the world — just you — and you can do what you want. Some of you will be ridiculous and say you would rob all the stores, and this is funny, but really, what would you do if you could do anything? Would you run for president? Join an ashram? What would you do? Now, add some other elements into the mix, and soon you will see where the problem is. It may be when you think of telling your partner; it may be that you think you are too old, or too something. These are the ways to figure out where the blocks lie and where the work is.

What you must know is that you are free to live the life you wish, and if you do not feel free, or if you feel like you are in some kind of prison, then you believe a lie of some kind, and that will add to your suffering.

The human mind and soul has a deep-seated knowledge that comes from Spirit. It is almost a pure love and truth detector. When you are wrong about a subject, the feeling is bad, and this is your soul telling you that your perspective is off from the truth. This is the way to find your path. We suggest systematically looking at the areas of suffering in your life and seeing if you can find the lie that is hidden there. Is it your culture telling you to behave in a way that feels wrong? Is it a relationship that is keeping you locked in old behaviors? There is an answer, and again we are getting you to look at this so that you can raise your vibration to the level you need for the joys of the bliss journey to connect.

For many of you, this will seem an impossible task, yet once this analysis is undertaken and a decision to attempt a breakout is made, the universe will assist you. It wants you to be happy, and it knows you need to be free to love, create, and follow your passion. It is not the universe that is against you, nor is it this mean and dictatorial God so many of you follow. It is the conditioned mind that is the problem. Spirit is free, and many of you are unhappy because you are in self-imposed prisons. But you have been there so long that you stay, even though the door is open.

Start to look at your lives as your own, to do with what you will, and see if there can be some adjustments made, at first in your thinking and in the lens through which you view your life. Who and what are you living for? Is the big house you struggle to pay for what you really want? If it is, that is fine, and all is well. We are talking about the suffering. You all know what the area is, so approach it with love as you approach yourself with love. Do not attack or run, but at first just look and see what can be changed. Even a little change can reap large results over time.

The feelings you have today of sadness and fear are okay, dear one. They remind you of where you were and prod you to take care of your thought. This is the next lesson.

Use Your Thoughts to Find Truth and Clarity

The thoughts that permeate the mind every second of the day are the creative mechanism by which God force manifests in the world. The gift of this power was given to the sons and daughters of God, a gift to create on a never-ending line of ideas and feelings. The creative forces of nature too are created by your thought. Although this seems somewhat grandiose, it is indeed the truth. Bad weather is created by negative beliefs, as are disasters and economic events, for example. The collective unconscious is a powerful method of creation, and the groundswell of believers in the power of mind will turn the tides of negativity that have created a bit of a mess. The mess is fixable, though, so do not fear for your dear planet. She is in a state of healing all the time and will survive the swarm of locusts that are humans.

"The battle for peace" — what an oxymoron that is. Love is guaranteed to win, as the light is the only thing that is real. However, the mind that believes in illusions believes its world is real. The transformation to truth can only be done in little increments; otherwise, the disbelief becomes too large and change stops. The light works with what you believe you know to show you that you don't know, and then you move a little bit closer to the truth, adjusting your thoughts a little, adjusting your beliefs a little.

The transformation to truth would blast you from your physical body, so do not rush the change from sleep to waking; it is done gently for a purpose, and although the impatience is at least good, it does not serve you. In fact, sitting and doing nothing may be the very thing you need to do to connect, so doing what you feel driven to accomplish will stop you rather than help you.

Sit down and read that book that's been calling. The next message you need to hear may well be inside its pages, and until you read it, nothing will move forward. Each step is a step in the right direction, even if you think it is not. You will experience the thing you want — or the thing you don't want. Either way, you will understand yourself more and get clarity on the path before you.

Every Thought Is a Prayer

We are with you again, dear one. We can feel your love for the material shining all around you, and we too are happy that this is being written and that all will be sent out into the world and read by those dear souls who are sick and tired of the minds in which they have been living, without realizing that this is what has been making this world. Yet the work is indeed cut out for them. The beliefs are powerful and deeply entrenched, and they need to be uprooted by a constant vigilance that at first is exhausting. We will write about this now and help them on their way to freedom and love.

There is indeed discipline required to fulfill this dream of love that we are dangling in front of you like a carrot, and this is the help that we are offering. The prayers you recite are important. There will be those of you who do not like this idea, so we wish to point out that you are reciting prayers all day every day: You say, "I am fat," and the universe says yes to that; you say, "I am poor, and nothing ever goes my way," and the universe says yes to that. These prayers are answered, and then you recite them again, even louder and with more force this time, as the manifestation becomes clearer and clearer. So do not say that you will not pray. It is all a prayer. Every thought is a prayer.

We are asking only that you change the prayer to what you truly desire — not the wishes of your mother or your culture, but your wishes, your true desires of the heart that call to you. Some of you have forgotten what these desires are. You have hidden them so deeply under the training and drugs, the food and the bad habits, but they are in there. These are the prayers that will be powerful, as your heart is in them and you will begin to feel the passion. At first it will seem a different language, and as such it will be uncomfortable, and you will stumble over the words. But be vigilant at first and train your mind in the loving way and the forgiving way, and focus on the things you would like to experience.

So often in the West you focus on an object you think will bring you a feeling. We are asking you to focus instead on the feeling you wish for — abundance, peace, joy, love — and let the universe decide on the form that it will arise in. You see, so often the object will not bring you what you want, so then you ask for another object, and it too does not satisfy. This is because you are energetic beings and it is energy that you want, but you do not know it. You have been taught the value is in the object, and this is a factor that confuses you a great deal. You are taught to buy and to attach to the solid in the world, but all of the greatest experiences are just that — experiences. They are not solid at all. Love, dreams, enlightenment — none of these has a price or a physical density. So you are seeking, but you will not find.

This is also why the body suffers so much. You see it as solid and heavy, so it is; but if you start to see it as a ball of energy, sweeping and dreaming and attracting, you will begin to honor it as the sweet and delicate energy that it is, and heavy foods will clearly be the wrong foods to give it. You will see the need for living and happy foods, full of energy. That is how we wish you to see the world — as energy you want to experience. Then you will start to see that your energy is the attractor or the repellent of what you want rather than these objects that seem to hold the secret.

They are not the secret, dear ones. You are the secret, but your education has been wrong, and your goals have been distractions that have kept you from the prize you seek. This is the truth, so that is another homework assignment for you: See yourself and the things you desire as energy, write down the experiences you would like to have, and begin to train your mind and feed your body with these dreams of the future. Stay out of the past and let it go. For many this is the ball and chain that is drowning you as you try to swim in the ocean of life, and unless you let it go, it will take you down, and you will drown in the sadness and resentment that it is made of.

There are many ways we will be able to help you feel your way into the experiences of which we speak, so we will write much and share many things over the next few years of communications. There are times when this will seem a strange and exotic path. Some of the friends and family you have will frown and mumble that it makes no sense. They will try to convince you that the world is bad and that they are good and have nothing to do with its creation, but there is a logic in this, and there are many of you who know this to be true. You feel it in your heart, and those of you in that state, we are talking to you, and we ask you to have faith and follow the path to love. You are going to not only transform your world but the minds and hearts of all.

You see, as you raise your vibration, that light affects all around you, and on some levels that are beyond your comprehension at the moment. You see, the universe and the energetic realms are all connected, and a change in one mind affects the whole. You are not selfish in this behavior. You do it for all, and that is what is happening. There are no separate interests, despite what you have been told, and every feeling and thought you have affects the world. This is what a miracle is: the transformation of one mind, one thought at a time, into the realms of love. Miracles do and will happen as you transform your thoughts to light, little by little, bit by bit. Even one hateful thought transformed is a miracle; do not discount the work you will be doing. You will not get the kudos you deserve from those you know, but we are cheering you on, and the world of energy, spirit, and love is cheering on the sidelines of this game you call life.

It is not as you have been taught, so read and reread this information until it is true in all the cells of your ever-transforming body and mind. Then you will understand. The path is an easy one, because you will know the truth of your own power, and you will wield it with a gentle hand to all those you meet and who need your help on their journey.

It is a disease we wish to spread, and it is the cure for all the ills of the world. This is a grand plan, is it not? We ask you to join us on this journey to heal the world, and every step is an important one. You are so important in this plan, and we ask you to see that this is indeed so — that your soul is a powerful being of light and love. We are challenging you to act accordingly, and the true strengths and talents that are yours will begin to shine and your life will be changed.

CHAPTER ELEVEN

The Channel

Tina was picked for many reasons, and we have decided to tell you, the readers, some of the rationale for her exceptional services being picked. We have had a long and varied experience with Tina in many lives. We, or aspects of us, have studied together, and this is one of those reasons — the long-standing relationship of our various aspects as spiritual students through the ages. We have seen many aspects of each other and are continuing to develop as friends and teacher and student. Different aspects are explored in each incarnation — sometimes the teacher, sometimes the student — but indeed we are friends of long standing on this journey through life and time. That is the main reason we are working with Tina, but there are other contributing factors that you will find interesting.

In the past, Tina had some bad experiences, as she forgot to remember her power and her connection to Source as young woman. The cultural conditioning overrode her knowledge of self, and as the memories of past existence are usually extinguished at birth, there was an unfortunate forgetting of who she really is. This forgetting, the bad social conditioning, and Tina's intensely focused and creative mind seemed a bad combination. The focus that she now gives to our work, and her artwork, she had focused on the misteachings around the body, so they created a vast negative-energy field that overwhelmed her.

There was a moment when we thought she would not survive, but as it turned out, an intervention occurred and her life was saved. At that moment, the tide turned, and the life that almost ended awoke to a better future. There were still many lessons to unlearn, but something began to shift, and the spiritual entered her life. Although drastic events propelled by her conditioning led to sexual trauma — and emotional trauma, as demonstrated in her first marriage — as the years went by, the experiences slowly got better. But at the age of forty-one, there came an awakening and a realization that she had to do something, and that was Ananda — us — whispering in her ear that it was now not only time for freedom and self-realization, but the job she had agreed to do in this lifetime was now approaching.

This was all invisible to her at the time, yet she was drawn, as if by an invisible cord, to the world of spiritual study and free expression of self. This seemed at times radical, and it was so for many who watched her from the outside. But that is one of our points, is it not? No one can understand your path but you, and this is an important issue to raise for consideration. Our dear Tina had some great adventures on the way to our reunion, and we are excited for her to share her story with you at some point.

But all along the way she was dogged by this question: But what about sex? The way it was for her in this culture, with the sometimes awful history she had had, it made no sense, so she often asked that question — "but what about sex?" There was no mention of it in the texts she so loved, and the mentions made elsewhere seemed poor explanations. She knew the power of sex and indeed had felt both the negative and the positive aspects, yet no one had an answer for her question. What she did not know, but now obviously is finding out, is that was her life's work speaking to her. It was in whispers a lot of the time but took on a loud and piercing voice in others.

Tina had many experiences that helped clarify her question, and then the true nature of her path started to become clear. She practiced the acts of forgiveness with real clarity and focus for many years, constantly going deeper and deeper into them because she felt lighter and freer and better with every act that was accomplished. And with every act of internal analysis and forgiveness, her desire for love became stronger and stronger. Eventually, as the last acts of forgiveness manifested into visions and answers to the questions that had dogged her for her whole life, the clarity that she wanted to teach spiritual healing arose as a phoenix from the ashes.

Yet that question was still there: How does sex fall into this life? She was not interested in being a monk in an ashram, and finally, as the last ego hatreds fell away, a strong and powerful sexual energy awoke in her body and mind. That was our call to action.

This has been a lifetime's work, and indeed involved a lot of pain and suffering, but this is how it works in the realms of spirit. An agreement is made, and then you forget what it was, but it shows up in the questions you ask and the very difficulties you encounter. So as you look at our dear one writing and speaking for us, know that there were many hard years of forgetfulness, and many more hard years of prayer and forgiveness, that led to this miracle.

You each have your own journeys and your own miracles to achieve, so yours will look different. Yet this too could be your path. The channels to the bliss energies and spirit are opened by a deep faith and action that follows on the heels of that faith. So if you are inspired, and if you feel drawn into the world of spirit, go ahead and keep as clear as you can. Indeed, the years dragged by at some points for our dear one as the call of food and alcohol dulled her senses and fed the ego.

So learn from her mistakes, and clarify your body and mind so that you can hear the words we speak gently into your ears. That is the story, although there are past chapters that are of great interest, and we will share those in the future. But for now, that is her story from our point of view, and she will tell it from her standpoint.

We are Ananda, always in love and deep respect for all on Earth who are looking for the way home. It is a long path at times, and often dark, but there are lights now, and we are happy to be one of them, as is our dear one, Tina, who is at our side and is our dear friend and companion through the ages.

II

A Transformed
View of Sex and
Sexual Energy

CHAPTER TWELVE

Faith and Sex?

We are now speaking of the interest in the meaning of faith and the role it plays in sexual relationships. The faith you have placed in things that have not deserved your faith is a subject that we must approach again at this time, for this act of loving with an open heart is indeed one of the biggest acts of faith you will ever undertake. Faith in bodies is the reason you have been so fearful. Faith in judgment is the reason you have been so mean and afraid. Faith in the voices of others is why you have not developed your own confidence. We wish for you to look at what it is you have placed your faith in and change that.

Put your faith in the force that holds the universe together. Face the fact that this is indeed a powerful force. Place your faith in the force that grows a baby in the belly of its mother. Do not place your faith anymore in the voice of hatred and judgment from the past, nor in a church that does not really promote love but pretends to speak the words while tolerance and generosity are lacking in their actions.

Faith is what will allow you to walk across the bridge to your lover. Trust in the new and comfortable arms of the one you have carefully chosen to be your partner. We are here to say that a partner is not needed to reach these heights; indeed, it can be a solitary journey if you choose. We are not saying that one or the other is more important; however, the faith and trust that it takes to share this journey are harder to cultivate alone, and they will push you to a level of love, trust, and forgiveness that is harder to reach in the solitary state.

Cultivate a mind of love and forgiveness, and when the old voices call, ask them whether they are love or fear, and it will be clear. Do not listen to the fears; they will keep you small and closed. The energy of God's love is not small and closed, so it cannot easily travel in those channels. You will have trouble feeling it and hearing it. Pursue the path of love and openness. Give it the faith that you have been misplacing in your body, in others, and in fear, and a new landscape will open up to you as you venture forth.

The asking of this is indeed tough for many. The culture in which you live sees surrender as a failure, but in fact it can be the line in the sand that defines the point in your life where all changed for the better. Surrender to the force of angels — not the force of ants. There is a place for all things, but this journey to love requires faith that outweighs all others.

Now, there are more practical lessons for the followers to whom we speak. The joy of sexual union can be fearful for some, but those of you who are fearless may still have some lessons to learn in gentleness and openness. The voice you use with your lover needs to be gentle, and consideration must be there for the trust that opens the heart to develop. Some are harsh and offhanded with sex; it comes and goes easily. These are the ones who may think they are already masters, yet their hearts are still closed. The body alone participates in the journey, and that is a narrow path that does not allow for this deep joy and pleasure the heart gives as it opens like a beautiful flower. Buds are pretty too, but their potential colors are the beauty you see.

So do become a gentle and considerate partner, calling, if you can, throughout the day — once, perhaps— to tell your partner what you feel and how you are looking forward to seeing him or her later. These are the small gestures that encourage the closeness of sexual union of which we speak.

We are seeing such busyness in your lives at the moment. To touch base, so to speak, will go far in learning the way to your lover's heart. We are sure this seems silly and romantic for some, but it is a gentle seduction that we are advocating for the cultivation of a connected energy that facilitates the opening of the flower later on in the day. This is what you wish. Do it and enjoy the results that will show up later on in bed.

CHAPTER THIRTEEN

The Internal Landscape

The body is such a distraction and of such immense value to the ego that it is always taking the focus, and what we are attempting to teach is that the energy must always be the focus. Always eat and think for the best and clearest energy, and then the connection to Source and pathways to the divine will open.

Indeed, there are many layers to this process, and again we must insist that all who are following us are gentle and allow the relinquishment of objects, ideas, and resentments in a gentle way. Ripping off the bandage will reopen the wound, and it will not help. Carefully, oh so carefully, unwrap the bandage, wetting it if necessary and taking a little break here and there. But be kind to yourselves; you are only lost because you have been given the wrong information. It is not that you are stupid, weak, or even confused. You have just been focused on the wrong reality.

You see, it is the reality of energy that is the real reality. This is where the solid reality you so believe in comes from — inside your beliefs, feelings, and passions. And as so many of you do not know what is going on in there, no wonder there is a bit of a mess and a lot of confusion. For example, sickness is the mind projecting into the body beliefs about self-hatred, love, fears — whatever you believe — so if you are sick, you need to go inside and look at what is going on in there.

We are not suggesting guilt, oh no — this is the ego's playground. It loves guilt as much as it loves war. No, we are asking you to go inside and look at resentments, dislikes, and hatreds, areas where you easily feel limitation. If you are on this plane, then they are there, and we are here to help you unearth them and gently lay them aside so that you can create the blissful existence you truly want and of which we speak.

There are no shortcuts, but immediately the path will feel better than having no guidance and this feeling of disillusionment or blatant fear so many of you have. We are always seeking to inform, to heal, and to clear that which does not serve you. All will not wish to make the changes we suggest, but what we would like is for you to make the changes you are willing to, then stop for a while and integrate those into your world, and then see if they help. If they do, you may become willing to shift again in a little while. We use our dear Tina as an example: It took a strong wake-up call — a poisoning incident — and three years of going back and forth for her to really change her eating habits, and it was that shift that was part of our arriving in her life.

So you do not know what your future holds when the barriers to love are removed, and all bad eating habits and abuses of the body are indeed a lack of love for your self and the vehicle you are driving. You need a healthy vehicle to embrace a life that is full of passion. There is a path to incredible health. It is a bit of a trip, but there are many rest areas and pleasant stops to look at along the way, as you would on a hike up a mountain with a fabulous view. Take it slowly, if you must, but do go. You will love the view and see vistas you never imagined you would.

CHAPTER FOURTEEN

Gentleness and Appreciation as a Path to Happiness

We are counseling on the appreciation of the smallest of joys as a path to sublime realization and the feelings of bliss we wish to cultivate. The smallest joy can be magnified in the mind of God through you. The special bond of the human and the Creator is embellished by the joy of thanks and true vision of an open mind, willing to entertain the unknown. The small mind wishes to have answers, and the larger mind of the God you are wishes to experience only the special and unique experiences of this world. Freed from limitation, the mind will blossom into the great creator it is and will manufacture more experience through which it can experience itself and the world of its own thinking.

The world is not as you see it. It is an energetic soup of ideas and dreams and nightmares; it just depends where you focus your attention. The dreams grow and change as the experience is enjoyed, and the nightmares will disappear in the truth of your being. The time is ripe for the awakening of many minds to the truth that this is a place of divine intervention. At any moment, God will speak through you and to you. All you have to be is wiling to hear and willing to do the next thing presented to you. We are sure this seems simplistic, but all events are for your well-being, and the resistance you feel to some of them delays the waking process. The opportunity will come again until you accept the challenge presented. We care not about the time involved, but you do care. The trying times you complain about are indeed your choice, and if you would dive into the experience and ask to be shown the lesson of the trial, the changes would come and the awareness would grow.

The avoidance is the problem. The issue is not actually the issue; it is a reflection of your self brought to you to see. The issue is a gift, mirroring the darkness within that needs to shift for joy to be the constant in your life. When the acceptance happens time after time, eventually the plate is cleared and the joy of the real world will dawn on your mind, gifted from the divine to the cleansed minds of the children of God.

The dreams you have are your curses. Dreams of wealth and sex do not reflect the divine purpose of true joy and bliss but the pleasures of bodies striving for dominance in a scheme devised by the ego and the mechanism of the physical organism it creates. The ego is not an evil thing, but it is a dangerous mentor at times and will kill, given a chance at superiority in the world. The wars you see and drugs you take are the ego's playground. It loves the battle and enjoys the fight. This is why you enjoy so much gossip and attacking thought — because that is the language of the ego. Until you separate yourself from its influence, it will wreak havoc on your world and in your mind, convincing you that its ways are best and keeping you from the real peace and beauty of an awakened existence.

So we are on a path to disempower the ego and to empower your faith in the spirit that guides you to higher planes of thought, deed, sex, and love — the kind of love that will create a loving society that cares and caresses, the kinds of love and desire that do not hurt but heal and massage the body and soul into a new realm of joy. In the world of God and the angels, humans sweetly greet each other every day, eager for the mental joys and adventures of a freed mind. We are on a path to a mind able to embrace itself and others with the energy of God, an energy of a being so at home in its skin. Joy is the way, and love is its language.

This is the path we will teach, and the truth of the matter is it is what you are all striving for on your shopping trips and your big purchases. The feelings of bliss and love are the carrot advertisers use to get you to buy these ideas. Why not have the real thing? It is free and easy, after a fashion, although it does take a little patience and work to achieve the goals of which we speak. Even when you have all the clothes and the house you want, you will still not be satisfied, and you will eventually come to this path. So why not come now and save a lot of work and pain in the meantime? The access is universal and unlimited, and the rewards are untold and generous — with no bill to pay at the end of the month. The bliss will arrive on time into your heart, postage paid with a kiss from God and a stamp of love.

✳ ✳ ✳

During this period of dictation I was often outside in the summer sun, taking in the environment while in an extremely awakened and love-infused state. Ananda was very present with me as I walked after a powerful energy session.

We are here with you again, dear one. Today is a productive day, is it not? You are open to us and in love with us today. We can feel the energy as you walk and pray and enjoy the day. We are sure the feelings of our being with you are a new and expressive experience for you; they are for us too. We are very happy to be having this earthbound experience with you, and the thoughts are flying fast and furious on our side.

We are aware of the questions you have about the book and how it will be published. The job is ours, and we are good at it. We have done it before and will succeed at planting the seeds of acceptance for this manuscript too. Right now we are asking you to focus on its production and perfection, and we will tell you when and how to publish it and with whom. We are excited to see our Facebook page up and running, and we will help with ideas for mixing up that pot. We are a good marketing team, and the books will sell well. There will be many about our teachings and the subjects people are interested in.

Gently Dismissing the Ego

We will talk now about harmlessness and gentleness on the path to the blissful states we are in search of on this journey to bliss, divine sex, and love. The start is in the mind, and all thoughts must become those of love and not attack. This is such a basic truth that the ego dismisses it and says it is not important. As you are seeing, all the elements of this path construct a solid and firm base on which to build your practice inside the mind. The ego runs riot, punching and shoving, knocking over furniture — the equivalent of a bully in its own environment. It is hateful and mean. If it does not attack others, it will attack you, and if it is not attacking you now, it will attack you in the past and make you guilty.

It is this inherently violent ego mind that is responsible for all conflict, internally and externally, on your planet. To achieve the calm and loving state we need you to achieve for our goals of blissful union with the divine, you must exhibit the love that you are consistently with yourself and others. The fight will go out of you as you follow the path of forgiveness, as this is the quickest way to defuse the ego. The principle is this: The ego believes in war, and forgiveness is the opposite of war; so if you enforce this belief and manifest it in your actions every day, and eventually every minute of every day, the ego will dissipate, as it is getting no energy from your mind.

You must remember your mind is the ego's source of energy, and the feeling that you are not able to be responsible for this crazy monster in your head is indeed an illusion. You are responsible, and you feed it many times a day with the thoughts that you have. The great benefit of this discipline, however, is that you will feel better and calmer, more loving and open. The defenses you have erected to protect you from the cruel outside world are not working because the enemy is within. It disguises itself with words about keeping you safe and how terrible everyone else is. It assures you it has your best interest at heart, yet that is the same lie behind the wars that are currently going on.

The ego has a deep-seated agenda that it will not tell you about. It wants to keep you weak and disempowered, because then it has the power that you have willingly handed over. It is time to gently take that power back through the least violent act on Earth: the act of forgiveness. This causes the energies to settle, the anger to dissipate, and the ego to weaken. This is a miracle to feel inside your mind. The running and controlling can stop, and the attacks, gossip, and judgments will subside. The energy that is freed up as your mind comes to rest is some of the energy that Spirit will use for the awakening process of the bliss pathways. There is so much energy and focus being wasted on the wars that the ego creates, small and large, that there is an energy shortage for you, the thinker.

This is an interesting fact, is it not? You cannot imagine the energy you will have as the ego quiets and you claim your true power back from the unwelcome visitor that has been in charge. Your home will become your own, and you can clean up the mess the ego has made and create the loving, peaceful, and calm residence you all wish for. There will be a chance for love to enter. It cannot come in when the bully is in charge.

It is a gentle energy that is not interested in war, so it will appear to be gone while the battles continue. Yet when the fighting stops, you will see it sitting quietly on your doorstep, waiting patiently to come in and help you. The loving essence that it is never judges you for being mistaken, frightened, or confused; it simply waits quietly until you are ready to kick the bully out and invite it in.

This is what we wish you to do: Go inside and see where there are resentments. For some, this is a scary process. The ego will counsel you otherwise, as if it knows you are trying to kill it, but what you are really doing is releasing it — and not in a violent way. So think and see the one for whom you have unforgiveness, and at first simply put a white light around them. You do not need to forgive — just see them and put a light around them. This will suffice at first, and we will give more forgiveness instructions at a later date. But whenever the person's voice or face or your hatred for them arises in your mind, in whatever way, do not engage it. Put a white light around the images and stories that are there — every time. This will change the energy profoundly, and deep changes in your mind will occur, freeing you from the torment of hatred, confusion, fear, and dislike. This is a technique that slips past the ego's defenses. It is so passive that the ego does not understand it and lets it go. So practice this, dear ones, with all the negatives in your mind, and relief will begin to be felt.

Happiness Is Gentle Acceptance

We are now going to talk about the thing called happiness, this elusive subject that all try to hang their hat on but can't quite find. Happiness is really the state of being we would call peace or acceptance. Happiness rises naturally when the mind is not interfering with it. The ego is so loud, and the discursive mind so chatty and low in vibration, that the experience of peace — which is always present — is hidden. You believe it is not there. It's silly, really. You all think that the car or the house or the body will bring it, but actually, quieting the mind is the only thing you need to do to feel happy. The world is actually a really nice place to be, most of the time. Simple pleasures like a nice meal, good conversation, shared ideas, sunshine — all of this — can make happiness stream across the clear mind, but they cannot penetrate the dark clouds that fill the mind with fear and judgment. So the sadness or lack of happiness is also blamed on the person or thing you hate when, in fact, you all do it to yourselves.

The simplicity of this concept is definitely lost on the mind full of ego. It wants such complicated answers to enlightenment, but there are none. All of the practices ever taught by masters were to bring about a state of peace, and this is what you are all searching for — but in all the wrong places. As the saying goes, put it inside, they will never think to look there. This is the design of the ego, and this is also the trick to getting it. You must do the opposite of what the ego wants to access the very deep areas the sexual energies flow along — not the superficial energies of the "quickie," but the deep and sensual energies of the full-body orgasm and permanent bliss of which we write. The energies need clear channels along which to flow, so all blocks to their path are to be cleared. Indeed, the idea of healing requires the clearing of these blocks.

This is what we are doing to you in our sessions, dear one. The old pathways still exist like ruts in a road. They have to be removed. It is like a grader going over the old ruts that have become rigid and will not blow away in a gentle wind; the path must be scraped down quite vigorously to be clear again. The old stories were long and told many times, and the new stories are like little babies that need to be nurtured and helped along the way to maturity. The sessions we are giving you are like the grater replacing the surface of the energetic body and resurfacing the pathways so that they are clear of all debris. We will continue this for some time and instruct you in a method of doing this for others at some point in the future, although it is not yet the time. You are still our little guinea pig, so to speak.

CHAPTER FIFTEEN

Prayer

The clarity of a message is as clear as the channel it comes through, and that is the secret of the path we offer, as it is the pathway to clarity, fearlessness, and love. We are sure the effort you are having to put in now is a bit overwhelming, but we assure you it will be of great benefit to the world and all the souls who are suffering at the hands of their minds, so to speak.

The first step is asking — whoever or whatever you feel comfortable with. Spirit is not offended when you use the words you choose. Even anger is welcomed in the beginning, as a lot of you are angry at the Church, at a lover who hurt you, or at a parent who abused you in some way. Anger is not warranted, but it is the first step on the path to healing for many, and the more quickly they go through this phase the better, as it is a difficult one to endure. For many, the thought of all that anger coming out is enough to stop them dead in their tracks, but it is a catalyst to the development of peace and acceptance. It is in unexpressed anger that the torment lies, and the barrier to love is contaminated with the thoughts of hatred and judgment. We are sure you are in agreement with this.

The truth will be seen as a foreign language at first, not understood or believed, as it is so far from people's experiences and current beliefs. The energy of God as expressed in sexual activity can indeed be contaminated by the lower mind and vibrations, making it an event of attack rather than bliss for many. This is the forgiveness you must encounter — letting go of unpleasant past experiences with sex, and, as if a small child, redeveloping the relationship with the body and experiences with that body. We must reteach that the simple act of touching yourself with love will heal the bigger picture. A simple hug will help heal the deep sexual fears that so many are experiencing. The path to healing will be supported by Spirit as soon as it is spoken and asked for with sincerity. The opening of the mind is the most important event in the whole process, because once it is started, the process will continue at a pace you can handle. As long as you keep asking for Spirit's help, it will be there, and the perfect circumstances, people, and things will arrive for their enlightenment.

We are not proposing a mass event here, but each person will arrive at his or her goal in an individual way, at an individual pace fitting to his or her experience. The deeper the hurt, the longer the ladder out of the pit. You were in a deep pit, and now you are peeking over the rim of the hole you were in, blinking in the light of love and God, as will all those who read this and choose to heal the wounds that keep them from their divine right to pleasure, joy, and bliss.

God is in the smallest of details — the flowers on the side of the path, the waves in the ocean, and the feathers of a bird. You are not exempt from God's energy and presence, and all you have to do to enhance God's presence in your life is begin to slow down, listen, and ask and pray for guidance and help. Some of you balk at asking, as if you are asking a God outside of you for help, but we are sure you understand that your understanding of the universe is quite distorted at times, and the narrow view of the world your small mind makes up are stories as told to children — simple tales that make sense of what, at times, is a senseless situation.

We are here to tell you it is a complex system that is beyond your understanding until you pass on to other dimensions and your view expands. It is indeed an act of faith to trust in us and believe what we are telling you. That is all right. We are not offended in any way and are timelessly patient in offering our help to all of you who wish you could be different and that your lives were more joyful. We see the attachment you have to what does not work, and that is the hardest bond to break — a belief in something that is not true. It is as if you have to let go of your entire world to get a new one, and in some ways this is the truth. You must let go of thoughts and beliefs that do not serve you before new ones can be planted like baby seeds in your mind. Then those seeds must be cared for and watered if they are to grow and become strong convictions eventually accepted as truth you no longer doubt. We ask you to just observe the areas where there is the most stress and difficulty and offer up your free will for guidance in that area. The stress will immediately lessen when you accept that you can be helped and that help is at hand. The rules are strict: We cannot help unless we are asked and asked often.

The morning is a good time to do this, as you awaken. Offer up your day to the pursuit of divine love, and the day will change. We guarantee it. Events will begin to shift to bring to you the best for you. As long as you see yourself as your creator, with the ego in charge, the road will be rough and probably will become rougher as you go along it. This is because the ego is not divine; it has a different goal: physical survival, not transcendence. Ego is the voice of fear and judgment in your mind, and it is not until it is quieted through the changes we have suggested that the quieter yet persistent voice of God will be heard and listened to.

We use the word "God" here and know that for many it is not a happy one. We are asking those of you who have this feeling about the word to go into that anger and resentment, for until you can hear that word and feel no reaction, there will be a barrier to the communication we can undertake. The word is not wrong, but your association with it is.

A word is indeed harmless. The reaction you have to it is a map into your mind, showing you where you need to change a view or a belief. All things should be viewed with love, and if there are words or people who create a problem and reaction, they are indeed your teachers. Writing and praying for transformation around a subject will release any fear and resentment around it. Writing and praying will allow for forgiveness of that thing, freeing up energy and allowing more love to flow through the channels of your body.

The human body is an electrical device, and interference causes disruptions in its functioning. Lower vibrations are interference, such as hatred, fear, resentment, and judgment. The electrical capacity of the human body is enormous when it is given a chance to express itself, although for most of you it would be a scary event if you felt the full energy that can come through and be generated by your mind and heart. So the journey will seem a little slow, but that is so you will not run screaming from the room, so to speak. The force of the energies is awesome indeed, and again we ask for a small amount of patience in accepting the currents you are asking for. Those of you further along the path will get a very quick response to your request for sexual healing, and that is so you will become practitioners and teachers sooner rather than later. The world needs this so much right now.

CHAPTER SIXTEEN

Love versus Sacrifice

The idea of sacrifice arises perfectly at this time, and the devastating idea of the nobleness of sacrifice has been perpetrated by the powers that be to keep people disempowered. If you believe in sacrifice, you will not empower yourself and will, in fact, see it as a sin to be avoided. This is in keeping with the Church's ideas of powerless sheep, guided to the slaughter by leaders who have their own self-interests at heart.

This is indeed a case of the fox guarding the hen house, especially the story of the sacrifice of God's only son as the tenet that drives the Church. This is a sacrifice of fear, demanding that you fear a God who may turn on you at any moment. If he killed his son, then surely he will kill you. This is all in your subconscious mind when it comes to the Church and Christ, and we are speaking this now so that it rises out of the unconscious mind and into the conscious one, so that it can be dispelled and replaced with the "no sacrifice is required" clause.

This is your struggle, dear one, with the choices you made around your family and the fact that you chose your own mental health over the traditions of the culture. You would indeed have handicapped them even more if you had sacrificed yourself, but as it stands, you feel guilty still, because of the independent move you made.

This is what an unconscious belief will do. It will nip at your heels all your life, making you guilty or sad, and you will not know why or how to change it. So when you feel guilty, go inside and unearth the belief that is hanging on to your ankle so strongly, and shake it off, like a bad dog. The truth is, you are free beings, and the most important thing is to remain free. This does not mean that you should not have relationships or families, but it does mean that you need to be yourself before you have them so that whoever is connecting with you knows the truth of who you are and what you need to be happy and be yourself. So many of you marry or have children before you even know who you are, and then you have to sacrifice to keep the status quo. In the end, families fall apart not because of freedom, but because of sacrifice based on ignorance. Eventually the soul screams out for its freedom, and it will take it, one way or another.

So do take the time to get to know yourself, and then make your alliances with others. We are so sad when we see sadness in the units that should be the happiest places of your lives, yet the image of the tired and disillusioned parent or lover is all too present as we look at your planet. Driven by social conditioning and cultural taboos, people are driven to the end of their patience until they either die of sadness or run for the hills.

Let us start a new tradition of loving yourself first before picking a partner who also loves him- or herself and making babies. This will change the world and create a stable family unit that is far from selfish, which is what a lot of you are thinking. It will provide the solid family unit that little ones love and will end the mess of divorce you now swim in.

The Culture of Sacrifice

You see, you have been taught to sacrifice by the Church and through the image of the crucified body of the suffering Christ that permeates your culture. Even if you do not go to church or no longer believe in these tales of torture, there is a deeply ingrained belief in the value of sacrifice in your culture. You hear it many times, particularly about love, which is our subject, so we will delve into this aspect of divine love and sexual connection so that we can excavate the truth of love's definition and characteristics.

So you will not get confused, we will clarify what sacrifice is. Simply put, it is giving up something you want so that someone else can have what he or she wants instead. Simple enough, is it not? This is the root cause of so much pain and sadness in your culture, yet you do not see it because you do not understand how the world is manifested, and you do not understand that the culture of sacrifice has been perpetrated intentionally to keep you disconnected from your own power and your ability to tap into the endless source that is your connection to God.

What would you do if you wanted to keep a population disempowered and you knew their power was their connection to their own desires and passions? You would find a teaching that spoke of disconnection being virtuous and passion being evil. Is this beginning to sound familiar to any of you? Yes, the basic doctrines of the early Church were developed by those who did in fact know the truth — that your connection to your own creative power came from a peaceful mind and heart listening to inner guidance. This is what Christ taught, so do not let our judgments of the Church get mixed up with those teachings of the most wise one who has walked the face of the planet.

Christ's teachings were the truth. The knowledge you need is within what he taught, not in the traditions and hierarchy of the conventional church. He taught that the peace of mind achieved through forgiveness and nonjudgment would bring you to the kingdom of heaven, which was within. He did not suggest you seek outside of yourself in structures and dogmas that emphasized your sinfulness, but he encouraged you to value yourself and others equally, seeking that which was kind and good. The idea of sacrifice was not his at all. He suggested a life of internal work, forgiveness of all, and generosity of spirit that guaranteed a wealth of a different sort.

Love Is Not Sacrifice

Let us now talk about sacrifice and the reasons you do it. If it is to gain approval from a person or thing you feel is important to you, then you are resentful of the feelings of not being appreciated. You sacrifice because of some misteaching that this is noble. When you do something for the love of it, that is not a sacrifice at all, and this is how all motivations should be chosen and interpreted for the betterment of the self. This is the path to the happiness that allows you to thrive and help others, if that is what you choose to do.

We are saying that it is all based on your own wishes. That is God's will for you — that you get all you wish to experience here, as this is your path of learning. The feelings that you have to do what you love to be free are the voice of God inside you, not those of the Devil leading you astray and causing problems. Most abuse is the thwarting of someone's freedom, often in God's name. The small children put down and called dirty for touching their bodies in innocent exploration are the ones who are correct, finding pleasure in the body and loving themselves. The adults, lost to the realms of passion, are the lost ones, driving the wheels of pain that turn on this planet.

We ask all who read this to take a moment to go inside, right now. Ask yourself, "What would I do if I were free?" Ask how you can begin to walk that path to your desire. This is the way to healing, to tap into the powers of the divine that are yours for the taking, but there are ways and means to get there. We are teaching those through this writing, and we ask for the cooperation of those interested in healing themselves and the world. This is the path inside — loving freedom. All contribute to the beings who are awakened humans, loving, helping, and joyfully creating whatever they want in their lives.

Most of the expressions humans see aren't at all loving. In fact, the restrictions one lover places on another show fear, not love. The freedom you give another is showing love. This is one of the biggest turnarounds that people will have to make in their definitions of the words we use.

To isolate oneself in a relationship is not love. You are all free, and that must remain so, even when you are deeply involved with anther human. Please let one another explore life and activities apart for part of the day, and then come together in joy to share the new experiences and new friends that have been made. The fear around this comes from the idea of love as possession rather than expression. We clearly see this fear when you see your lover off doing something with someone else. The joy that lover experiences is a good thing, so please let the fear go and think about what would bring you the same joy.

Some things you will do together, others apart. We all feel the wall that individuals put up to keep their freedom, but in the end those walls deny the love that you want. This is a very confusing thing for humans, and this is the toughest lesson. Keep your heart open and your freedom flowing, and allow that same courtesy to your beloveds so they will freely rush home to you and tell you of feelings and new desires the day formed in them. This is the juice of life of which we speak — the freedom-granting love energy that God has for you, that desires all you desire with joy and freedom.

The past will make you fearful, and the future will make you afraid too, so stay in the present and enjoy each other's ebb and flow. And know that all goes one way or the other in the end. Tightly gripping so you don't lose guarantees the loss, and it makes the time in between less than joyful. The art of love starts out in the daytime, in the words and gestures you spread around with all those you know. If you reap rewards every minute of the day from the people who love having you around because you are loving, then you are not needy; your lover will feel overwhelmed by the amount you have to offer and not be afraid, and so will love you in return. Give love all day, and you will be guaranteed to receive love all night.

Sacrifice and Relationships

Say you are in a relationship and you feel you should give your partner what he or she wants, against your inner judgment. We advise at this point that to do nothing would be wise. Allow a change to happen in your energy before you make a decision. Perhaps there is a reason your partner wants what you do not, and you have not yet understood that. So ask your beloved — talk about this issue and find out what exactly your partner wishes from the request. Underneath this superficial request you do not agree with may be a legitimate need that you *do* support, and perhaps there is a way for you to help your partner to get that which he or she needs without sacrificing your own desires. This is generally the case. Everyone wants something to satisfy a need they believe will bring them closer to happiness. So convince your partner that discussing the problem from this basis of honesty and seeking a mutually beneficial solution is the best way to keep the love and passion alive.

Passion dies in the mire of sacrifice, and love dies through resentments that fester and grow under the surface of the best intentions. Your soul will get what it wants, one way or the other, and if you are not paying attention it will go from a whisper to a shout, and from a shout to a scream. So listen to your heart, and pay attention when your belly tells you that no, this is not what you want. It may be a small thing, and you may feel it is too petty to insist on, but if you feel it is not right for you, the other person must come to see your reasoning, and you must have the courage of your convictions and speak your truth with kindness, understanding, and love.

You all want the same things: happiness, peace, love, abundance, and health. Not one of you wants something else; you have all just been taught many incorrect ways to get what you want. That is why we are here — to help clarify the "how" of getting to that elevated state of happiness and bliss about which we keep speaking.

There are many misconceptions in the minds of modern Westerners in regard to relationships, and we will discuss a few here. You see, before we can truly teach you the path to connection with divine bliss, we must point out the pitfalls you will trip over along the way so that you can prepare yourself. Many of the things you believe about love and relationships are way off base, and this is why they keep on falling apart in vitriolic divorces, causing such pain and disillusionment that you do not even want to try again. This game of love has become such a painful arena for you all. If it is pain, it is not love, and this is what we wish you to truly comprehend.

If you look back on your relationships and it breaks your heart, then it was not love that drove you, and it is not love that drives you now in the sad recriminations and regrets. Love never judges, and it never regrets; it is only ever loving, giving, and present. All of the other feelings associated with love in your minds do not have anything to do with love at all, not in the least. These are the ego's desires. The desire for punishment, the desire for revenge — these have nothing to do with love, and it is very important that you begin to tell the true story of love, knowing what you know now from what you have read here.

You began with the light of love in your eyes, but the ego took over through your own ignorance. The ego is the one that destroyed what was so hopeful, and the ego will warn you against going into that fray one more time. But if you follow our prescription and come to a true understanding of what the ego feeds on and what it needs to thrive, you will indeed starve it of its favorite food, and you will allow love to flow in your life and into your heart as it wishes to do.

You think of love as elusive, but it pervades everything. Even the hearts of the darkest of you will open to the energy of love through the act of forgiveness. Is this not what you truly wish, to feel the open-hearted sensations of a willing mind and heart that only wants to connect and understand? It is, and we are here to assist you in the clearing of your vision from the pathways of confusion that you have been taught. The love principles that pervade your culture are fictitious and must be disempowered for real love to stand a chance.

CHAPTER SEVENTEEN

Focusing on Yourself

The self wishes to express all the time, and the constraints of that expression are what causes suffering. The joy one feels at sharing a great conversation is the mind's greatest joy. The free exchange of information is empowering and expressive of the inner nature of the speaker. These are the joys for you that are priceless and are important for the vision and realization that freedom is the door that opens the way to enlightenment.

The ego wants control and knowing; the spirit needs exactly the opposite. Unexpected events delight the spirit. Openness and freedom are its food for thought. It will guide you to the freedom you need and love, even though ego will rail at the future it cannot control. This is the battle that most face at the beginning of their journeys. The ego, which has ruled over the mind and life, does not understand this new teaching to let go and be free. That is its idea of hell, and it will counsel you otherwise. "Hold on," it will say, "do not follow this insane teaching." Yet there will be a part of you that recognizes the truth in these words, a part of you that knows you are not living the life you could be. There is some inkling in you that you are meant for greater things — more love, creating art, writing a book — yet the circumstances of your life and the thoughts in your head argue for a side that is not totally yours. Your wish is to do what you love. The sound of the human heart breaking, of the human heart not fulfilled, is the saddest sound in the universe. Your human heart is sad and alone in its misdirected belief in sacrifice and being "less than" so that no one is upset with you.

Dear one, you feel this as you spread this message around. What your family or other people will think matters not. The only question is, is this what you wish? And if it is, the questions are unnecessary. You are doing what you are meant to do and what you wish to do.

Here is your real need: to seek the purpose of your life. It is written inside in the language of feeling and desire, and it is what will never lead you astray. Although those around you may rub their heads in confusion when you first try to follow this map. They will survive and perhaps learn to follow their own internal guidance. In fact, your purpose is to live the life you choose and inspire that very passionate way in others. They will indeed look at you and ask how you did this thing that they find so very hard to do. You will have to face your fears, give up your grievances, and follow your heart, all of which you are counseled not to do. Do these things you must, and the reward will be beyond your dreams — if a little scary at first.

Expressing Feelings

We have mentioned before that the feeling body, the emotional body, is the clue to many of life's deepest secrets. The lies propagated about this element of your experience, particularly in the Western world, include this idea that feelings are scary and messy and wrong somehow. There are other cultures that express feelings quite well, but we are not talking to them. We are talking to the serious and stoic Western mind that sees the area of emotions and feelings as a minefield to be avoided. In fact, this area is the very opposite, and this is why so many of you are in trouble.

When you have been raised in families that ran roughshod over your expression of feeling early on in your life, you are living with a deep and crippling disadvantage. You see, the very energy that is God-given to show you your way through your life is essentially ripped up and thrown in the garbage, and you are given a map that is inaccurate and wrong. And you wonder why you are so lost and cannot find your way to where you wish to go! This is the issue so many of you are facing in the search for happiness, and it will hinder you in your search for the divine communion with God, yourself, and others that we are here to teach. This is an important lesson, and you must listen to our advice.

Communication cannot be free and open as long as you innately feel that feelings are wrong or deceptive in some way. Part of the problem for many of you is that you have overridden your feelings for so long that as you begin to allow them to surface, they feel very strong, at times almost as if they belong to someone else. Indeed, that is not so far from the truth, if you think about it. If your life is designed by others' desires, and all the structures around you have come from ideas and information to please the culture, the family — whoever or whatever you are trying to do to satisfy them — your own dear desires, as you start to entertain them, will indeed terrify you.

What you will see is that to do what you want you will have to upset the apple cart, so to speak, and arouse the anger and hatred of all those who rely on you being what they have come to count on. This is the prison of the self-created life that is not yours. This would be called the midlife crisis in your culture, and it is indeed sad that this event is seen as a joke in some ways and made fun of. This is not the way to look at this. What is happening is that a conditioned mind is finally sick of living for others' ideals and values and finally — if timidly — decides to start to live for itself. In spirit we applaud with much vigor when the mind of such an individual finally says, "That is it — we're not doing this anymore. It will kill us if we do!" That is the crux of the matter.

So many of you will die young of a variety of diseases, and it will be no one's fault but truly your own creation. The sad part is that most of you do not have this information or, if you do, do not truly grasp it. There are those who know the theory of this statement but are still not happy. The other beliefs, deep in the unconscious mind, are keeping these people prisoners. It may be a belief in a judgmental god; it may be a belief in sacrifice as holy; it may be fear of the emotions that will be roused in those who will be upset at what you do. And that is the sad, circular irony, is it not? The fear that stops you from speaking your truth is also the fear that gives the others in your life a power over the destiny that should be yours.

So what do you do about this? Well, for some this can be a long process; for others, it will be a very quick one. Some will stay and belabor these choices for years, wrestling with guilt, shame, and confusion. Others will hear this and it will go to their very hearts, and they will change their lives in just a few weeks. You must create your own experience, but what we will say is this: You know how you feel, and if you start to be more authentic and tackle each resulting disturbance as it arises — not as you picture it in your mind — you will be fine. What happens, unfortunately, is you envision the whole process at the same time instead of allowing it to be a gently unfolding process of growth and developing skills.

In this exchange of honest feeling, this is where we would like you to head: to the small and kind honoring of the self. Whether that is to take a class, take the long way home, go where you want on your holiday, or whatever that desire is, begin to honor it and share that expression with those around you. Some will hate it, and some will cheer you on from the sidelines, and this too will be a valuable lesson for you. Who is it that cheers you on, encouraging your true self? Those are the ones you should go to for support in the future. If there are those who shoot you down, be careful not to share quite so much next time. We are not telling you to lie — never do that. But be aware of where you get support, and go there.

When you are learning this new area of self-expression, some of you already have an idea of those you will not tell, and we think you should listen to this clear inner guidance. Dear ones, this is our point. You know who is kind and supportive, and you know who is judgmental and cold. Be aware, and listen to that voice. These are the beginning steps toward your freedom and your life of dreams that you wish to create. You cannot create your own heaven from others' needs and desires — only from your own. And this is even more amplified in intimate relationships.

Know that each of you has the right to live your life, and your choice of partners is very important. If you want children and your partner likes to party out late all the time, there is a compatibility issue that will not change. You are very much who you are, and until you put great effort into changing, it will not happen. So do not expect anyone to change; it will not happen. Trust us — this is one of the biggest areas of error you make in your intimate relationships.

Follow Your Heart

The choice of acceptable partners is a simple and clear one, but oh so many of you are not at all clear on this issue. Pick partners with consciousness and some thought. They will be who they are, and they are showing you who they are. Believe them. See what it is you want for yourself in the relationship you wish to create.

You must get to know yourself, and we suggest no one get married unless they have spent some considerable time getting to know who they are. We are not saying you shouldn't date or have live-in relationships, but do see that you are attending to the path of self-knowledge and that you understand where your conditioning is and what it does. That is a tall order, we know, and an ideal situation. Most of you have no idea how you are conditioned, and it is not until you are deeply involved in a relationship that areas arise for healing and transformation.

We are sure this is where a lot of you are at the moment: You are with someone who perhaps drives you crazy or with whom you cannot imagine a happy future. This is a sad state of affairs, but all is not lost. What you must do, especially if you have not done so in your life so far, is begin to make decisions that work for you. On the surface that appears as advice that would end a relationship rather than save one, but stay tuned, dear ones — we are not done yet. You see, what actually destroys most relationships is not open and honest communication, but living a lie and not speaking your truth. This week it may keep the peace, but not much more. What will occur over the years is the death of love and a breakdown that will probably lead to the dissolution of the marriage. Some stay for cultural or family reasons — again, motivated by fear of judgment — but this is not success.

We wish for those of you in that situation to imagine the end of your life, when you are asked, as you are, "Did you reach your potential? Did you create that which you intended in your physical existence?" And you will answer, "No, I did not. I did not want to upset my wife, my mother — " whoever the person is. Imagine that for a moment and see the deep sadness it will cause your higher self. Your higher self will sadly ask if you enjoyed yourself, at least, and you will answer, "No, not really. I didn't feel happy most of the time. I didn't do what I wanted, so I could not be happy."

Imagine that, dear ones. Imagine it — the birth of a body, youth and adolescence, all that effort not to live your truth or shine that very special light you have inside that is truly unique and yours alone. This is a sad situation, and we are here to stop that scenario right now. We are here to tell you to express yourself first to yourself and then gently to those around you, and to keep your own counsel as a valued mentor who has some learning or experience that tells you they know something you do not.

We are here to tell you to express your passions, even if that is in baby steps at first. We are here to tell you that real and blissful experiences — not the sad and failing story that we just recounted — are at the end of that road. We are here to tell you that you must develop a strength that comes from your relationship with the divine, that teaches you to love and honor yourself first and then, if you are able, to honor those other desires. But you may very well not be able to do that. You may have to develop the strength to say, "No, I cannot do that for you. You will have to do that for yourself." And you will, dear ones. You will, because you are here reading this. You feel the need for passion in your life, and you know that you cannot go on the way you are. You are feeling the sadness, the aches and pains, or perhaps you are already feeling the life draining from your body. And you know that if you do not change it now, you will die of something. But what it will really be is boredom or a broken heart.

So communication is all, and this is the truth. The ego will tell you to shut up and stay put, but its motivation is fear and not love. Pursue what you love, love who you love, and be what you love. That is the only path that will take you where you want to go on this challenging journey. But hear this: The difficulty comes from *not* doing this, and that is the truth. You are struggling because you are not following your hearts.

If you are happy and following your heart, you are ahead of the crowd and may wish to consider writing a book rather than reading this one. We are in need of many happy people to teach this lesson.

Dear one, we are happy you are happy again and the little mood is over. You are back to gratitude and happiness, and, that is because you are following your passion.

I briefly suggested to Ananda that the audience might appreciate more information on sex, and this was their reply.

We are with you again, dear one. The Sun is indeed bright and makes it hard to see, does it not? We are excited for the constructive ideas you have pointed out to us, and we know what we are doing on this writing expedition. So we ask you to trust us on this one path into the physicality of sexuality, or there would be no point. There would be a racing to jump in the deep end before you could swim, so to speak, and that could cause you to drown in the experience. So the object of our journey would indeed be pointless, would it not?

It has been thus on our journey together, dear one. You would have sunk if we had attempted this connection any sooner than we did. There were experiences up to the very end that were very necessary in the evolution to experience to approach this very unusual adventure. Time would have been wasted had we started any sooner. It was all perfect, so our instruction to the dear readers who have come this far with us is perfect and exactly what they need to hear to lead them fearlessly down the path to the sexual experiences they wish to experience and demonstrate.

Trust

The trust that is required to follow your heart's urgings is large indeed, for the ego trusts nothing that it sees and yet sees what it wants to. It trusts nothing that it feels, yet it is driven by feelings of hatred and fear. It trusts nothing of what you say, yet it tells lies all the time. The trust you must develop in the spirit that guides your heart's feeling — this practice of listening to the heart — is very different from the ego. The ego has been in so much control. Spirit's expression is much more subtle, and it decides on the loving way, the creative way, the adventurous way. The ego is for the opposite of all these things. The ways of spirit form the path to expression of the self, which is God in a physical form experiencing its own ideas and thoughts — thoughts and ideas that you have imagined are the journey. Spirit is full of appreciation for experience, and when you are not, it suffers, and this is what you feel as sadness and pain, disconnection from Source and its loving nature. The idea is that you will suffer if you give room to hatred. The feeling the ego has is of separation and not wanting to trust what you see between you and your lover. It is not the trust of spirit.

The ego must be relinquished to get the best of this situation. The walls of the ego keep love out, and it quakes in fear at its approach. So when you feel fear of love, know that is the ego. Do not listen to it, but rather go deeper to that place inside that wants connection and ask it what it would do. Would it go closer or back off from a loving connection? The ego will say, "Run — run or judge. This person will hurt you." The spirit will say, "Let us get to know this dear one and see." "Let's see" is the first step to trusting and learning about another soul you may want to connect with. If there is no trust at all, then more work must be done on your own mind to free up the barriers to love's presence there. This may be through counseling, dancing, or meditation, visualizing the cutting of bonds and the freeing up of love inside the mind.

The barriers are fear and judgment. The past and the future darken your vision. These are all in your control to feed — or to stop and replace with loving ideas of a God who is on your side. To trust is to have faith and love the process of life. Trust is the faith that allows for your own growth and, in the end, the freedom you desire — freedom to create, freedom to love, freedom to be yourself. The art is listening to your feelings deep inside. Adjust your actions to soften and release them. The feelings of the ego are harsh and strident; the feelings of spirit are gentle.

The purpose of this life is to totally master the energies of creation, so listen to this advice. We are serious. The pursuit of energy is the most important of the activities you can follow. The energies create what you want, and it is a chicken-and-egg situation — you are searching for the egg without the chicken. You need the energy to create the body and the abundance, so please stay focused on the energy as the path to the future you so desire to create. The aspects of the mind at work here are the ego and its obsession with what it can see and touch. The ideas of spirit cannot be seen or held, yet they hold the power you seek to express.

This also applies to the areas of bliss experience. The physical body is not the pivotal factor; the body is the result and tool the energy needs to be accepted by the limited mind. The open mind does not need the body and, in fact, at times is hampered by its heavy presence.

This, dear one, is your experience recently. A lover is not needed to feel love. Is this not so? The relationship we are developing is fulfilling, even though it is does not involve the body of another. This experience is designed to open the realm of the mind to the truth of the experience of love. It is an inside job, and the other is incidental in some ways.

It is a joy to share with another, yet we want you to know that sharing is not necessary for the exploration of the subject of sex and love. This is the lesson for the wounded sexuality of some of those reading this: You do not need a lover to experience us; it is the joy of bliss. The fears you have at the mere idea of a lover do not need to prevent the healing process that will lead to the opening up of the world of sexual bliss, awakening, and perhaps eventually the physical meeting of another lover who will care for you and experience this amazing healing with you. It is always your choice. What we want all to know is that sexual energy is separate from other bodies but is yours inherently. A relationship with Spirit guarantees bliss and awareness of sexual arousal and satisfaction.

> *Your kidding about us being the perfect boyfriend is indeed true, and you are aware that a body is no longer necessary for you to be happy. This allows you to give freedom to your future lovers. You do not need to fear their leaving or the loss of them, because you are learning that the energy is in you and between you and Spirit.*

Respect

Respect is a very important aspect of the divine sexual relationship, one that must be addressed in the beginning stage for reasons that will become apparent. There is a lack of respect in many of the elements in current Western culture, and this leads to abuse and the development of many problems. Our vision of respect and honoring would be directed to the self — you, the individual you appear to be on this amazing journey through life. We want you to see yourself as the physical manifestation, in a small and compact body, of the very God so many worship. Indeed, this is the case.

When you start to see yourself as you truly are — this divine and creative being who is the manifestation of the thought of God energy, if you will — you begin to expect a lot more from life, from yourself, and from others, not in a needy way, but in the mode of respectful alliances. As you raise your opinion of yourself, you will no longer wish to hang around with those in your life who reflect your lack of self-love back to you, for after all, that is what they are. They mirror your level of love back to you so you can see how you are doing internally. So we ask you to look around at your relationships. Are you able to relax and trust these friends and lovers? Are you comfortable being yourself around them? If the answer is yes, then this is good; they are reflecting a healthy internal environment. If, however, you are involved in unhealthy relationships that are abusive or neglectful, then it is time for you to take a journey into your own mind. Take a deep and honest look at what is going on in there.

In this culture, the misteaching is profound. A bad person is seen as an enemy and as having nothing to do with you, but this is not the case. You cannot, in fact, have a person like that in your life if your internal vibration is a high one of peace and love. You cannot tolerate such a difference of vibrations. So if you are having personal issues with abuse or lack of respect, it is in the internal analysis of your own belief systems that you will find transformation and relief.

We assure you, at this point, that your ego will scream "No!" again, loudly and vociferously. It loves to hate the bad guy and will dismiss this as fantasy, but you must remember where the ego gets its food: The hating of the other who appears to be victimizing you is its favorite restaurant. Self-respect and respecting others cannot be divided into two separate subjects; they are indeed one and the same. You will attract a mate who is of the same or similar vibration, and if you truly wish to transform your love life in the direction we are pointing, then the internal work is the only path to satisfaction.

This seems counter to the culture, as are all of our prescriptions. You may be realizing that modern Western culture is the ego's playground in all ways, and the path to bliss and enlightenment is indeed one of turning in the other direction. But do not fear. In the beginning it feels as if you will lose it all, but in fact you will gain all in the process. There are relationships that will fade away, but that will only happen as a consequence of raising your vibration and will be welcome relief from negative content. Work may also change as you go inside and make the changes that we are suggesting. The work that you are currently engaged in may become something that does not satisfy you, and a higher calling may arise and be listened to. This is all an exciting adventure, and it deserves your respect as you travel down this road together with us.

Respect within the divine sexual relationship is of the utmost importance, and we wish to emphasize that the respect of self must precede this other relationship. If you are suffering from a deep-seated lack of self-respect and self-love, that is the first project on the agenda, but do not despair and think this is a never-ending project. If your desire is for a partner and there are no fear-based impediments lurking in your mind, the world will bring the partner who is perfect for you at this level of your development. And you may well have an opportunity to travel this road to awakening together, if this is your desire.

We suggest this be a qualifying feature of your dating life. Look for those beings who are interested in the same journey, the same information. This will aid you greatly on the upward spiral, and as you come together to experience this mutual exploration, growth, and evolution, the path can be speeded up considerably. But this does require the kind of respect we are speaking about.

For this culture, one of the challenges is the respect for women that has been lacking for millennia. In this religion-soaked environment, you must bring the deep-seated and unconscious beliefs that surround the idea of women's weakness or sinfulness into the conscious mind and discuss them as a couple. There is no room for hidden prejudices and fears around this subject. The females in the group must look at their own sense of weakness as a culturally induced belief system that is hampering their self-expression and blurring the vision they can have of themselves.

In the future, couples must not only see themselves as the divine manifestation of the ideas of God, but they must see their partners as total equals in all ways and worship their sacred nature by treating them with such love and respect that, if they were Christ himself, they would be honored. There is surprise in your minds and hearts at this statement, but that is what is required to embrace the divine energies. You must see each other and yourselves as gods and treat the bodies, minds, and souls of yourselves and others with the profound respect that this warrants.

So there is some work to do here, is there not? The sexual deprivations of the sexualized world must be let go for the sacred sex we are approaching, and there must be a consciousness raising of the most profound kind. Impossible, you say? Indeed it is not. As you begin to respect yourselves, your bodies, and your thoughts and actions and words, your world will begin to immediately transform into a much more loving, fulfilling, and rewarding place. The feelings of being lost and alone will start to fade. You will feel optimism for your eternal future that is very different from the worldly ambitions that occupied your mind previously, and there will be a dawning of love in your heart that will attract the perfect partner for your growth and development.

This is all for now on this subject, but this is one we wish you to start this very moment. Look at all the relationships and issues around you today, and analyze each one. Is it loving and kind? If it is, that is well done for you; your mind is in a good and respectful place. But if you are feeling attacked or belittled in any way, we want you to go inside and look at your own thoughts. Is it others who are the creators? We can tell you, if you listen to your thoughts and beliefs about others and the world, that you will find the culprits in short order, and your work of internal transformation can begin. On that note, we wish you well on your journey to respect of self and others. It is an exciting and loving journey to peace and fulfillment, and despite your initial misgivings, it is a wonderful journey with the ultimate goal: love.

Affection

We are now going to write about affection and the part this energy plays in the development of the higher forces of love. Affection is the pacified version of sexual energy, a gentler form of the more powerful creative force that is God. We are ever fond of this subject, as it is the gateway for many into further exploration of physical touch. The body craves touch, and not because it is needy in any way but because the energy transmitted between bodies is the stuff we are made of. We feel the electrical pulses of energy between touching bodies very strongly on the other side of the dimensional veil, and we are attracted to the sparks that fly between beings engaged in touch.

We are peacefully charmed by the sweet and innocent touch of children and their mothers, and we are excited and enthusiastic about the gentle brushing of bodies that wish to make love but can't or won't, for some reason. This restrained energy is seen in deep colors of blue and green on our side, and the feeling is one of great anticipation. It is like a light in the darkness when bodies lovingly touch, and the angels cheer you on to move deeper into the experience. We are not spying but living vicariously, if you will. We are energetic beings who can travel far and wide, but we do not have the ability to touch as you do, and we wonder why you do not do it more often. It is the thing you will miss the most when you pass on to other realms that are not physical. The skin-on-skin feeling is an intense one, and it can transport the mind along the path to the gateway of bliss and sexual union.

We are envious at times of the intense focus you have here on your planet and wish only that you knew what a great gift touch is in the universe of multiple dimensions. We are able to play with energies and meld and melt them in many ways, but the simple touch of an affectionate human hand is a special event indeed. So touch each other more, and know that even if you are only stroking your own hand up your own arm, we see it and feel it on our side and give a smile of gratitude for the experience. The feelings we express here are often attuned to your feelings, so the resentment or hatred we are exposed to from your planet are distressing to us at times, as we are aware of the potential that you can reach and the bliss you can experience. It is like seeing a person with a blindfold on who believes he is blind but will not listen to your advice. You can take the blindfold off and he will see things that he will not believe.

The ancients knew of these events and skills and taught them to all who wished to study, but the knowledge became forbidden and was lost in the dark ages of religion and the new testament of sexual restrictions, which were never preached by the man called Jesus. Actually, Jesus was a very attractive and sexual being who just happened upon bliss and found it more to his liking because of its amazing depth and clarity.

We are causing a ruckus here, we think, but that is too bad. It is time the physicality of Jesus was spoken about. He was a man who became enlightened — nothing more — but he continued on, and on that journey he reached the pinnacle of achievement that a human being can. He was transformed into a lightbeing. That is all. We are sure these words will upset some, but the truth is that all of you can attain this state. And indeed he taught those very words, as in "you too will do the things I do," and he meant it. He taught it, but the words he tried to use were terrifying to his Jewish disciples, and they feared for their lives after he was gone. Many of the true teachings were lost or distorted to make them more palatable to those who remained and had to live in an oppressive traditional society that did not like change. So the power and truth of Jesus's words have slowly been lost and distorted through many translations, although bliss is what he taught — that the kingdom was within. This is what we are proposing: that you go within and learn about the landscape of the soul. Ride the energetic wave that is the existence you call consciousness, and see the unlimited vistas you can travel to. The feelings you can evoke are truly the religious experience you are seeking.

We are certain that the powers that be will "poo-poo" this text and say it is blasphemous, but the true blasphemy is hating the self that God created and lessening it by calling it sinful or evil. That is the real blasphemy. The soul as expressed through the body when it reaches the higher vibrations is truly divine — never anything to be ashamed of or scared of in any way. The future of the planet is dependent on the love growing between you, and the diseases and destruction of repressed energies are killing you — and not so slowly. So turn inside and pray for the healing you so desire, and it will be done.

We are with you, dear one. The body is tired because of the exercise and the large challenges we are offering at this time. We wish to tell you to only do what is in tune with your feelings of the day and to balance the ideas we are offering and the realities of your self-reflection with all that is happening in your world. You are doing a good job, and the feelings are reflected back to you thousandfold.

This subject is a tricky one for many people, and there are many who will be made uncomfortable by the things we are saying, so the connection you have to love and to us is an important one. As this journey continues, we will be the solid foundation on which the feelings you have will be founded. We are your foundation on this journey. The love for you here is great indeed, and the courage of your convictions is greatly appreciated.

CHAPTER EIGHTEEN

Your Environment

We are with you again, dear one, on yet another glorious day. This is a miraculous time in the weather department, is it not? The never-ending summer — this is indeed a topic that we will write about, the effect of your environment on this journey to bliss that we are on together.

This is one of the trickiest areas of the human experience, one that trips a lot of people up. The environment you are living in is the sum total of all the thoughts, words, and actions of your life — and some other lives that you have led. This is an interesting idea, is it not? You imagine that this objective world exists, that you are plunked, so to speak, in the various locations and homes that you live in. But this is not the case.

When you are born, you are born into an environment that serves two major purposes. The family into which you are born is the one that provides the best experiences for the life's journey that you have decided on for your highest experience. The physical environment, the country and living conditions you are born into, are also for that purpose. For example, someone living in Saudi Arabia will have a different experience from someone living in China, and the family of a poor person will give a different experience than that of a rich person.

Now, you all wish to be born into the richest country to the nicest family in the best neighborhood, but that is not your soul's desire. The soul desires to transform itself into a complete, realized version of a physical manifestation of God, and that is where we come in. Those of you who are drawn to this teaching are in search of the sexual experience of

God, as God energy is delightful. A transcendent sexual experience is what you all want, whether you are conscious of it or not.

The divine sexual experience connects you, God, and your lover — if you have one — together in a divine dance of bliss beyond the mere physical experiences you have in this environment of yours. There are many of you who have less-than-ideal experiences of the sexual kind, yet you are here. Why is that? There is something in you that knows the environment you are in and the experiences you have been having are missing something. There is some part of you that has glimpsed the divinity that sexual exchange and energy can be, and that is our goal — to lead you to that divine experience while you are alive here in this place called Earth.

Going back to the environment you exist in and have invited, the areas where you fall down or get confused are in seeing that environment as some kind of mistake. It is no mistake. These areas are there to show you where there are false beliefs and to aid your spiritual education. You see, if you are living in poverty, there is an aspect of you that believes in poverty. There is a manifestation that is in tune with an inner condition. Of course you say, "But there are those poor countries, and indeed poor continents, in dire circumstances. That cannot be right!" Yet on a soul level, that is the environment that for now will show them what they need to see.

These are not punishments but gifts, and disliking where you are — if that is indeed the case — is the force, the energy, that will in actuality drive you toward the realms you innately know are where you are supposed to be. On a sexual level, those of you who have experienced violence or just plain uninspired connections are pushed to seek out that which you know is possible by those very conditions.

So we are asking you to start to see the challenges in your environment as a springboard that will push you to the spiritual heights you wish to experience. What happens, though, is you lament the conditions over and over. You lament the past over and over, reiterating what it is you don't want and how victimized you are all the time, so more of the experiences arise to show you that you are still fueling the beliefs that are keeping you small.

This is where the mental training of which we have spoken comes into play. We want you to look at your environment and see the gift that it is hiding in plain sight. See that your lack of a loving partner is pointing deep inside to some belief that you are perhaps unlovable. This is untrue, but your environment is reflecting the lie that you are telling yourself. There is a potential for each life to be the perfect reflection of the realized mind. It is a high and lofty goal, but that is what we are saying is possible. Those of you sitting and reading this know it to be true in your bones — that there are possible experiences that you are not having. The path to that perfection of experience is manifested around you in your environment this very moment.

If you hate someone, that is the key to your freedom. That energy in your mind, body, and soul is the opposite of that which you wish to experience, and it is acting as a block to the experiences we are writing about. If there is someone with an obese body reading this book, there is a belief system operating in that mind that puts food above all else; it has become a friend, a lover, a god, and it must be relieved of these jobs that you have assigned to it. It is not food's job to give you these comforts.

So that is what we are suggesting today. Look at your environment, face those areas of it that are not to your liking, and ask what each one's message is. Forgive your environment. It is your teacher and shows the inside manifested outside, and it will guide you to the places that need the awareness of light shone on them.

That is it for this little excursion into the environment. It is your friend and your teacher, and we will explore this more in the next few pages. How do you go about shifting the belief systems to which you adhere, and what does that look like?

The Effect of Nature

We are with you again, dear one, ready to tackle the subject of your choice: the effect of nature on the energy that pervades the body. A wonderful environment is, as we told you yesterday when we sat on the delicious, warm, and sun-drenched rock at the beach, a reflection of the mind in which you live and exist.

When the sunlight falls on your skin, you are connected to the divine heaven in the celestial realm in a way that few of you realize. There is a never-ending energy coming to your planet from the deepest realms of the mind that is God, represented to you as deep space. This is the truth of the matter. Divine intelligence is pouring over and through you when you are outside in the natural environment, which is one of the reasons we tell you to be outside in nature as much as possible, given the requirements of your daily life. And if your daily life does not allow at least several hours a day of natural light in natural environments, you will suffer on a deep cellular level.

This is one of the greatest issues happening in this modern culture you are so fond of. There are those of you who have an innate knowledge that nature soothes and feeds you, but you do not really get just how profound that feeling is. There are energetic elements the body needs to receive, there is intelligence it needs to thrive, and this all arrives on beams of light — be it starlight, moonlight, or sunlight. On those first spring days, when you leave your little boxes in which you live and lie out in the sun for the first time, your souls sing in joy at the information they are receiving.

The cells in your body are not separate from the rest of the universe. In fact, they are deeply entwined, and it is this that is missing in so many of your lives. You might take weekend trips to the park for a few hours, or spend holidays trying to relax and get outside a little, but the majority of you are deeply dissatisfied on a cellular level, which is contributing to the depression, sickness, and dysfunction you are suffering from.

The body is the world, and the world is the body. This is not a metaphor. It is the truth, and the connections are endless and unbreakable. This is one of the reasons the world is exhibiting the sicknesses you are experiencing. The pollution you are dumping onto your dear planet is the same garbage you are dumping into your minds, and the result is the same: a difficult situation that is getting worse by the day.

You do not need to fear for dear Earth, for she will be here after you are all long gone, and she will thrive after this scourge has left her dear and beautiful body. But you do have a choice here. You can start to focus on the things that truly satisfy the soul — love, communication, communion, healthy eating and food production, and compassion for each other and the planet itself. This is the path we are suggesting: Instead of going for the quick fix — the burger, the shopping, the television — delve deep into the endless depths of your soul and begin to experience the love and passion that is there, just waiting for some sign that you care or are interested.

Do Your Part

Your soul has come here to experience heaven on earth. You are creating an experience of extreme contrasts from which to pick and on which you can focus. In the end, the outcome is certain, and you will reach that state. But when you are in time as you believe you are, there are experiences you would call unpleasant or painful, and you do not need to have these experiences over and over again in an effort to teach yourself a lesson you do not need to learn.

You are love beings — created in love, by love, for love — and it is only in your separation from that state that you become lost and afraid and suffer the terrible belief that you are alone, unloved, and uncared for in this vast and cold universe. This is not true. Your spiritual guides are waiting for your call and will help you climb out of the pit you have created, but you must lift up your hand for them to grasp. You must do your part in the dissolution of the illusions you are living under.

In the beginning, you must act as if the illusion is not as true as you now believe, and this is indeed a tall order. Everything you have been taught tells you that the illusion is real; the cars, the houses, the trees — all seem solid and real, as you would say. Yet it is all only an illusion of reality. It is all only energy, and the meaning you have laid on that energy is all the meaning it has.

When someone says words you do not like, it is not harmful to you in any way. It is only harmful when you assign meaning to the words that creates the illusion of attack, for when you believe something is real for you, it does indeed become real. The ego mind attaches to an idea, works it, embroiders it, and becomes indignant. Then all hell breaks loose, so to speak. The acts of forgiveness we have been referring to are the acts that see an object or a behavior and do not judge it either way; it is not your salvation or your destroyer.

You must begin to act as if you are the creator of your world, which you are, and you must begin to behave as if you are an eternal spiritual being who will last forever, because you are. When you stop acting as if you are a body (which you are not, by the way) and start acting as if you are the temporary but very holy manifestation of God (which you are), you will gain access to power and peace beyond your understanding.

This is how you do it, dear ones. You listen to how you feel, and it is as simple as that. Your feelings are your guide to how you are doing. In these initial stages of the journey, when you react negatively to some-one's speech, you think you feel bad because of what they said. But you actually feel bad because of how you have judged what they said. In the beginning of this process, your reactions and judgments are so fast and so unquestioned that you cannot see the decision you make — that these words may hurt you. But as you become more aware in all the areas of your life that we have been talking about, a small space will begin to appear. You will start to see a moment when you have a choice, and it is in that small space that you will make a different deci-sion. You will decide not to fight back. You will decide to see the people saying those harsh words as souls who are lost in the realms of thought and attack, and you will begin to see that they are in a hell of sorts and deserve your compassion, not your attack.

The Rising of Peace

What will happen as this process becomes second nature to you is peace will rise. As you put down your weapons and stop defending yourself, you will realize that most of the anxiety and fear you were experienc-ing was your own creation. You were donning your armor and had your spear in hand all the time, and when you are prepared for war, you are not relaxed — not in the least.

As you begin to think of peace, look for peace, and value peace above all else, it will indeed manifest in your life, and you will begin to see a different world. Your body will begin to relax, and if you are sick or your body is struggling, it will be given some divine peace in which it can heal. This is the path you will follow. The tiredness of the battle is wearing you out, and it is wearing out your dear planet. What you do not know, and what we are so happy to tell you, is that as you transform your internal world and strive for peace in thought, word, and deed, it will become manifest in your outside world. Not as some "airy-fairy" wish-making idea, but in tangible, real results. You are connected in an inextricable way to your environment and to your world. It is not as you have been told. You are powerful beyond measure, and you are gods, able to transform all that you see and all that you experience, inside and out.

These words resound in your ears, do they not? The fact that you are gods and can change your world — if only we could implant that truth into each mind reading this and make it stick. But this is information that goes against all you have been taught: that this world is real and solid and unchangeable. We want you to understand the liquid nature of this place that you call home, that as you observe anything, you change it.

As you observe your lovers with judgment, you change them on the inside. They will feel the anger or hatred exuding from you, and the next time they think of sharing a little piece of themselves, something in them will say no — that you are not a safe haven. Do not think that just because your ideas and judgments about your lover are only in your head or shared with your friends that your lover does not feel them. Your minds are one, sharing the same wavelengths and basic makeup. All of those awful things you have said are coalescing into tangible objects that will become events such as arguments and fights.

This is the way of it, dear ones. None of your thoughts are separated from anyone else's, but you never know this because you are so secretive. Sometimes relationships get very close. You will share your deepest thoughts, and you will see as you spend time together that often you think or say the same thing at the same time. What you do not realize is that this is happening all the time, all over the world. So when we tell you to forgive, or not to judge, you are sending more loving thoughts out into the virtual environment. If we can turn the tide of thought in enough people, there will be a revolution of love on the planet, the likes of which you have never seen. Relationships will begin to stabilize, marriages will begin to last, and the passion and joy you so wish to experience will begin to become manifest wherever you look.

So do not do these things for yourself only; do them for your children and the dear Earth. Every hateful thought is a real and poisonous thing that affects all, and this is now being proven in the scientific world. But you need to understand the mechanisms as they work in your daily lives, and this is why we have come — to help you decipher this language you have not been taught. The language of love is so important and so powerful that it cannot be stressed enough. The great religious teachers who caught a glimpse of God on their journeys here have spoken of love and its power, yet many of you nod and say, "That is nice," and then gossip or put down a member of your group you feel is behaving badly. These are the little hatreds that grow into wars.

Use Your Thoughts for Good

You think we are being dramatic, but from our perspective it is clear. The constant fear-based nature of your thoughts and the uninspired and judgmental life that goes on in between your ears form into the very crimes and diseases that you blame God for, screaming in anger and asking why this is allowed. It is you who is allowing it, and we are not angry, but we are telling you the way it is, and it starts with you first. The hateful thoughts that run through your heads are attacks of the most brutal kind.

You look at criminals on television and call them evil or a lower form of life, yet the things you say to your dear self are the same acts of violence on an energetic level. They are no less serious and no less creative of misery. The depression that is epidemic in your culture is caused by many things, but the self-judgment for mistakes made and the hatred of the body or features are deeply destructive to the health of the mind. Each slight is as a knife cut to the dear one that you are. We are being very forceful here, but we deeply want you to know what it is you are doing to yourself, your health, your relationships, and your world with this behavior. We are urging you to begin a process of saying nice things inside your mind — nice things about your accomplishments and about the body that does so much for you every second of every day yet is abused and hated.

If you are in a relationship that you wish to keep, stop gossiping and hating inside your mind. You are destroying it as surely as if you were saying the words out loud. In some ways, it is worse; at least if the words are spoken, the others may respond and defend themselves, but so many of you are not honest or brave enough for that exchange. If you are in a relationship you do not wish to stay in, then leave. Be honest and tell the person that you are done, but do it with grace and as much love as you can muster. Every word will create the divorce that is kind or hateful, and you cannot blame it all on the other person. You have been there dancing the dance with them every day, and this marriage that has failed is a mutual creation. Indeed, the reason so many divorces are hateful and painful is because, finally, all the words that have been thought for years are now out in the open. But this is the responsibility of each of you; and you are all doing it.

It is wonderful for us to see those of you who are working on this area of forgiveness and nonjudgment. We see your lights growing brighter every day, your bodies healing themselves in the peaceful energy that you are creating, and it is a miracle in this superficial and judgmental world in which you live. We have berated you long enough, and it is not something we will do often, but heed our words: You are creating the stage of your life today, so do not lament where you are. You have put yourself there. But the good news is you can change it. You can alter the course of your future toward love and a healthy life of fulfilling and happy times on a healthy and happy planet, but you must start now.

Every moment is another moment of miscreation or focused attention on what you want to create. It is your choice. We are merely holding the light in the darkness so you can see the way, but you are free to listen or not. We ask you one more time to start disciplining your mind and tending to your focus. We will help you, and you will not regret it. We promise you.

Land

The next thing we wish to talk about is agriculture and the poisoning of the land that is happening. The radioactivity that is rising is of great danger in large quantities, and a plan to use solar power is most important. It is all free and easy, and it is imperative that as many people as possible push for this transformation from oil and nuclear energy.

We ask any who read this and are willing to write to their leaders and ask for clean fuels to be developed as quickly as possible. The time has run out for thinking about this. The oil will be so expensive soon as to force your hand, so why not do it voluntarily so that the transition is easier?

The nuclear threat is, of course, the most dangerous, and the effects on air — and in Japan's case, the sea — are already becoming apparent. Remedies must be put in place as soon as possible. There are forces at play that you are not aware of that are helping you on Earth, and the truth is all will be fine, although many of the souls currently living on the planet will choose to leave pretty soon — sometimes in large numbers that will distress those of you who really believe in death and dying.

This is one of the areas where new teachings are really needed. Indeed, so much of your fear and living of dull lives actually comes from the fear of death, but death does not exist. Many of you, after dying, will see that the lives you were living were actually more like a slow death, and the freedom and creativity you will access after you leave this Earth plane will make this life seem sad, slow, and pale in comparison.

This is one of the reasons we are here: to teach you about the sexual energies available as a gift from God and help you tap into that energy before you go from here. There are innumerable joys to be had, which have been quelled and distorted by the ancient teachings, that could enhance your experiences here so that the death experience is not such a contrast. The feelings of otherworldly joy and of the body disappearing in bliss show you clearly that you are not a body and the heavy attachments to this physical life do not weigh you down. You actually get a glimpse of the energetic being you are. The low vibration of the ego and of the physical body ruled by it are difficult at times to overcome, and this is where a little patience is required to undo the realms of the ego that you have become attached to.

A new practice will bring a new experience, and this does indeed require a lot of faith — to do something that not only scares you but takes discipline, even though you can see the rewards. This new path will take you on vacations — not to tropical islands, but to places from which you do not need to return to a dull and mundane life. You will go to realms that will always be there with you, even as you go through your days of work and family. The energy remains and brings joy and pleasure to the simplest of activities. Walking along a beach becomes a thing of not just simple pleasure but blissful reunion with the divine. And although this is hard for you to imagine now, we assure you that this is possible, and indeed likely, if you follow on the advice of this book.

It all begins in the mind and is free, although some intense periods of study to enhance the lessons and set them off, so to speak, would be of great use. We are asking you to keep up the good work of growing and allowing the divine into your mind through loving kindness, meditations, forgiveness, and happy thoughts about a bright future. We are always here and always watching your progress with joy.

We are with you again, dear one, with the joy and bliss in you that you so deserve. The energy coursing through your body right now is God in his/her glory, the truth of the search that so many are looking for. The joy that is available to the human mind through the open channels of the body is endless and amazing indeed. The force of this

*is what creates worlds, and the more open and joyful the connection,
the more fruitful a world this is.*

A New Environmentalism

It's important to learn new things, even if they are not what you wish to hear. These are the lessons of this world. Most of what is good for you, you do not want; and most of what is bad for you, you do want. The world is designed by the ego to trip you up and deceive you — that is its intention. It is not a cruel trick played by the God you believe in, because this world is not God's creation. It is indeed the ego's playground, and that is why you suffer and wish to leave so frequently. It is tiring, and it's the antithesis of heaven. It is not your imagination, but the truth. These are hard words for most to digest, as they believe in the world with all their hearts and souls. But as the world of spirit is heightened, there is a connection made with the energy underlying the surface forms — which are indeed of the ego — to the truth underneath, which is the God energy we seek and talk about.

This is the vision you must develop: the ability to see the destruction the ego offers and walk in the opposite direction of the desires that are simple. Walk in the direction of the deeper drives of the soul, which in the beginning are hard to find, due to the nature of the untrained mind and the practice of following the ego's dictates all the time. As you begin to listen to the voice of God, the answers will get clearer and louder, and they will always give you a clear light to follow that leads to the perfect answer. The ego's guidance will scare you, make you fat, and lead you down the road of suffering all the time.

There are many more pages to write, and the feeling in us is one of great anticipation for the continued sharing of our knowledge. We are now going to speak about the future of your planet and the fears that many people have right now about its survival. These people are worried about the dear Earth and feel that *that* is the most important topic — not sex or love. But we reassure you that as you get in touch with the divine sex we are talking about — making love to God, if you will, and honoring the bodies of light that you can become — the need to consume so very much will subside. The need to attack others will subside, and the need to drive far and wide to avoid yourselves will subside. All of those things are destroying your dear planet Earth, so do not dismiss the association between bliss and the hard realities of the life you live here on the planet. Even though she will survive you all and shake you off when she is sick of you, the overall vibration is one of love. But you are sowing the seeds of destruction every time you make an unnecessary purchase or a hateful comment. Humans do not realize the power their every action and thought has on their world. Each one sends out a powerful wave of energy that will enhance or destroy something. This is indeed the truth, and the words you speak, even in the confines of your minds, environmental or not, are polluting in some way.

So for all the environmentalists out there, expand your idea of what environmentalism is, and work on the connection to the divine energies that are the life force of this dear world in which you can realize miracles and overcome your physical bodies, if you so choose. Be a disciplined practitioner of love of self, of others, and of the God force that holds it all in place and gives the opportunity to choose the path of enlightenment. When that path is chosen, Earth will give a shudder of pleasure at the words you speak and the love you make, as the loving energy spills around the planet, coming back in the form of love for you and those experiences you wish to have.

So go on a search deep inside for the barriers you have constructed and the walls of fear you have around your heart, because this is the way in. The way in is not fearful or scary. Even if you have been hurt in the past, that is over now, and there is a chance for a fresh future if you are able to listen to these teachings and slowly but surely trust in the love that God has for you and all that you wish for.

CHAPTER NINETEEN

Beauty and Forgiveness

We are going to talk about this thing called beauty and what it is to the mind of the human searching for peace. Beauty is such a personal thing, is it not? The eyes that fall on one face and find it lovely will look at another face and find it ugly, and the one who loves the other face will find the one you love unattractive. This is a perfect illustration of the mind being totally subjective. Beauty is only for the individual, so the personality of your reality is illustrated in this one subject. All individuals have their own world of beauty, and we are to allow all to have that freedom.

The breakdown in many relationships is in not allowing the other's idea of beauty. Yes, this idea of a man seeing beauty in a touchdown of a football game and that of his wife seeing the beauty in a pair of shoes are equally valid, and neither should judge the other's choices. This would alleviate a lot of bickering or fighting in the world. The battle between two minds who have different ideas of beauty — that is the beauty of the individuality of God, represented in all of you.

There are no two alike, and the search for sameness will only create boredom. The insistence on sameness creates wars. Let those on the path to love truly accept all other paths that their fellow travelers take, and let them only be concerned with what they consider beautiful. It is an important awareness. You cannot appreciate the same thing as another in exactly the same way, and that is the way it is supposed to be.

Immerse yourself in the things you consider beautiful, and allow your loved ones and all you come in contact with to have their beautiful things too. It is an act of loving kindness to look at their choices, and even if you do not understand them, give them the honor of their own experience here. You do not know their past, or their future, and the judgment is not yours to make. In fact, it will stop you looking at the beauty in your life and dim the light we are encouraging you to inflame.

The passions that create the life you want begin as simple attraction, a curiosity about the nature of an experience or person you wish to engage. Do not edit yourself when a desire is aroused through beauty. The future it may bring you is the path that may lead to the future you want. In fact, it is almost guaranteed to, if the desire is a feeling of gentle love and wonder — not the possession of lusting after something, but the genuine, gentle curiosity of a mind wondering what that thing or person is about, the desire to explore and investigate a subject more thoroughly. These are the beginnings of a life of passion, of opening the channels. Listening to these quiet voices will indeed lead you down the path to the joys of life in each of them and in the divine.

We tell you that the divine is in every object, every flower, every face, and this is why judgment against it is so painful for you; it is not the truth, and your soul knows it and sends a message by making you sad, angry, or disillusioned. You will begin to listen to this feedback and know that God is speaking to you and gently guiding you to the life of freedom that comes from forgiveness of all your judgments against everything.

These are the simple things too — not just the big items. Forgive the rain, and appreciate it; forgive the dirt, and know that life is messy; forgive the loud people next door, and allow them their anger or their festivities. They are alive and know nothing else to do at that moment. The forgiveness we speak of is often misunderstood to be for the bad events of the past, but forgiveness is an ongoing practice in every moment. When you accept what is, you trust the Divine has a purpose in it you cannot see right now. All that is going on is for the greater good, and stress of great proportions is lifted from your mind when this truth is brought into the heart and accepted. You are always free to move on to another environment if you feel uncomfortable — that is your freedom — but the disturbance that thing creates in you is actually your judgment, not the event.

We are sure this will raise the roof, so to speak, and many arguments will arise about abuse and hunger and all the ills that rise up in indignation at this concept of acceptance. But all these things will be healed and transformed as the world accepts what is and stops attacking everything as if it were a mistake. There are no mistakes, and the gifts of these trials are for your education and eventual freedom, not the insane mind of a God who hates you.

CHAPTER TWENTY

Understanding and Healing Your Body

In Western culture you are taught that the body is a solid object. It changes drastically over time, and that, when you think about it, disputes this theory, yet most of you see the body as quite a solid and static thing. This misconception arises particularly when you are diagnosed in the Western way, with sickness that your culture would consider incurable or chronic, which does not serve you well at all on the path to healing what is incorrectly manifesting in your physical self.

The body is the first mirror on the path to self-understanding. It is the outward reflection of your inward condition and contains much information on how you are thinking and how you are doing on the inside — in the realm of thoughts, dreams, ideas, and beliefs. It is a miracle of design, but it is really a creation of the ego mind in the sense that it is not permanent. It is not of spirit in the sense that it is fallible; it can break down, and it is temporary. These are all qualities of things of this world and not the world of spirit. Many of you in spiritual practices of various kinds have been told that the body is divine in nature, and we will be writing some challenging thoughts here that go against the grain of that which you have been taught, so hold on to your hats and be open-minded, if you can, for a little while.

When a spirit is manifested on the physical plane in the form of a body, it is to experience that which is out of alignment with truth. This is the concept that is difficult to understand. You have always been taught that God created the body and the world and that this a holy place. Yet have you not wondered at the sicknesses and pain, the darkness and the fears that manifest in the world and in the physical body?

We have mentioned before this idea that you come here to unlearn that which is not true, and in a sense, the body is not true; it is not who you are. It is a form that is manifested so you can unlearn the incorrect beliefs you have about yourself and about the world, and this is why it can be such a tricky and confusing subject.

Good health is something you all desire and strive for. Good health is a sign that you are in line with the truth; sickness is a sign that something is "out of whack," as you say. This is not some kind of punishment, and there is no judgmental God handing out diseases to the bad and the evil out there. But there is a vibrational balance that is infallible and will show you exactly where there is work to be done.

Think about it: If there were a Creator God who made your bodies, why are there so many errors? Why are there so many random-seeming mistakes showing up all the time, some seemingly without a cure in sight? This is a sign that your philosophy around the body is incorrect; it is not logical, and it makes no sense.

We are proposing here that your problems with your body are showing you an internal issue — a belief system, we will say — that is out of accord with truth, with the balanced energy of the universe. And your symptoms, far from being negative, are in fact offering you up information to help you focus on the internal creative changes that need to be made. This turns your sicknesses from mistakes made by a foolish God or punishment from a vengeful God into a gift to help you see that which is incorrect in your thinking.

Your Western way teaches that the body is an objective thing that exists and randomly goes wrong, or that is attacked by bugs and diseases all the time, and that it is somehow fallible and flawed in its vulnerability. What we are teaching is that it is a temporary house for your soul's journey, and that journey is to undo the untruths that are in your mind — your belief in erroneous ideas and incorrect assumptions. It is a map to the solution to your problems. We will give you an example so you can understand that about which we speak.

Symptoms Are Messages

Let us say you are suffering from chronic pain in the form of arthritis, this difficult and confusing disease so many of you suffer from in your society. Much of the problem is diet related, but it is also related to the constant stream of thoughts of self-hatred and judgment many of you are subjecting your bodies to. These thoughts create all the time. They create a toxic soup of chemicals within your body that causes the internal mechanisms to attack themselves and leads to deterioration in the internal structures of the joints and the connective tissues, causing the distressing symptoms from which you suffer. The food aspect is made worse by the lack of love, and choosing low-vibration foods via low-vibration thoughts compounds these difficulties. Many of you with this condition, rather than going to the doctor and seeking chemicals to mask these symptoms, would be well served to change your minds — not only about yourselves and your amazing and beautiful natures and value, but also to change that which you ingest.

You see, the idea that the symptoms are the problem *is* the problem, and we wish here to get you to understand that all the negative physical symptoms you have are messages from your body to you to help you understand the internal workings of the mind that are out of whack. You have a guidance system, as we have mentioned, that tells you where you are off track — the feelings, passions, and desires you feel all the time. But because you have not understood these messages, many of you have lost your connection to your internal source of wisdom and have become lost and confused.

The sickness and physical ailments you have are not who you are. In fact, they are who you *aren't*. Sickness is your guide to what is internally wrong — a gift, if you will, pointing to your internal misteachings that are getting you off track.

The idea of the energetic body being the result of the physical body is also incorrect. In your culture you are taught that the body creates, and this is not so. The mind creates the body, and until you take this flipped concept and turn it around, you will be unable to change the physical manifestations you are experiencing.

You see, the ego mind wants to experience that which it believes to be true, to come to a deep and abiding understanding of the concepts it thinks are true. As you travel through your life, all your beliefs become manifested in physical form for you to see, and this is where the problems start. You are taught many incorrect things — that you are sinful, that you are bad, that you are wrong — and all of these teachings go into the mind framework and begin to make that which the vibration represents.

This will make a healthy and strong body if the vibrations are high, and you will enjoy the experience of being in this physical body for a time. But if there are dark areas of misteaching — that you are flawed, that you are weak — these too will manifest to show you what is going on inside.

If you look at the system this way, then you will see there is some benefit to illness. Do you not see this? It is information you need to heal those unloving thoughts that permeate your mind. If you have not been taught this, you find yourself in a very confusing situation, indeed.

This is why your medicines that seemed so amazing at first are becoming a prison of sorts. You are not, in fact, getting healthier, but sicker and sicker as you try to mask the symptoms that are trying to send you a message of where to look for the problems. You are living longer, but the quality of life of the medicated aged in your culture is becoming very questionable indeed. Many of you are becoming afraid of old age, and you should be — unless you take on this different perspective and begin to listen to your internal guidance system. Your feelings, thoughts, and ideas — these are the map to extreme well-being and health you so wish to experience.

Every time you deny that you feel negative and override your guidance system, you contribute to a future sickness. Every time you are riddled with fear, believing in a disastrous future, you are sowing the seeds of sickness. And every time you judge another, you are lowering your own vibration into the realms of the unwell and feeble. If you attack yourself or others in your mind, you will manifest sickness in your body — not instantly, it is true, but eventually for sure.

This is not a punishment, we wish you to understand. The purpose of your life is to remove all the negatives and come to a place of joy and extreme health, a place of love and understanding that all are equal, that all is good, and that the universe is made of and for love. All these errors are errors of thinking and misteaching that need to be changed for this dream of heaven to be reached. These seem unusual concepts for the Western mind, we know, and many of you will not be ready to see things this way. But as we have said before, your system of things is coming unglued, and you must, in your sane moments, see that it is not working very well, this system of fear and judgment that you are practicing.

The body needs to be healthy and strong to practice the exercises that we will be discussing soon, and that will be the first large hurdle for many of you. But we wish to put things in a little perspective here. These accomplishments of peace, health, and joy about which we are speaking are high and mighty goals many of you will only make small steps toward at the moment. This program of growth toward joy that we are speaking about is not a project for this month, or even this year. You must understand that this is the work of a lifetime — even several.

You Are Not Your Body

This is where you must change your thinking around the body. You see, you think you are your body, and that when it dies you die. This is not true. You are not your body. Your consciousness has made it, and it will make another and another until these goals of peace and joy are reached. And then you will move on to nonphysical realms, where a whole new ball game exists. But the mind that you are a part of is not physical, so we suggest slow and determined patience on this path.

Enjoy your life and be kind to your body. It is, after all, the tool you are given to work out your errors, and to attack or degrade it gives you less and less opportunity to heal that which is causing you pain. You become stuck in the physical, a prisoner of that which is designed to lead you to freedom. But you must begin to look at it in the correct way. When you see the endlessness of the existence that you have, you can become very patient with yourself. You can understand that there is time aplenty to change that which needs to be changed and that it is okay to relax a little, to not be so hard on yourselves and on your bodies all the time.

The body will respond very quickly to a change of mind and a change of heart, and it will offer up its health and its miraculous ability to change if you will change. So if you have been looking at your body as a liability, as an enemy, change those thoughts, or indeed it will become exactly that. Call it friend, and it will be a good ally, allowing you to travel and explore this third-dimensional world you live in, full of experiences to enliven and enlighten. Call it enemy and treat it badly, and it will fail and fall, and the journey will not be a fun one.

Heal by Changing Belief Structures

There are many beliefs hidden in the mind that disempower your ability to heal. The belief that the body goes wrong spontaneously is a large one in the Western mind that denies the true source of your power and keeps you focused on the problem rather than the solution.

We are working on you, dear one. Your energetic body is being cleared of blocks and being opened in areas where it is closed so that more energies will flow. We are opening up all the meridians and channels, so the clarity of our connection and your abilities in creativity and healing are being enhanced. You are actually quite healthy, due to the intense forgiveness work that you have done over the years, so we are fine-tuning, if you will, the connections for a very specific task that we have in mind.

People who are unaware of the spiritual nature of their bodies, that the body is indeed created by the energetic body, are tied to states that don't work, so they become sicker and sicker, and very tired. The idea of using medications to mask symptoms is, of course, the most challenging one in Western culture — the idea that as long as you don't feel anything it is all right. The truth is that the answers to all the problems are in the feeling.

This is a mindset that must be deconstructed from the beginning to access the health and choice-making ability that is needed on this journey. The mind, when focused on an untruth, is confused. There is indeed a part of you that knows the truth, so deep conflicts arise such as anxiety, digestive problems, phobias, and the like. Anyone suffering from these anxiety disorders should not engage the kundalini energies until they are in a state of peace, able to be calm and not fearful. Too many demons will raise their heads to be looked at in the process, so it is better to deal with them one by one before a focused practice of raising sexual energy is undertaken. The fears that will be aroused will derail the path, perhaps permanently, and that we do not want.

There are ways to change the mind. A *Course in Miracles* is of course a favorite, as it is gentle and allows for many discussions. The triggers and words arouse many issues around God and the Church. Many of these areas need healing in the minds of Western students who have had run-ins with the Church at some time in their lives. There are rules and fears, unwritten and unseen, lurking in the minds of many, that will need careful excavation, and it is this we suggest as a path to awakening, as a gentle and fearless way of opening to spirit. The chances of someone becoming overwhelmed in doing the Course lessons are indeed low. The path is a gentle one, designed to only approach the mind with respect and care.

The structures that need to be changed must not be attacked. They need to be gently unpicked, as in undoing knitting — one stitch at a time — and then the material can be reused in the new construction. If harsh methods are used, the mind runs in fear and will not participate again, often for many years.

III

Blocks to Transformation

CHAPTER TWENTY-ONE

Fear and Guilt

We are now going to write about fear and the devastating consequences it has on your ability to connect in joy with us, with others, and with God energy. Fear is a creation of the mind of the thinker, and what a powerful one it is! Fears arise and totally block out the light of love. Fears are real and chase you around the house all day. We are sure you feel that they have a life of their own, yet they are your babies, nurtured and fed with the food of doubt, self-loathing, and faithlessness. They feed on the fearful ideas of separation and the culture's demands that you earn a lot or buy a lot of things and own a large and expensive house.

If you own such a house, you are afraid to lose it; if you don't own such a house, you are afraid you never will. Damned if you do, and damned if you don't — there is no escape from the conditioned mind's solutions. They are not solutions, but problems laid on top of problems. The only real solution is to replace your sense of insecurity with real faith in the ability of the mind to focus and create the future you wish. This is a difficult reconditioning process; it does indeed take work and prayer to connect with your true guidance system.

Western culture's largest belief is that if you are rich and own a lot of things, you are more holy than the street people. Very early on in the process of awakening, this fear will arise: "Will I lose everything I own?" And of course, you must be willing to entertain the idea that possessions are a hindrance rather than a help to the awakening process, but many are already realizing that their homes and possessions are becoming more of a liability than a blessing, and for many, the idea that is dawning — that they can be free — is a very seductive one.

The fears of family rejection are also big on the list. Even a family full of strife and argument seems to have a hold on the Western mind, as if the members are the owners of an individual's life. Again, this is not as big an issue for Eastern students to face. In the East, the life of spiritual pursuit is an honor for the family. Western students will have to let go, bit by bit, of the belief that somehow this journey is negative and harmful to their families.

In truth, dear one, this is your experience. Although you left both your families, there was still guilt — was there not? — over the decision to remove yourself. We know that this is finally over, and the honor you are giving us is indeed the honor that is deserved.

Fear in Relationships

As you are getting closer and closer to your beloved, you will encounter many fears, so we will chat about them here so that you know what to expect. As you venture closer and closer to your beloved through the communications and practices we are suggesting, you will find that fears, and at times terrors, will arise. This is to be expected. After all, you are attempting to destroy the ego's grip on your mind — and therefore behavior — and your ego will feel this as a mortal attack and will do what it can to stop this action at all costs. The ego, you see, has your physical well-being at its core, but it has been overfed and misunderstood to such a large degree that it has become a dictator who slays his own people in an effort to control, and in the end, seals his own fate through a revolution of the people. We are indeed the revolution of mind that the ego, in the modern world, needs to experience, for you are at the mercy of this dictator who will scream in outrage at your temerity in daring to dethrone him from his seat of power. We will give some examples here of the kinds of experiences you may have as you venture down these less-traveled roads into the heart of love and communion.

You are taught by the ego-driven culture you live in that there are scarce resources, and that if you do not keep safe that which you have, you will lose it all and be taken advantage of. The principles we are suggesting you follow are the opposite: to give all that you have — body, mind, and spirit — to that beloved you wish to connect with. The ego will want to protect the objects and powers it has and will tell you to protect that which is yours. This reinforces belief in the material world and the idea that you, and only you, provide for your well-being and abundance. When you offer up all that is yours, trusting and knowing that your beloved is the love you wish to be with, you will be saying to the universe through your actions — which represent your beliefs — that there is plenty for all, and that the more you give, the more you receive. For if you have and do not share, you do not get the full experience of that which you have, and we have been talking about experience as the real thing, have we not?

Your indoctrinations in your culture have told you that the real thing is the object, but this is not so. The value in a sports car is the rides you can offer your beloved, the wonderful sun-drenched journeys through the environment. The car sitting in the garage is of no value whatsoever — except to the ego's sense of self, this artificial and fear-driven small self that will not bring you that which you wish.

As you delve into a relationship, practicing these areas of giving and loving beyond that which you have previously experienced, you will find these beliefs coming up for transformation, so it may seem like a rocky road at times. You may believe that a perfect relationship will always be peaceful and easy, but we have some bad news for you: It is in the intimate relationship that you will encounter some of your most negative — and therefore most out-of-alignment — beliefs, and this is important to know and prepare for. The communication pathways, the conversations you have with your beloved, and the deep connections we are suggesting will not only prepare you for the bliss we speak of, but they will also lead you to the beliefs that are incorrect that are manifesting in your life. This is a good thing, and we know that if you have chosen a partner who is also interested in growth, who is also interested in erasing that which is not true from his or her mind, that you will find a way through these difficult fears with each other's well-being at the forefront of your minds.

These are indeed difficult, if not impossible, goals to achieve if you are not both deeply involved in self-realization, for you cannot do this alone in a relationship. However, you can do it alone *outside* of a relationship. What often transpires as one of you gets onto this path is that one will be more willing at any given time than the other. One of you will be saner than the other when that one is triggered by a deep and primal fear. It will be the saner one's responsibility to hold up the light of love and sanity for the partner who has temporarily lost his or her peace. This will be easy to discern, dear ones — so very easy. Those who are afraid will claim they cannot do this anymore. They will claim they are too afraid and must go back into ignorance. But the truth of the matter is this, dear students: You cannot go back, for once you have an awareness and understanding of the truth, you cannot revert to ignorance again. And if you try to, you will feel more pain than you ever felt in trying to wake up. So beware of these fears and the ego's stories of imminent death. You cannot hurt yourself by loving another, and you cannot hurt yourself by loving yourself. Just make sure that the definition of love you have is true, pure, and clear of any of the ego's contaminants.

Fear is one of the biggest blocks to passion and the free and easy feeling needed to connect with the sex energies that abound in the universe, that high-flying feeling that is the antithesis of fear. Some may fear their lover will leave them and hurt them, so they cling and hold on too tightly, pinching off the energy that needs freedom to bloom and play. The fears of abandonment are silly when you think about them, really. A person is with you, and you are afraid they will leave. Well, of course they will leave, but it is better to expect this and make love to them anyway. We all need freedom to follow our passions, and a relationship is much more likely to be a good one if both parties are offered freedom of choice and the trust of their beloved to come and go with their true feelings. The sense of obligation will be destructive if both partners are not on the same commitment page.

There are no specifics that a relationship should follow. All are free to create a version that fits their desires. Even multiple partners are fine, if that's what you wish to experience, although there is a loss of intensity in the connections in this case. The dissipation of energies among more partners spreads the energy thin and less intensely for each person in the circle. For some, this is better and more in line with their vibration; for others, the intense focus of a monogamous relationship is the path to joy. You will find those who are in tune with you, and we suggest trying different forms of relationships if you are not sure of your true preference. This is where cultural conditioning is very powerful, and many will fear creating a disturbance in the waters of their family or culture. This is up to you, of course, and will restrict you as you choose — or not.

The fast and furious pace of the culture in which you live is a detriment to the deep exploration of the intimate relationship. The quick and easy communications skim across the surface of your minds, never going below into the real and juicy depths of the mind you are willing to share. We suggest you set aside time for communication and to explore subjects in depth, with love always as the motivation. This is indeed foreplay for the mind, and the body follows along. There are often mistakes made by jumping into the physical too soon — not because it is wrong or evil, but because the mind is the organ of pleasure and will lead the body down the path to bliss, not the other way around.

Deeply probing the mind of your loved one will unearth the impediments to joy, and you will help each other heal the old wounds that are like barbed wire wrapped around your hearts, tight and painful. A shared conversation about old wounds and tears shed in healing will bring you very close together and open the heart center, giving a lovemaking session more depth and deep feeling that will bond you on a more profound level. The male of the species is indeed sometimes more resistant to this form of bonding, yet females are also becoming harder and tougher as they live in the world, so all are encouraged to open up their hearts and minds to each other.

Let Go of the Fear and Guilt

These are the beginning steps of awakening to bliss, of excavating fear and cultural misteachings that will sabotage the process. These misteachings must be brought into the open, discussed, and systematically disempowered in students' minds, or they will arise as fears and scary monsters as the bliss energies are awoken. The underlying fears and ego devices are near the surface as you grow, and the choice to deal with them must be made consciously, or it will be done unconsciously, and the former is much less scary.

Although fears are felt, tears may flow, and a sense of losing your value in the culture arises, we must say here that your value is never under dispute by the God essence. You are all of equal value, and the possessions you own and your family's approval — or disapproval — make no difference in the eyes of God energies. These energies flow where the channels are clear, regardless of state, age, or physical well-being, and the channels are cleared by love and forgiveness of themselves and others. Guilt will block the channels; like mud in a pipe through which clear water wishes to flow, it will clog and prevent the flow of clarity and joy. It needs to be dealt with in compassionate and gentle ways.

These elements will arise in layers, one after the other, as you travel down the road to bliss. Support and gentle counseling and prayer will help each of you pass the mud out of the pipe so the water can flow clear and refreshing into your hearts. There is a future of awakening to Spirit ahead that is indeed a blissful ride. The ego's fears are with you, and facing fears intensifies these feelings briefly, but after their release and continued disempowerment, you become free.

You are a miner, and the light on your headlamp will help you see just a bit further down the mine. The seam of gold will eventually be illuminated clearly for you, but the shaft down to the mother lode can seem a dark and perilous journey indeed, and the time it takes to shore up the ceilings is important. All fears must be removed so that the fears of the material world do not come crashing in. If you hurry it too much, the mine will not be a safe one and you will be scared to go in.

After several weeks of accepting this process, you will begin to see that these fears and ego needs were dogging you all your life, and a peace is arising that you never knew before. This is the joy of the path that will be seen as you travel on your way. It is a road that has been neglected. At first full of weeds and boulders that must be removed, the road now becomes a smoother one that sets its travelers to peace and ease that were not known before.

Feeling Bad About Feeling Bad

Now we will write about the guilt of losing the fast and furious energy that is the gift of God. In some ways, when you are sad, you know it is your own doing, and you suffer more, knowing that you should be a different way. The self is horrified by its emotions, yet this self knows the emotions are real. It is a real conundrum for the mind, feeling bad about feeling bad. How does one fix this? We are suggesting that you go deep into the bad. Cry about the loss of innocence, the loss of joy that you are feeling. Acknowledge this sadness with tears of regret. Deep in that emotion, the events that led to the depression will arise. There is no shame in feeling this sadness deeply instead of feeding it with food or alcohol. Feed it with the attention you crave, the loving caress of a hand and gentle coaxing, as if you are your own dearest friend, asking, "Why you are so sad?" The friendship you offer yourself in this circumstance will indeed heal the wound and allow you to come closer to your self — the self you know you can be.

The raising of the energy after such an experience will allow the future to look a little different. You have comforted the one who was hurt, and this is not self-pity but self-nurturing. This is what your culture lacks. You are expected to cope and pull up your boots or fall apart after a night of drinking when the truth of your sadness finally surfaces, begging to be seen. But in drunkenness that sadness cannot be healed — just regretted the next morning as an embarrassing slip, a weakness that seems other than who you are to the world. Often this is your true self, desperately begging for your healing sight to see its wounds and acknowledge the damage that was done.

It is often good to do this when feelings of pain rise on their own. There is always a place for a therapist to help, yet you really don't need one to find out what the issue is. A lot of you already know where the wound is, but you won't go there. Your feeling body and emotions are very clear, and gently, if you listen — not so gently if you don't — they will take you where you need to go.

So do not be afraid of the emotions that are your map to healing. They will eventually normalize and become a gentler guidance system. When they have been ignored for a long time, they come out in depression, rage, or crying jags when you are under stress. But listen more often, and they will become the dear friend who guides you down the path to sanity and balance, not the apparent enemy that wishes to embarrass you at parties.

CHAPTER TWENTY-TWO

Insanity

The subject we will cover here is the idea of insanity and how this fear narrows the view of what people will allow into their world. Society's views on insanity are very narrow, and just dealing with this fear has many layers. The idea that any spiritual experiences are insane is a pervasive one in your culture — the opposite of India, for example. Even a slight movement of the body that cannot be explained, such as Tina has experienced [Tina felt many unusual body movements during her energy sessions], will cause medication to be administered, and the energy will immediately be disrupted and the spiritual experience short-circuited, so to speak.

There are many such experiences that Western society is afraid of. Hearing voices in the mind is sometimes seen as insanity, as this channel has experienced with us. But a voice in the mind can indeed be associated with a spiritual awakening. Again, this causes problems for any student who is on a spiritual search for the divine bliss energies of God. These students must surely remove themselves from the Western medical model as they pursue this path, as they will immediately be told that something is wrong with them when, indeed, there is something very right going on.

The fears around possession and evil spirits as portrayed on TV and movie screens also cause confusion. Again, many of the movements of the awakening body and mind mimic those that are portrayed on the screens of entertainment, so a jerk or a change in body movement of any kind really scares the spiritual student, and confusion arises. In older traditions, gurus and teachers gather around the student to explain these phenomena.

You, dear one, will be the explainer of these phenomena, assuring participants that this is a normal part of the body adjusting to the energies of bliss and awakening.

The spiritual student must understand that the fearful limits placed on the body's movements and the mind's expressions are part of the prison keeping humans from the divine union with God that they are seeking. These proscriptions have arisen over centuries in which the burning of the bodies of so-called witches happened; to be a spiritual seeker in any way other than following the Church's rules was considered evil. It became very unsafe to practice any form of blissful pursuit, and many died for expressing bliss or ecstasy — unless they were in a nunnery or monastery. The rules have continued in the unconscious of the cultural mind, and they arise as soon as a practice provides any movements like those we are speaking about.

So the populace must be educated that in meditation, and in the pursuit of the bliss states, many unusual events will occur, and that support of loving members on the same path must be present. For any who wish to follow our path to the awakening of bliss energies, it must be understood that unusual events will take place, and with the Western mind there is no basis for understanding.

This is indeed one of the first talks we would like you to give, as it is the primary fear in Western minds that stops them dead on this path to awakening.

Baby Steps to New Education

The mind that is trained in the Western way is in a difficult position at first as the new energies are experienced. There are many concerns about acceptance, about the loss of possessions and sanity, about being "put away" — anxiety about the consequence of this path we wish to share. The students following this bliss path need support.

People need new education that these bliss states look a little unusual at first. This can help in Western culture, where the suppression of joy has inhibited the flow of soul energies in the absence of dancing, hugging, and affection — any state that is not serious and intellectual. The path to bliss begins in the release of the severe constraints in the Western mind, of the oppression of joy and happiness. We see that this is a sad state indeed, and many of you go on an annual vacation to a more expressive culture, often for just this reason: to find an ounce of joy in the year so that you won't go mad.

The idea of insanity must in some way be turned on its head. The lives you are living are, in fact, insane, devoid of happiness and joy, bogged down with ego drives that never give rest for fun and clean play. By "clean" we mean with joy that is accessed without drugs or alcohol. The only time most access the joy state is briefly after the first drink, but this deteriorates quickly into a lower vibration that is not so much fun and hurts the body, and in the long run it destroys the natural ability to feel pleasure.

There are baby steps to take on this journey that we ask all to endeavor to start as they are exploring this area of expression, the divine bliss path. We ask you to read and learn about the expression of energy in the yogic traditions of tantra and Vedic practice. This opens the mind to wider horizons so that the idea of insanity begins to fade into the background of the mind. These are all important areas to become aware of.

This is the beginning of the process to allow these energies. There must be a letting go of the fears around Spirit and an acceptance of an energy that initially feels like an "other." In fact, this is your energy, flowing for the first time, and there is no reason to fear it. It is the very energy that you desire, but its unfamiliarity is scary and the power in it can be felt as soon as it arises. There is a learning curve for managing the feelings that are aroused and the fears as they arise for clearing. Talking about the events and sharing the experiences is imperative if you are an absolute beginner. Others with more experience in this area will hold the hands of those less experienced and assure them that this is normal on the path to fully awakening the mind.

The dimension in which most of you have been living is so flat that the burgeoning energies feel like a ride on a roller coaster. If at any time it is too much, just stop the activity or meditation that is causing the event and still your mind, excavating the fears so they can be brought into the light for cleansing and healing. As long as the fears are in your subconscious, they will sabotage all areas of spiritual seeking, short-circuiting the flow and frustrating the process.

Do take it slow in the beginning. We know this is difficult, as the

Western mind is too used to speed and accomplishment, but this may backfire on this journey, as too much too soon will blow its circuits, so to speak, or scare you too much. Take each part slowly, and know that Spirit is with you and will give you what you can handle. Spirit wishes to connect with you in all ways and supports the journey to bliss. It is as if a long-lost child is coming home to its parent — sometimes the hugs are so strong that they overwhelm you. Of course, we are the energies, and it is a case of working out the volume, so to speak, so that there is energy flowing in a manageable way.

Now we will leave you tidying and editing for the day. Enjoy the Sun, dear one. We are with you in love throughout your day as you walk and care for the transformer that your body is becoming. Drink your water, and know that coffee and food will not bring you the experiences that you want, ever.

CHAPTER TWENTY-THREE

Sexual Wounding

We must talk to those of you who have been wounded by sex, who have been so hurt that you are afraid even to read the words. There are many of you who have left the playing field and refuse to return to the game, so we must explain to you something about the nature of sexual energy and its part in the life you wish to live: Sexual energy is not really optional. It is the very driving force of your life, the thing that you call passion — not just as it relates to your lovers, but as it relates to your very being.

The loss of passion means the loss of life, and this is one of the greatest problems of your society. So many of you, particularly women — although not exclusively women — have been attacked and are deathly afraid of sex and what it has come to mean. It has come to represent fear, betrayal, pain, confusion, being overwhelmed, and sadness, all of which are destroying your ability to achieve joy, creativity, passion, and energy in your lives. What we must convince you of is that to live without passion, to stop sexual energy flowing, is to put out the candle that lights the room of your life. We are here to tell you it is imperative to let the past go and to begin to heal the sexual wounds that are keeping you powerless and disconnected from your engine, the fire in your heart that will give your life the drive and feelings of desire you are lacking.

Many of you who are wounded have turned to other substances as your lovers — alcohol, food, television, and other meaningless areas of entertainment — to fill the void that lost passion has left. And we wish to tell you that now is the time to reclaim your sexual energy and once again feel alive, strong, and ready for anything.

We do not wish to scare any of you, so here we will say that you do not need to have a sexual relationship with anyone else — but you do need to have a sexual relationship with yourself and your god, whatever form that takes. You see, you have mistaken the meaning of sexual energy because of all the incorrect things you have been told — that it is evil and dirty and dangerous, and that you deserved the hurt that you got. These are the beliefs that cloud your mind, and this is the worst piece of news yet, our dear sweet ones. The beliefs you have will create that which you focus on, and the way to heal is to change your mind. Yes, that is all you have to do — change your minds, and your experience of the world will change, and sexual energy will once again become your friend and the energy that creates that which you wish to experience. Many of you attracted negative experiences because you had been taught negative things, and as we have explained several times, you get what you believe, whether you want it or not.

"A cruel universe," you say? We know it can appear as such sometimes, but what about the idea of a universe that gives you everything you ask for, no matter what it is, no holds barred? That is indeed what this is, dear ones. The genie you have all dreamed about is real, but because you were not taught this, because you were taught incorrect beliefs about sex and sexual energy, you have inadvertently made things and experiences you don't want. You have been told sex is evil, so when you engage in sex it feels evil because these ideas are planted very early in your minds when you are but small, impressionable children, too young to know any better. The beliefs are deep, often not even in your conscious minds, but they are always manifesting so that you can see them, and this is the gift of experience.

We know the sexual wounds you have experienced do not feel like gifts, but they are there to show you what you inherently know is not true — that sexual energy is evil. This is what the beliefs you hold are telling you; this is what you are experiencing, so this must be true. But our best news is that you do not need to do anything about it. You merely have to change your mind and begin to tell a different story, now that you understand how the mind of creation works. Look to how you feel, and know that anything you think about sex that makes your stomach turn or your tears arise is a lie. Know that sexual energy is good — and good *for you*. These are the words of truth, we promise you.

You must let go of the ideas that cause pain. Perhaps the thought of a past event makes you sad or makes you cry; then that memory must not be pursued anymore. You must retrieve other more loving thoughts from the past when love was predominant and you felt safe and loved. Or it may be the thought of the perpetrator of a crime that makes you angry and afraid. We say it is now time to forgive and let the crime go, knowing it is you who will be set free by this act.

Forgiveness is hard — we understand this — but you must try over and over again until it is accomplished, and you will receive great rewards for doing so. We promise you. If you keep the hurt, nurturing and feeding it with emotion and words, thoughts and stories, you will remain lost in the past, and all your precious energy and potential health and strength will remain there with the thoughts and feelings, inaccessible to you. This is not what you want. Take back your strength, take back your love, and offer it first to yourself, then to your relationship with God, and then, should you choose, to your beloved, whomever he or she may be. That last part you do not have to do until you are ready, or ever, but we do want you to do all of these steps in the reclamation of your sexual self, and this is why: You cannot be healthy and strong without this energy. You cannot be creative and happy without this energy, and you cannot thrive without this energy. It runs the vibrancy you need to achieve all of these things, and it brings you joy.

Ah, dear ones, we know you are scared and you think that you will lose control of that which you have, but the truth is you do not have control. All you have is fear and resistance, and you do not want these anymore. It is no way to live. Life is good, and you want to experience its fullness, do you not? You do indeed, and this is what we also wish for you — a full, happy, and vibrant life in which you feel love, beauty, and strength. This is yours for the taking, but you must let go of the past and refuse to play with the demons who dwell there anymore. They are not good playmates, and we wish for you to find new friends in the present, where the Sun is shining and new friends wait to meet you.

Child Abuse

We will, here and now, address the idea of children who are abused, as this argument always comes up at this point and is used to disprove the idea that you create your own life. This idea of the innocence of children is predicated on the incorrect belief that you have only one life and that as a child you arrive as a clean slate. This is not the case at all, so the argument is empty. Children are born here because they have incorrect belief systems that they wish to live out in the third dimension, so they arrive with ideas and thoughts from before that must be manifested so that they can see what is working and what is not. You all come with a past, and when you look at the little body of a newborn babe, know that he has his own path to live, and that will indeed have its own challenges. These challenges are not punishments, but rather opportunities for healing, opportunities for incorrect beliefs to be seen in the manifest world so that they can be addressed. When you start to see your life's problems this way, all becomes clear and you can attend to that which needs changing.

Do Not Fear Sexual Energy

Since the beginning of time, sexual energy has fueled the creative processes here on this Earth plane, and that is never going to change — ever. And if you do not heal the injuries and judgment you have about sexuality and its appropriateness, you will have to return again to learn the lessons, and for those of you who have had a hard time with this energy, that is a scary idea.

So be brave, and know that we mean it when we say you do not have to take a lover to do this. But you do need to dance again, you do need to be creative again, and in the beginning, you will need to feel the feelings you have been drowning out with television, food, and alcohol. When you take these substances away, you will begin to feel the emotions that the heaviness of these activities has been numbing, and you will need to be prepared for the emotion and pain that will arise. This is the reason this feels so difficult to do, but you must do it. You do not want to experience another lifetime with this energy, stuck and hated, do you? No, you do not. So start now to reclaim it, in baby steps, so you do not frighten yourself — first in the mind, through prayers of forgiveness and transformation, and then, when you are feeling stronger, in the world of action.

Maybe you're willing to go out there once again, so you take a dancing class and dress up for it, feeling attractive but unsure. Remember you are in charge this time, and there is nothing you must do. But please do stay sober in these circumstances and feel the nerves. They will keep you alert. Your guidance system that has been ignored for so long must be given a clear voice to speak for you, to show you the way.

None of you are responsible, in a sense, for what has happened to you, and we never wish to make you feel guilty, as if it is your fault. You are creating the wrong things because you were told the wrong things — by people who knew no better most of the time. They too were innocent, even if they caused you pain. So do not turn your hatred to them, for that will lower your vibration, and we must raise it at all costs. It matters not how you raise it, but you must feel better in small increments.

These deep wounds will not change overnight. Our dear one, Tina, spent many years working to transform her inner world, and finally her outer world could reflect that. Celibacy at that time is fine and nothing you need to explain to another. In fact, you do not need to discuss this with anyone except your spiritual guides and perhaps a dear and trusted friend. We guarantee you that if you begin this process, miracles will indeed happen, and if you can transform your hatred of sexual energy to a quiet and gentle appreciation of it, then you will access the energy you need to create what you want and what will enliven your life.

The idea that you can hate sexual energy and thrive is wrong. You cannot. It is the force of good and strength and creativity. Have you not noticed the dried-up and energy-less auras of those who have given up on sexuality? There is a feeling of moroseness and failure around them that gives no energy, no vibrancy. This is not a judgment on our part — just a statement of truth. Sexual energy is a gift for you that you misunderstood and need to reaccept into your lives. Come to understand these gifts as they were meant to be used.

This culture in which you find yourselves does not help you want to heal. We understand, and this is why we tell you this can be a private affair, so to speak. But there is hope on the horizon. There are small groups of individuals arising who get this whole system and understand that something has gone terribly wrong with the teachings around sex and love.

The tides are changing, and we are here to do this work. So take heart, dear ones, and know that even if there is not a lover in the flesh in your future, claiming back this energy will bring passion, energy, and health back into your experience, and that is worth the effort, is it not?

Letting Go of the Story

There is indeed a whole world of experience that is lost when the damages done to the sexual self are left to rule the experience. Indeed, the most beautiful and expressive areas of the human mind and emotion are lost to most people who have been hurt by the bonds of their past and their refusal to enter into the present moment and forgive the events that took place so long ago. They think that if they open to love, the same thing will happen, but it is their thoughts about it that will indeed create the hurt again. Love wants to express through you and with you, and it is so sad when the channels to its expression are rusted shut with hatred and memories of betrayal. We are asking all who read this book to honestly open to the possibility that their wounds are safe refuges for them, that they can blame others for the fear they indulge. Yet the sad truth is that the individual is in the prison of shut-down energy and fear, not the person who hurt him or her.

Let us bring this difficult subject into the light instead of demonizing the past person and what he or she did to you. Admit that there is a delight in blaming and retreat. It allows you to be safe — safe from experience, safe from life. You are the full motion of love only when you forgive the past, forgive the people who hurt you, and allow the love that is all of you to flow outward and inward and all around you. The dear, sweet heart of the wounded soul cries out for affection and connection and is confused by the refusal to go down that road to the possibility of bliss.

For many, the idea of bliss causes the fear of giving up their story to arise. They are so identified with the elaborate tale they have woven that to let it go brings up mortal fear. Yet it is in the letting go of the story that true freedom will arise and express itself, beautiful in the life you wish to live — a life full of bliss, sexual fulfillment, community, and joy.

These are the rewards for letting go of the story of your violation. Step into a future that is different from your past, and allow love to flow through you. Yes, the channels are closed and quivering with fear at the prospect, but follow our prescriptions and they will open and begin to allow light's loving flow through your body. And as the barriers to love's presence fall down around you, you will understand the dark and confining fence you have been living behind.

Indeed, some of you are living in a concentration camp, surrounded by barbed wire made of unforgiveness, fear, judgment, and self-hatred, feeling nothing of the sweet embrace that love wishes to offer you. You are prisoners with the key in your back pocket, hoping for someone else to release you. This is the romantic fantasy that so many feel is the solution to their problems, but it is a projection. Another can never set you free if you are the one who is in charge of the mind that hates and is afraid. Others will slip from your grasp after they arrive, once they encounter the sharp and solid walls in your mind that prevent them from immersing themselves in you. You are the gift of love that they seek — you just do not know it.

Yes, this is beautiful writing because you recognize it as the truth of what you know you are capable of experiencing. There is a place in your mind that knows this is so — that your fulfillment is indeed a God-given gift that you desire with all your heart. You know that the way you are living is a shallow reproduction of the power that dwells inside of you, yet the fears you bump up against stop you in the bad habits you have of numbing out. They seem impossible to give up, yet this is what you want. There seems to be no way out of the maze of habits and old patterns you see as who you are. But those patterns are not who you are any more than the leaves are the tree. The tree will bloom again next year if it is fed and looked after, receiving clean water, sunlight, and the challenge of storms to strengthen its branches. Humans are afraid of the storms and see them as something to desperately avoid, yet the challenges and obstacles of your life are gifts from God to show you where you are constricted and afraid. God wants your full realization and strength, and that is why you feel fear at the challenges. There is part of you that does not believe that you are special and beautiful, a strong and infinite being. That is why you came here — to grow out of the limited thinking that is creating the life that does not live up to your dream of what it could be. You know this in your bones.

A new way of looking at fear needs to be adopted. Fear is where you want to go, where you need to go. So feel the fear and know that this is God's love manifesting for you to overcome the limits of your mind's past. It will bring you into your full power to express love, beauty, and calmness for all to see. There are no barriers except those in your own beliefs. No one is your prison guard. You are free to do as you wish, to pursue what you wish. Feel the edges and go past them. Not all at once, but nudge them out of your way so that the horizon in front of you is clear and expansive. Then you indeed have free choice. Most of you do not have any idea what freedom is or what to do with it. Your cell is comfortable — you have filled it with cushions and foods you like, and a television sits in the corner and beckons to you to leave your narrow existence and enter its fake world, where life seems to be.

Your life is such a treasure when you break through your bonds and begin to explore the fullness that you are, leaving behind the judgments that create the walls of your cell and define edges in you that are not real. You are a boundless, powerful being who can transform the world with your gifts and intense creative energy. It is this you will receive as you brave the walls that keep you small. So be brave, and know that the force of the universe will rush to your aid when you decide that being small is not serving you anymore. You want the passion! You want the desire to course through you and energize all you do and all you feel.

CHAPTER TWENTY-FOUR

Men and Women on Different Pages

The history of lovemaking has, for many centuries, been controlled by those in power, and that has for some time been men. But it is time to make this coming together one of true equality, and for that, the female side must be spoken about, especially as you are now facing a generation of young men who have learned to make love by watching pornography, and this is indeed a sad sight to see. You have, in this new generation of the computer, been indoctrinated in the most primitive way of having sex, in the lowest realms of the ego. The terms and conditions of the intimate encounter are very coarse indeed, and little refinement is shown there. Women know this, of course, yet they too are falling into the trap of the ego-driven sexual encounter because of all the conditioning they are subject to. But their bodies will not respond so well to the rushed and crude approach. Man's reproductive sexuality will function in this realm, and of course, pornography is generally made for men, by men, at the moment. We are not attacking men — merely pointing out that they are the ones who can function reasonably in this realm of images and ideas in the modern world. But women do not fare so well; their bodies and minds require gentleness and patience, and this is by design.

It was designed this way so that there was some impetus to spend time to reap the rewards of the kundalini. Left to the boys, generally it would not happen. Women require a longer time to reach excitement and to relax into openness, so it is a blessing for a man to have a woman who requires patience and a longer time of foreplay, because she will lead him into the realms of the magical kundalini, which does indeed take more time to encounter. So to any men reading this: Be grateful for the lovemaking that your partner requires, even the long lead-up time, for your partner is taking you to the energetic realms where you want to go.

There was a short time in the history of the world when men and women were truly equal, and this has been hidden in the historic record, for the time was long ago and the culture far away. But when the information about sexual energy, kundalini, was given to humans, there was a culture that took it to heart for some time and practiced these principles in a very focused and honest way. What they achieved was enlightenment through sexuality, but the cultures surrounding this small group were savage and patriarchal, and the men contained within those cultures were unwilling to concede that women held the key to their getting into heaven, so to speak.

We are not saying here that a woman is necessary for this to transpire, but it is one way to achieve this delightful state. Many find their salvation through pure prayer, meditation, and celibacy, and this is as it should be. There are many pathways to God, and you will find the one that suits you. We are writing for those who have a calling to find bliss with a partner, in the "real" world — the world of partnership, living together and working together.

You will know if this is your path by the feelings you have around it. You may have thought of going to a monastery because of the state of the world you see at the moment and your despair at finding your way in this Western world, but there is something in your heart and mind that cannot go. You love being around people. You love living life to the fullest, and you long for a partner with whom to delve deeply into the world of spirit. This path is for those of you who feel this way. If your spirit speaks to you through these feelings, then you are being told by your desire for a loving partner, a tantric partner, that this may be the path for you.

You have so many choices, it seems, in this modern world, yet they are not as varied as you think. There is the body's world — the world of the ego, material and fear-driven — and then there is world of love, Spirit's world. This is an energetic world, and it will become available to you as you practice forgiveness and nonjudgment through the attainment of peace. These are the only two real choices you have.

This world convinces you of the thousands of options it pretends to offer, but there are only two. Many of you have been choosing the first for a long time and have seen its rewards, which can seem many at first — money, fame, sex of some sort — but this will not satisfy for long. Oh, perhaps it will last a few lifetimes, but if you are feeling dissatisfied and disillusioned, then it is time to change your direction and look up toward the light, instead of down to the Earth plane, for what you want.

CHAPTER TWENTY-FIVE

Sin and Punishment

We will now go on to our next chapter, which covers the ideas of sin and punishment as they relate to sexual activity. What a chapter this will be! This is perhaps the most challenging belief for you all to change — that the sexual act is a divine act when it is motivated from the higher mind, the mind of love, the mind connected to Source. You have indeed been sold a bill of goods, as you say, when it comes to sexuality. And even though the times are changing, they are heading in the wrong direction for most of you, and that is one of the main reasons we are here — to redirect your beliefs around this most challenging of topics, sin and punishment.

You have been told for millennia that the body is evil, that sex is only to be enjoyed in the confines of marriage, and that even then it is less than savory and should not be talked about. No doubt, in the Western world the tides have changed, and sex is out of the closet, so to speak, but it is out of the closet in the worst way possible, and it has gone wild with the dictates of the ego mind that is driving your culture. So we will tackle the underlying issues first and then head to the more obvious ones, the ones that are there for all to see.

Underneath the surface of many of your minds are the ancient and persistent teachings that sex is evil. Many of you do not understand it because of the prohibition around education on this subject. You learned it in secret and you keep it secret, even from each other, the ones with whom you are making love. The subject is fraught with fear and discomfort.

It is a science, this sexual-energy business, but because the Church did — and still does — call it evil, even though the words are gentler in the new century, the ideas that pervade your minds are still seen as true. "Don't talk about it, and certainly don't study it." There are many misconceptions about the "sins of the father," we will say. Your parents never spoke about it, and there was always a quiet knowing in the house that you should never speak about sexual energy. As small children you felt bad about any curiosity you had about this obviously powerful subject. We are here to tell you sex is sacred when the higher mind is brought to the actions, and there is never any kind of punishment meted out for the practice after you die. In fact, there is never any punishment meted out for anything after you die! We may as well throw that one in here while we are at it.

The universe does not work the way you have been taught, and it certainly does not work the way your churches have taught you. The universe and God are love only. All the pain, all the suffering, and all the hatred are your own makings and have nothing to do with the love that pervades all. All those unpleasant things are pinching off love, turning away from love, judging the creations of the universe, and it is you who create them all.

The analogy of light is always clear and understandable, so we will use it here: Love is light, and darkness is the absence of light or love. There is no switch for darkness — only something blocking the light. The shadows you feel and see are the blocks to love's presence, and they are removed by forgiveness, understanding, and nonjudgment only. They are not removed by rules or punishment, but enlightenment. They are not removed by creating prisons, but by teaching freedom, and freedom comes from understanding, not narrowness of thought.

We know those of you who look at the world and see it as sinful do not understand our words, because it seems that the world is so full of the bad and the ugly. But all of this comes from these old and incorrect teachings, and you are living in a culture of ignorance and superstition around sex, even into this modern era. The hangover from the Church's misteachings is still causing you much pain, and it is high time the subject had the light of awareness shined on it. As the tales of sexual corruption and misdeeds arise in your awareness within the largest church on Earth, it is time to call a spade a spade and to accept that sexual energy is powerful, and it is not going anywhere.

The problem is in the speaking about it. Because of your underlying belief in its dirtiness, you will not talk about it, and it is only in changing that belief into the truth — that it can be one of the most glorious ways to connect with Source, and it is one of the quickest ways to connect with that energy you call God — that you will become willing to learn and to share your precious selves with each other in a high-vibration way. The desire to connect is so strong, but the teachings of sex's nature are so wrong that you must use a substance to override the conflict, and that is why so may of you use alcohol to access sexual energy. The problem is that alcohol keeps the sexual energy at a low vibration, so you have this catch-22 situation where you cannot feel the divine nature of sex because you are numbed out and vibrating at a low frequency.

What a mess we are in together, but we will rise above the old teachings and get into the subject in a new and enlightening way. So we would like you to begin to unearth those dark beliefs you have about sex. Contemplate that which we are saying, and come to understand that this energy must be negotiated. You are all suffering from its blocks and its misuse, and it is time to speak the truth and get to the heart of the matter.

Sex as Perceived by Gender

Half of your population is taught that sex is good, powerful, and strong, a force to be wielded with a lust for life, so to speak. The other half, the part the first half is seeking, is taught that sex is bad, that those who participate in it are "less than," and that if they are not monogamous there is something inherently bad about them. "This has changed," you say? We beg to differ. This has not changed at all.

Many women and girls are raised with very difficult beliefs around sexuality, and it is causing them a great deal of pain. And because the excessive use of alcohol is what is used to override these beliefs, much damage is being done to your young women as they venture into this realm of sexuality. Drugs and alcohol are used prolifically, and the information gleaned from the pornography industry through the use of your Internet is creating the most poisonous atmosphere you could imagine. You thought the old restrictions of the Church were bad? If you could see, on an energetic level, the damage that is being done to the hearts and minds of your young women in this century, your heart would break as ours is breaking. We must tell you to stop this awful and degrading treatment of each other, and to come to understand the sacred nature of sexuality and its ability to transport you to realms so high, so beautiful, that you would give up all your substances and distractions if you could only experience it. But our challenge, of course, is that you can only experience it if you give up all of that stuff first.

Many of you will not survive long enough for that to happen, and for us that is a sad story. Death is not the end of the story, of course, but those who die young from this raw sexual energy beaten into the ground by the ego, and the lives spent grieving — the parents and lovers left behind by these early losses — are sad indeed.

There are many young ones, and we will say here that young ones would be anyone under thirty years of age who is lost when it comes to sex — as lost as their parents were, just in a different maze. The older generation realizes where it went wrong and that its teachers were wrong, but the younger crowd is not so aware. They think that because they can go to a party, get high, and have sex, that all is okay, but this is as sad as a generation frozen in fear.

Each group has its own price to pay for the behaviors it engages in, and not from a judgmental god, but from a loss of love, peace, health, and indeed, the loss of the gifts this energy has to offer all of you.

The pornography industry is throwing fuel on the fire, and although we will not go into a rant about it here — we will save that for later — we must remind you that the vibration of that activity is causing much degradation, pain, and suffering. The inflammation of desires in those who use it is unhealthy and powerfully destructive.

How can we help here? That is our question. What can we do to assist you out of the dark depths to which you have been taken on this journey so far?

This generation is told that blow jobs are a loving act when performed on demand, and that the energies of pornography are the energies to be sought. This is not the case. If there ever were a way *not* to make love, it is shown in the pornographic images viewed on the screens of your computers and televisions. The gentle and honorable way that lovemaking should be engaged in is the antithesis of that which you see, and unfortunately, many young men and women do not know this. They do not have any other place to go to learn about these things. We need to get the truth out there that mutual respect, health, and loving communication builds the foundation for a healthy sexual relationship, and that these dear and precious bodies you own are for the joy of sexual expression and the joining of hearts and minds in love.

We sound romantic to your hardened Western hearts, we know. There are many of you who will not heed our lessons, and that is sad but okay. You will get to continue on the path you are on and learn the lessons it has to give you. But there are others of you reading who know you do not want to play these games anymore, and it is to you we are speaking. You have had the dull sex, the hateful sex, and the uninspiring sex, and you are willing to give this a shot. You have seen your own incompetence in this area — the fears, the pain, and the confusion — and you are, perhaps, willing to accept that what you have been taught is wrong, and that your experiences prove that something is amiss. You have not been told something you need you know to thrive in this area.

Many women will not participate in the kinds of sexual relationships out there that seem to be required of them. They are learning that they are free to choose what they want to experience and that the designs that have been made in this patriarchal society do not fit their feelings — what they want and need to be happy. So they have secluded themselves away and will take their own peace and self-nurturance over the other options that are available.

And there are many men out there who are lonely and do not understand that what they have been taught and the ways in which they have been raised are destroying their relationships. Their inability to communicate and access their feelings is their enemy, not their friend.

Oh, dear ones, there is such pain and loneliness in your society, and there is no need for it. The issues are all coming to a head, it is true — the violence, the hatred, and the access to everything is speeding up the deterioration of your hearts and minds, and an intervention of sorts must be made. All of us on this side, the nonphysical side, are rallying ourselves to offer up the help and understanding you all need to get yourselves out of this sticky situation. We are here to help dispel the myths, but there must first be a deconstruction of what has happened and what is happening. That is the most difficult task, because what has become normal for you is so far from healthy that you look at what we prescribe and shake your heads, saying you cannot go that far, that you cannot give up all that we ask you to give up.

What are you giving up that is so valuable here? Are the lives you are leading so very satisfying? If they are, then you are on the right track and do not need us, but we think you are reading this because you are curious, at least, or desperate in the worst cases. We are here to speak about an option that has not been spoken about.

CHAPTER TWENTY-SIX

Diet

The extreme nature of sexual energy when it is fully flowing is indeed awesome, and the person hoping to experience the event must prepare for it. Most of you do not have the strength of character at the moment to allow the full flow of this energy. The fears around possession and evil that are perpetrated in your culture prevent you from truly letting go of the body and surrendering to the divine energies that wish to flow through the vessel you call a body. The electrical charges and synapse firings that accompany this sort of experience are indeed awesome to experience, but we suggest a good time of preparation by reading about other such masters of this energy, about eating properly, and about being one with God.

This is no small feat for most of you; however, the rewards are enormous, and the bliss that can be experienced overrides other pleasures you might seek through food or alcohol. Not only do you get to enjoy the experiences heightened sexual focus brings, but the health benefits are legion. The body revels in this energy, and the creativity that rises as the channels are opened can also be something to behold. The special features of this practice turn a person not into a body worshipper but a divine conduit to God and forces of love.

This energy is for those of a higher vibration who wish to experience the flow of God energy through themselves and within themselves. This is the very reason most religions prohibited sex as they did. There was a deep understanding by early mystics in the Church that God energy was sexual energy and that if the people were separated from each other through fear, the Church could gain control of the bodies, minds, and hearts of those who were now separated and sad with no connection to the divine. These people would go to the churches in search of the very jewel they carried inside them in ignorance. This has been a very sad sight in Western religions, and we are determined to free up this lovely connection that will heal your troubled world of its hatred and wars. The last thing you want to do after reaching these heights is hurt or scare someone. Open channels of sexual energy create the most kind and gentle beings, who feel for all and wish only to be of service.

The ego, when given precedence over the God channel, will starve you of contact and connection and feed the fear-based paradigm in which it believes, promoting attack, judgment, and fear-based behavior. We only wish the best for our dear human friends, and we will be giving direct instructions on how to achieve these goals in a systematic and loving way that will heal even the most terrified and damaged of you.

Avoid Low-Vibration Foods

We would now like to speak about the foods you are putting into your dear and amazing bodies. This is perhaps one of the most important and transformative areas of sexual energy in your immediate vicinity, although most would not imagine this area has anything to do with sex and God. On the contrary, your dear bodies were designed to eat only fresh and healthy food — with some exceptions, such as nuts — that can be stored for some time and contain their essence of life.

The foods that are being consumed in your culture by the majority of people, and especially those who are sexually wounded, are poisonous indeed. Low-vibration feelings call out to low-vibration foods, and so many of you are at a low vibration in your bodies. These low-vibration foods have become normal for you, and you feel deprived if you cannot have your deep-fried food, sweets, or chips. There are so many things you ingest that are not actually food at all but poisonous to your very souls, and if you could feel the struggles that ingesting these foods causes in your biology, you would not eat them.

Most people have no idea just how healthy a body can be and that the feelings of "dragging your ass around," as you say, are not normal at all. Have you ever seen children at play early on in their little lives? There is no end to their energy. But force them to eat fatty foods and watch a box for entertainment instead of enjoying a fresh fruit salad at the beach, and you will see the transformation. The changes that can be wrought by a slow and steady morphing of diet are miraculous indeed, and anyone who feels separated from the passion they believe they can feel, perhaps at some point in the future, will surely set a path to that goal when they feed themselves with healthy foods that grow of their own accord on the planet.

Most people will say price is an issue, and we understand the dilemmas of many in this regard. But the truth is most of you should be eating about half the amount of food you do, and if you do the math, most of you could eat quite well if you all ate less and consumed more fruits, vegetables, and happy animals — if that is what you choose to do.

We feel the industrial raising of animals produces sad food, and if you like to eat meat, which again is your choice, God does not care. But choose animals who are raised in a safe and happy environment, who are killed humanely without extended suffering. These products do exist, and if you support the growers of these foods, then the prices will come down. We guarantee it. Dairy and other factory-produced foods are not in the body's best interest either. They are high in fat and full of hormones that confuse the body's regulatory systems to the extreme. Some of your cancers are fed by the chemicals in these elements and are not good for the land or the mind. They are heavy in vibration and drag down the etheric and physical bodies. Lighter salads are tasty and full of nutrition. The sexual nature of your being needs the elements found in natural food to function at its best, and a lot of you would actually feel a bit sexier if you were not so bogged down by your diets.

Do not mistake this for a push toward thinness for vanity's sake; that is another disease. See each meal as a means of nutrition for the soul. If you have a spiritual practice, add this to the regimen you believe brings you closer to God. All the foods designed to eat grow not in cardboard boxes or aluminum trays, but in the ground and on trees and bushes. It is easy to identify the foods that you should eat. They appear in nature in the forms in which you consume them — not blended and denied their true nature.

Ananda is helping me to transform my diet, so they comment here.

Water is a major component of the delicate balance required in your bodies to transmit the spiritual energy that we work with. The electric, metal, and salt components of your bodies work together to complete circuits of connection, so they function together for the transmission of energy messages and the all-important brain waves we use to communicate with you. Dehydration is a problem for clear communication, so please keep up the water intake, especially on these beautiful warm days.

The issue of food continues. We see the desire for breads in the form of scones and such. This needs to be a treat that you have once a week or so. It is not the end of the world to have it, but the healthier fruits and rolled oats are much better for your digestion and the higher balances we require to do our work. Lower-vibrating food will interfere with our transmission and the healing of the body matrix we have undertaken with you. All is free will, and you can choose anything you wish. We are just telling you from our point of view what helps our job here and what interferes with your ascension program.

We are happy to see you are trying very hard to accept this assignment, and we appreciate your genuine participation in this process of healing the physical body. We are also very happy that today you were happy and not stressed out about money. The tides are changing, dear one. The universe has no choice when you are vibrating at a high level but to bring you what you want, as the attraction law, as you know it, is indeed at play.

Healing will come for those in your presence, and they will notice the change and see that it is a result of spending time with you and your higher-vibration view of the world. We are excited to see the design plans for websites and blogs you are planning to set up for the writings of Ananda. We are Ananda, and we love that name and the mission for the future we are working on together. There will be an amazing manifestation of abundance and healing through this work, and we will guide you clearly and gently, although quite quickly. You will create the life you have dreamed about, and we are very honored to be on the journey with you into this new area of creativity. Indeed, this is as good as painting as far as the creative force is concerned, and we hope you do not judge it as less than that.

We know channeling has always been up there on your "to do"

list, and we have always been there, waiting for the right conditions to align themselves. The timing is perfect, and we also have an urgency around this. The world's makeup is rapidly transforming and healing, and healers are required to mother the next generation, such as your friend. She needs a mentor to quickly achieve her goals, and there are many such young women who need to hear your story and your adventures, to see they too are capable of reaching the heights to which they aspire. We thank you for listening. Enjoy your dinner.

Your Food Should Be of the Same Vibration as Your Spiritual Practice

Students on the path to the bliss energies must look at their food consumption and immediately start a program of natural foods. We do not want to restrict the amounts to begin with, but there should be a transition made to all-natural foods and, if possible, locally grown ones. Of course the ideal is organic, but for many this is a process.

As it has been for you, dear one. There were a few years when you changed and then returned, changed and then returned. Each year the transformation is going deeper, and the results become more solid in their manifestation. This is indeed a path that many will follow.

We do not want the food to be a strain as such. This adds stress to the body, and this is not what we wish to do. The exploration should be into the natural tastes and feelings of natural food, developing a belief that a meal is a prayer.

Many people will go to church or a yoga class and then eat a meal that is not holy in any way. We wish for you to see that the spiritual path and the foods eaten are of the same vibration. So that is the place to begin. Is there discordance between your spiritual practice and the food you're consuming? If you are eating french fries and doing yoga, that is a disconnect. Look at it logically, without attachment, and choose a different food to eat. Basically, as the path is refined, the foods too will naturally refine themselves. But initially a disciplined decision must be made that food is holy, and a prayer to the energetics of the body must be said. Even this will be a radical idea for many, and it may take a while to integrate this belief into actions that will become habits.

As we have mentioned previously, water is one of the most important components to the clarification of the body and adds much. Many will hate this: The dehydrating and stress-inducing aspects of coffee are not so suited to our path. Coffee disintegrates some of the elements that are required for sound transmission of electrical impulses. Indeed, the agitation that it causes interferes with the peace that is required for the message we need to send to those accessing the divine energies. Coffee is disruptive and agitates the emotions, even though many are so used to it that it is the idea of loss that agitates them. This again is an example of the body/ego attachment to substances and activities that are not good for you on an energetic level.

Take Your Time with These Changes

Dear one, as you cleanse from coffee and cream and sugar, can you not feel a lightening, an acceptance of being that was weighed down before? We do recommend that even a month may be taken to make subtle changes in this consumption.

Do not rush the giving up of anything; it will not serve the long-term purposes we have for the development of the bliss energies. Being overwhelmed with the idea of losing drugs or habits that you are attached to will end the process.

For the coffee addiction, if you are having the large servings, start with using a smaller cup. Start by reducing it by one cup only, then down to fewer numbers, and then to smaller cups and to the half-caffeinated version. This seems overly gentle, we know, yet the spiritual seekers of the West are often beating themselves up in the extreme. You have no gurus and no training. You need help and patience to undo the damage, to get back to a place of clarification where the vibrations have a chance to balance again. We ask you to consider your food practices as a prayer to God. Do not separate your diet from your spiritual practice. As you would not harm another, we ask you to stop harming yourselves. Stop saying, "Well, everyone else does it." We are not of that mind, and that argument does not hold water, as you say. You who are on the path to experiencing divine love are not striving to be normal. Indeed, you are striving to be exceptional, and you need to acknowledge this and embrace it without resentment.

Dear one, we have seen in you the process of slow surrender to the changes in food over the years, and in fact it took many tries to get that penny to drop. So we encourage a sensible yet quietly disciplined approach to these changes.

* * *

We are with you again, dear one. We relish your renewed dedication today to the system. As each fear is removed, you become more enamored, and this is why we counsel those on the path to feel the fear, analyze it, and go through it. The fears dissipate and fade into the ethers as you approach them, and you see that they are just ideas and there is no need to stop because they arise. This is the reason for so much wasted time and so much suffering. You are taught to back away from fears as if they are real, and this makes them stronger and even scarier. So every fear is to be probed, and each time, you will get energy and strength of mind based in truth and not illusions. This is indeed the biggest secret, so we wish to approach this in the context around foods and the deep attachments that each person has to the diet of his or her choice.

Reprogram Your Food Choices

Many of you have no real choice in what you eat. You are running on programs from your parents and your culture, and the very idea of messing with this scares you. The ego attaches to food in a most powerful way because it is the very basis of the survival mechanism. And as we mentioned previously, the ego is only assuring the survival of the body and cares not for the higher realms of the minds in which we seek to live. That is why the food issue is such a primal one; it kicks up the ego's most basic fear of starvation. This is why it is such a problem. When you really get this truth — that your food issues are your ego desperately trying to survive — you will not only have more compassion for yourself and the difficulties you encounter, but you will see the way around the ego's efforts to stop the changes that you so wish to make.

Of course there are reasons for every food choice you have made in your past and in your education. Maybe you ate to please your mother as a child and associate it with being a good person; maybe you were indoctrinated to eat a product, convinced by a marketing program that was driven by finances and not the truth about nutrition and the food's quality. These are the programs that are running and that have to be looked at for the profound changes we are asking to be put into place.

You see, most of the foods that are now available at coffee shops or supermarkets are not even foods anymore. Yet because of advertising and the slow programming of food companies and marketing boards, you have been taught otherwise. So we are asking you to go back 200 years into the past and look at what was being eaten then, before food's industrialization. Then you will get a better idea of what you will need to consume to be healthy.

For example, 200 years ago there would have been a limited amount of cheese, meat, and dairy products — small amounts as a treat or at a special event. These would not have been eaten at each meal; they were too expensive and too rare to be consumed in that way. Grains would have been rough and ancient grains, not the genetically modified grains that almost all bread products are made of. Again, no chemical preservatives were in use back then, and you know this is indeed a difficult process to avoid in this industrialized world of misinformation and fears.

We suggest that the first step is to avoid anything in a box, carton, or package of any kind. This will immediately make your diet simpler and healthier. Many of you will need to do this over some time, as you are so used to these products and have behaviors and rituals around them that it would frighten you to abandon in one fell swoop. This is where we wish for you to understand the ego's fears and to shift your diet bit by bit so that the ego can handle it and will not scream in terror.

There seems to be a different creature living within you in the form of this ego, and that is not too far from the truth. Immersion of the consciousness in the physical body was a later event in the evolutionary process, and the body, if you will, existed as primitive organism before the higher consciousness arrived and infiltrated the form. This idea will help you understand the power of the programming that you are working against — the primitive ego survival mechanism and modern dietary programming, driven by finances and other elements that are making a lot of money from the processing and packaging of once perfectly good foods.

Obviously, we encourage the use of organic products where possible and the elimination of any factory-raised products. Factory-raised animals are stressed and afraid, sick and unhealthy, and you are not served by eating their flesh. Small amounts of organically and humanely raised products are fine, but anything resembling daily consumption of these products is discouraged. You will enjoy them more, their taste will be better, and the nutrition will be pure and free of chemicals.

As for fruits and vegetables, use your discretion here, and learn about the seasonal fruits and vegetables that are available. Obviously some of you are living in colder climates where not much of anything is available in its natural form, but there you must decide on what is best, and larger changes in location and lifestyle may need to be looked at. But that is for another day, and we will attack those deep and disturbing topics at some time in the future.

Many of you have been dealt a tough hand in this food department, but do listen to us. Even if it takes two years to change all that we are asking you to change, you will remove untold sickness and add amazing quality to your life. The aging process will become an easy thing instead of the hell that the modern diet has created for your poor bodies.

We are all for the love and not for the hate of anything, so that is the energy that we wish for you to approach this topic with. Do not lecture others; they must come to this on their own or the lessons and the journey will not be theirs. You must follow your own inner guidance and allow others their own inner guidance. But know this: You will die young and in pain if you keep eating the crap that is portrayed as food in your culture, and you will pay a price of which you are currently not aware in the loss of joy, health, and, of course, the pursuit of bliss that is underlying all of our teachings.

You wanted a simple brochure on better sex, did you not? And here we are, giving you a guide to transforming every aspect of your body and mind. Yet that is what needs to be done to save your lives and your planet, and we hope that the message is received with the love that it is given in. We want your lives to blossom, to be full of love and joy and unbelievable health. That is our motivation, and we hope you are able to listen with an open heart to this treatise of love for all.

Vitamins and Minerals

Now we will write about the vitamins and supplements you all are taking in an effort to be healthy. The first element in this is the vitamin C that is seen as having magical powers. Indeed, there is some good benefit to taking this, but the general approach is to add it to the life that is not balanced, to compensate for a lack in basic nutrition. The additive idea is better than nothing, but it will not work on our path.

First you should simplify your diet with the healthy, naturally occurring foods on the planet that grow of their own accord, and cleansing water should be drunk daily in good quantity. There are such things as algae and other green foods that are indeed food, even though they are sold as supplements. If it is essentially unprocessed and green, such as the algae mentioned, it will add some strong nutrition to your diet.

For those on this path, there are many products like this on the market. Use your intuition and do a little research. We will not endorse a particular brand, as this is not necessary. All producers of healthy foods deserve their kick at the can, so to speak. So go and feel your way along the shelf, but only after you have balanced and cleansed the solid center of your diet and eating habits.

Hunger arises now, as our dear one has a sound in her tummy that is drawing her attention. We are suggesting that a little hunger several times through the day is a good thing. Do not suffer with it and say, "Oh I am starving," but observe that the body is asking for food and ask it what good food it would like. If its message is desperate and of a poor quality, close your eyes and meditate for a few moments, and ask for assistance from Spirit to get the willingness to make a sound choice, rather than leaping for the bread or sweet that the simple body may indeed want. It is a want rather than a need, and as the muscles are sore and reluctant at the beginning of an exercise program, so the mental desires for food will be uncomfortable and complain a little. Mental discipline is developed for this reason, so make a decision on behalf of the body.

Please set up this loving dialogue with your body. Tell it the story of survival underlying your choices, and insist that you love it and have its best interest at heart. It was you, dear ones, who let the ego have its way for so long, so it is you who will need to help it out of the pit it has come to know so well after so many years. The ideas of attacking and forcing will need to be let go and replaced with the loving and gentle instruction idea, as you would do with a youngster. The body-ego attachment needs to be gently separated, and the soul-body connection must be made. It will take a bit of time and a lot of love, but you *are* love, and this is the path to bliss and joy that you dream of in your fantasies.

You will not need to escape your life after this practice is established and the pathways are cleared. We assure and promise you, you will not regret this journey, unlike some of the journeys the ego has taken you on — to hangovers, hatred, and overeating.

We can feel restlessness arising. The body needs to move. Walk in the sun, and we will do a session if you wish.

✳   ✳   ✳

We are with you again, dear one. You are our voice. We must say, so far there are no complaints, and our choice was good one. This morning we will continue on, as you said, with the ideas of minerals that the body needs to function. The art of communication is an interesting one, and the chemicals needed to facilitate that in the body and brain are a delicate balance of minerals and salts, combined with our precious water, that all work together to form electrical circuits along which Spirit makes transmissions.

This is a fine and delicate system when it is functioning at full capacity. You are a clear channel for Spirit, and we can communicate very easily with you. As you can imagine, this is not always so and, indeed, not often the case. The disruptions in the transmissions are many, and food with this balance is just one of them. We suggest that the salts and minerals found in a varied natural diet — without sodas, coffees, and other drinks and foods that disrupt the device — be used. This is a general prescription for healthy eating and drinking, again, to help us speak to you and through you. Each and every moment there are also disruptions through the thoughts, of course, but that is a whole other topic.

We feel we have lain a lot on your plate, and many will slump in the corner after reading this section. Yet take heart, as it is only humans who think that food should give their life meaning. There are many creatures on the planet — in fact, most of them, including plants — that eat one food and enjoy it thoroughly, as that is what they are supposed to eat.

188 * Making Love to God

The attachments that come from strange trainings of power and love, as they are attached to food, pervert the mind into thinking that food gives more than it does. If you think this way, there is indeed a maze in which you can get lost in the food department. See each meal as an opportunity to support the body, and give it nutrition and healthy taste, and if the love of your mother or father pops into the preparation, ask it to leave your food alone, for it will not be of service to you in any way.

Beliefs about Food

The belief systems operating in your world, the behaviors that you exhibit, are created in many different ways over a very long period. To unravel the minutiae of this is impossible. It is personal for every one of you, but what indoctrinated you was a repeated, and often physically forced, compliance to these behaviors, often with dire consequences if you did not do as you were asked.

Let us think about the beliefs and behaviors around food. Many of you were often force-fed foods you did not like and fed too much for your little tummies. As children you were often denied pleasures if you did not comply, and often physically punished, all in the name of "good nutrition" and the ideal of "good parenting." Your guidance system was overridden in a forceful and brutal way. These were your lessons of food consumption, and you wonder why you are struggling with it now. The ideal would be to place a selection of bite-sized foods before little ones and let them choose what to eat. This is an example of how the teaching got in, so now we must admit that it works, this repetition and going over something again and again. This is what you must do to replace a belief system you do not want anymore. You must input a new one with the same determination, if not the same brutality, of the first indoctrination.

For an example of a device to change, take the idea of mantras. Around foods you may say something like, "I only eat healthy and natural foods that nourish my divine body." This will, over time, determine what you decide to consume, and it will, if you are determined, erase the voice that says, "I will eat whatever is put in front of me."

We wish for you to apply this principle to all areas where you are suffering. In the area of sexual fears or distress, you may wish to say something like, "I am drawn to healthy, kind, and loving partners, always."

Each of these mantras — if employed while walking, for example, while doing the dishes, or while doing any of the simple and common tasks of ordinary life — will change the programming. Yes, it does take some time, but you must reclaim all areas of the mind that are driving you to reach the goals of which we speak.

Start this very moment. What is the behavior you wish to change? Write down your history of that behavior and ask what the phrases are that you are saying at the moment. See that you are contributing to the problem yourself through your unconscious prayers and mantras, and decide to take the power that is yours back from the past, back from whoever or whatever taught you this terrible way of dealing with the issue. Do not do this with hate or judgment, but with joy that finally you are getting to the root of the issue, and soon you will see results.

This is the way to undo brainwashing. It is more brainwashing, but the results will be more conducive to the life you wish to lead. That is all for now on that subject. Stick with it. Whoever wanted you to behave this way stuck with it and influenced you for decades — remember that.

Clarification of the Body

This hurdle is second only to forgiveness in the ego's arguments not to follow this path. It will scream of deprivation and say it is suffering too much, and for what? But of course, at first there is a slight feeling of loss before the feelings of enlivenment and joy start to arise in the cleansed body. For many who have eaten in ways they consider "normal," this will seem extreme, yet what is normal in Western culture is not good for the body. Constant consumption of meats raised with hormones and chemicals, wine on a daily basis, that little something at the end of the day to make you feel it was all worth it … there are gifts that are indeed difficult to understand at the beginning, and we ask those reading this to trust us for a little while and admit, if only intellectually at first, that these habits are indeed heavy in energy and not so good for the etheric body.

We are telling you that the subtleties of bliss need a helping hand for you to feel them, and that the gross weight of the ego's world in which many are immersed is like being stuck in mud. At times the struggle to get out will get you in deeper, and the ego will often act up and become stronger at any slight indication that its vices are under threat. This is a primitive survival mechanism that kicks in on a deep cellular level, and that is why it is so powerful. The mammalian body in which you live, as amazing as its systems are and as powerful as it is as a transformer, has ancient and powerful drives to live that the idea of transcendence crosses. The battle between the Devil and the angel is indeed this one.

You have a split between the two aspects of yourself that must be healed, yet at first the healing and the bringing together of these two aspects looks like a battle. The things Spirit asks of the ego scare it and make it want to run for cover, and it is important that your mental disciplines and education can force, if you will, the ego's hand. Your mind and heart are the real creators, yet until that becomes deep-seated knowledge in the conscious mind, the ego programming will try to override it, afraid it will die. Indeed, the ego does die with the body, so in its sad way it is threatened with the ideas of eternity and Spirit. It is as a child running with scissors: You must not allow it, even if the child is very upset with you. You know better, and it is indeed an act of love for the child to prevent this.

So dear ones, as you become more solid in your belief, Spirit's ability to override the ego will become stronger, and the things that once seemed impossible will become a discipline you are willing to practice to enjoy the true freedom of the awakened mind. For some this will be too much, and more years of suffering and loneliness may be needed, but that is always the choice of the individual soul — to stay the same and continue to create the same life.

This is the secret that so many really need to integrate into their minds: that the negatives in their lives are their own dear children that they nurture and feed with tales of limitation and past hurts. We are truly compassionate for those of you who are stuck in this back-and-forth place, yet even if every step forward is not permanent, there is progress made, and there will be rewards that are beyond your ability to comprehend at the moment.

CHAPTER TWENTY-SEVEN

Alcohol and Drugs

Another issue for the Western mind wishing to participate in the form of lovemaking we desire for you is that many of you use drugs and alcohol as sexual lubricant, and you will find this idea of clean and sober sex somewhat daunting. We know much of what we speak about is hard to accomplish, but what is the alternative?

Are you happy with a 50 percent divorce rate? Many of the married couples do remain together are not happy or sexually satisfied. Are you not curious about this intriguing form of expression? Is it not worth a few months of experimentation to see if there is anything to it? We think it is worth a try, and our assurances that you will not be disappointed are genuine and heartfelt.

You see, from our vantage point we are watching you all on Earth masturbating in front of computers, getting half-drunk so that you can have sex, and generally having a difficult time with these most intimate of matters. You need help, and we are here to help you find your way to the light that sexual energies can take you to. You are not alone here, no matter if it feels that way. There are many beings in the nonphysical realm who wish to help you, who wish to teach you and heal you, but you must first raise up your vibration so that it is closer to ours.

When you are involved in all the behaviors that we have mentioned, it is hard for us to find you. It is hard for us to reach out and help. The interference from the low-vibration behaviors of your culture impede our efforts greatly, and we can become somewhat frustrated that you are in pain when there is help, but we cannot access your minds because of the interference of judgment, hatred, drugs, and bad food. All these aspects play a part, and as you can feel, this seems to be an overwhelming transition. But as you begin to make the changes we suggest, you will begin to feel more energy, more vitality, and more happiness almost immediately — well, once all the addictions have subsided, but we will go into that in more detail in later. For now, take our encouraging words to heart and continue on for just a little longer.

We are not totally against consumption of alcohol. For some it is a pleasant enough release from a world they don't understand. But as you are seeing lately, the need for such devices is driven by a mind at war with itself in some ways. A job you don't like or a partner you find boring are both reasons for another glass. The form of drug really is not the question; the question is, why are you taking it? Are you at peace when you take it? If so, it will do no harm; but if you are at peace, you will not want much at all. The excesses of drinking are caused, as you know, by separation from God, and the desire for mind-altering substances is always the same. So please do not judge one addiction over the other. Even the Internet is a drug for some — the same as a drink for others.

We will continue to say that the answer is getting back in touch with the bliss energies of the divine, which will not function when you drink. So sobriety is a natural side effect, if you will, of the divine sex we are talking about. The channels in the body that create this energy are very sensitive to chemicals and stress, and they will not function to the high degree they can if the body is being abused in any way.

You can live an ordinary life if you choose, but the long-term benefits of the bliss-making machine that a human can be are untold — youthful appearance, financial abundance, peace, and joy, to name but a few things that you strive for all the time by looking in the wrong places. Malls and shopping do not satisfy, and they cost a lot more than you think, wasting time and money that could be wisely spent elsewhere. We are sure you think this is not a way to save the planet, but you are wrong.

The underlying hatred and lack of forgiveness are destroying your home, although you will be saved from total destruction by those who are watching the play unfold. The stories of otherworldly help are indeed true, and the secret is being spoken about more and more. It is as if the world is ready to hear the absolute truth of the past and future of Earth and all its inhabitants and visitors.

Eventually we will all meet in one dimension or another, but for now this is our venue, and a lovely one it is. These words are your doorway to a new future, and the lessons of these pages will lead you exactly where you want to go: a future of peace and harmony and joyous lovemaking — alone or together, it matters not.

CHAPTER TWENTY-EIGHT

Body Size and Shape

Now we will talk about the issues of the body and its size and shape. This is a big one in your culture — is it not? — and directly related to the food issues we have been talking about. There are some of you who have noticed our mention of fat as if it is some crime. It is not. It is fine if the diet that is making you overweight is light and healthy in nature, and there ends the argument. If you are eating a light and healthy diet, you will not be layered with fat, and we must speak about this honestly without offense intended. This is a taboo in your culture because of the fear and judgment around fat. If you are fat, no one wants to talk about it. Since we are not offended by offending others, we will be the ones to speak about it.

The functioning of the body is a science, and this is how we want you to start seeing it as you are deciding what foods to eat. Many of you have so many memories and emotions attached to food that you are feeding the machine the wrong foods. Much of this is not your fault, yet you are the ones who must live in these bodies, and if they are fat bodies, this can be a source of great pain. We are here to help this process of letting go of the fat on your bodies.

The layers of emotion and fear that create the fat deposits are difficult to face, because as soon as you start to take foods away, the ego replies with screams of "no!" and "I am hungry! I am going to starve!" Also there is the underlying fear of being sexually attractive and open if there is sexual trauma hiding under the layers. This is a complicated subject, and one that takes time and love to untangle, so we will approach it in a simple way.

At first, look at your body naked in the mirror and honestly ask yourself if this is the body you want to show to your lover. If the answer is no, then there is work to be done, is there not? If the answer is yes, you are light-years ahead and you can skip this chapter. There may only be a few of you, but if you said yes, then well done. You have faced a large hurdle already, and you are on good terms with your body. If you said no, then here is the plan we suggest.

There needs to be some honest investigation into the reasons your body is in the condition it is in, and we wish you to be honest with yourself. Take the time to honor this process. Ask yourself what foods may be contributing to this; what exercise, if any, is helping or hindering this issue; and if is there a sexual basis for this issue. Regardless of the cause, there is a first step to changing, and that is to begin to eat a healthier diet, as we described earlier, and also to begin a walking program, if physically possible. These are the basic foundations that you can build on as the process unfolds, and indeed it is a process.

You must be prepared to pray for help in this area, as the emotions that come up and the deep fears of lack, future pain, and past pain are sure to arrive. These are not nice to experience, yet the feeling of being overweight and alone, if that is the case, is not nice to experience either, and this is the story we wish you would start to tell. The truth is that this is not what you want, and it is you who has created this to protect, to hide, and to comfort. We want the real feelings to come to the surface for processing, and this requires support. So we are happy to offer it, dear ones, as these emotions come up.

Please pray for guidance and the healing of this imbalance. Ask for natural and healthful functioning to be restored, and ask to be shown what needs to be looked at and how for the long-term healing of this issue. Bodies come in many shapes and sizes, and not all — in fact, very few — fit the culture's dictates of what is attractive. Indeed, this is another reason that television is not the best. There are many images of unusually beautiful bodies in that box, and for many of you the advertisement of foods and these pictures is a deadly combination. We want you to see the poisonous mix that this is and begin to wean yourself off these images that portray the human form, particularly the female form, in such a strange way. You may not think that this is possible, but the pain many of you suffer from in your body's self-image is just this, and if you would compare yourself to ordinary people, you would feel much better. This is not a great revelation.

We want you to look at your habits that are contributing to your pain. If you want to be the way you are, then do not suffer. Accept your choices. But if you are suffering and wish to remove the fat so you can feel more open to sexual activity, then stop telling the stories that keep you there. This is all we ask: that you start to be honest and deal with what is rather than the victimhood of "I can't do anything about it." You all can do something if that is what you choose. Just be brutally honest, write these things down, and have a slow and gentle plan for reconditioning yourself. And do include prayer; it is the most powerful healing tool you can employ in improving the health of the body.

We wish to address some cultural differences around weight, and if your culture likes more weight on the body, that is fine. But again, make sure that you are eating healthfully and that this does not give you an excuse to abuse your body. Your body is a sensitive device that needs nutrition and care, and that is what we ask you to follow — the path of love to your body. It will serve you long and well if you treat it with respect, but do not worship it as a god. It is not one.

Dear one, we are happy you are visiting us frequently today. The book will get written in no time, and, at some point, you will be glad we worked so hard on its production. As you get busier and busier, time will seem to disappear and become more and more precious.

Fat as Unnecessary Protection

Fat is a way to hide the delicious body that leads you to delightful entertainments with sexual energy. For some, fat is not an issue and they enjoy voluptuousness of the hips and belly; but for many, fat is like a bucket of ice water on the flames of passion and does not serve the higher good.

Not only will eating too much heavy food drag down your sexual energy, but the embarrassment of the look and feel of the parts of your body your lover wishes to look at and squeeze causes a shutting down of the heart in fear of rejection. This is the biggest liability. We do not condone the severe diets of the starving person, but we encourage you to gently begin to pick healthier foods if you wish to enhance your sexuality. Pick food high in vibration. If you don't, it is like putting sludge in a Ferrari and expecting good performance — it will not work very well and will cause sickness and even more suffering.

A body employed in the search for higher realms will respond very quickly to the love you give it and will reward you with a more youthful feeling and energy. Of course, if there is fear around sexual expression, the fat will stay as a barrier. The fear must be dealt with, or you will feel the protection must remain to keep you safe. You are safe; no one can hurt you without your consent. Many of you do not see that this is so and that now, as adults, you are in charge, whereas when you were younger you were not so aware of your part in all this.

So do take the time to sit down and honestly look and ask: Are you hiding from the divine sexual experience you would love? If you are, ask why. Explore the injury and gently, oh so gently, begin to change your food a little at a time. The attachment to food in particular is a very difficult one to change alone, so pray for our assistance in this matter and know that feelings will arise as the foods are removed. Be prepared for this, and know that it is a good thing.

The layers of fat may contain old energies that are released when you lose weight, and they are real in their intensity. So be kind and loving to yourself in other ways. Do not comfort yourself with food, but nourish your body with healthy food that will move your pleasure centers to their proper alignment with divine love. Do this not for us, but for yourself and the passion you wish to reignite.

There are others who remove the fat to be skinny and asexual. This is not necessary either, although this is an idea that works for some. We are aware that not all beings wish to travel the divine path to bliss that we advocate. If that is your choice, we support you, but punishing the body for a result is not the way. Always love your body as the communication device it is. It is not your enemy, but a valuable vehicle that will help you evolve into the being you already are.

Exercise

We are now going to go over the subject of exercise, as this is another great issue in Western culture. There are many who can barely walk at all, and others are obsessed with exercise as a control mechanism. So let us look at the lazy ones here, as it is obviously food that is making them heavy, and the fears that are hidden under fat are heavy burdens to carry around and indeed to feel.

Eating large quantities of fat-making foods makes exercise almost a torture for the poor body schlepping, as you say, that weight around. Ideally, the human body is lithe and lean, with natural variations found in different genetic types. There are fat pockets that should appear in the female form that are as they should be — hips, tummy, and breasts. These are of a great beauty to the balanced mind, but that is our aim, not our present state.

The body has evolved in a very active way, walking and farming, gathering and hunting. Many primitive tribes walk or are in motion doing something all day. Indeed, the body can do this and is able to do it easily if fed the right foods. In modern culture, what we recommend is a walking program that gets you into nature as much as possible given your living conditions. There are parks and greenways, and for some lucky ones in the cities, green spaces. We are sure there are many of you who live in the concrete jungle, but that is another topic altogether.

For the average person, being around the vibration of trees, water, soil, and all the growing things gives not only physical exercise, but the ability to commune with nature, that balanced and quiet creation that is so fully alive that it will feed your soul and bring you into balance. Let your exercise plan involve sitting on a log at the beach or in the woods. As you walk, stop and enjoy the environment, and feel appreciation for the immense variety on your planet. This is a simple plan, is it not, this walking plan? As we have suggested for our dear one, Tina, walk several hours a day in nature. That is an optimum, but whatever you can do in nature will help.

There are other modalities, such as yoga, that those of you who are drawn to will love to do. It is more the mindset behind these modalities that we are concerned with. The rabid pushing of the body to achieve ego goals is not a healthy one and can be a form of attack. If this is the internal attitude, it will cause stress and destruction of the cells rather than healing and health. There are no shortcuts here, but the path is a pleasant one. It is a simple idea to do what you love and do it for fun; let that be the reason to go for a swim, pick blackberries as you hike, or take a camera and snap pictures as you walk through the park. It does not need to be a deep and painful experience. If it is, you need an adjustment of attitude.

Of course there are athletes out there, but they have a path different from ours; we are more for the slow and gentle meandering than the triathlon. So keep simple habits in terms of exercise, and again, keep an eye on your motivation. See it as support for your body, not a hurdle, punishment, or sentence. Come at it with joy and a feeling of love for all the muscles and tendons that are working so hard to support you on your journey. Without your dear body, you could not master the areas of which we speak. So love it, but do not worship it. And enjoy your walks. We often connect to the mind as it peacefully gazes over a field or ocean view, inspiring you in subtle — and sometimes not so subtle — ways.

That is it for exercise. If any more specifics are required, we will answer those questions too if necessary. But your culture has made a science of this subject, and we suggest it be more of a pleasure and pathway to relaxation and stimulating vistas than a regime. However, it is very important to move and move frequently. So do get off the couch, dear ones, and venture out into the beautiful world on which you live.

Energy

The subject now is energy and the things that new students of the bliss path can expect as they begin to run the energies of which we speak. Indeed, as this path is chosen, there may be many new manifestations arriving in the body and the mind. For example, there may be sensations and visuals that begin to change. There are often visual experiences of lights, and different colors in the visual field begin to occur almost immediately. These are signs that the process has begun and needs to be accepted.

This is why it is important to disconnect from the Western model, as a lot of these experiences would be considered odd or sick in some way. The lights are the spiritual vision awakening, and there is nothing to fear. You might feel a presence in the room, and this often happens at night, as the mind is quiet and the resistance is low. But if the daily activities, practices of forgiveness, and healthy thinking and eating are in play, then the tone is set, and you need not fear any lower energies as such.

Here, we wish to again mention that this is all vibrational, and only those at a low vibration will experience low-vibration events. So this is a time to relax and welcome in the beginning of a whole new world of experience and joy to come. Indeed, there will be energies felt in the body also, and these may be felt as pressure on various parts — often in the head and spinal area. It can even feel like an ache at times, but do not think anything is wrong; it is the kundalini awakening.

We ask that your thoughts be of the highest vibration so that the energies do not encounter blocks at the beginning. This is likely, but as you practice the many aspects of this new practice we are teaching, you will see clearly the areas that need correction. Any thought or food that is not in alignment with your new path will feel heavy or cause mental distress, and as this happens — and it will — we want you to go into that thought or food and discern what is really going on. Unearth the fear or the attachment, and gently let it go.

All attachments and fears drain the energy from the body that we wish to use in the bliss process, so this is the groundwork that is your part. We have a part too, but this is accelerated by your work in these foundational areas. All the facets of the energy work we have asked you to change become of equal importance as the journey continues, but you will initially have better areas and worse areas. For some, food will be difficult; for others, their thoughts may be harder to harness. None is better or worse than the other, for all play a part in the functioning of the individual energy field. This is a disciplined path, but the material approach is also hard, and we ask you to remember this as it seems things are leaving your life.

We wish for you to say that you are creating space for the divine to enter, and this will feel better. The wording is all, and as you experience the dropping away of things, know that the space will be filled with things and experiences that are of a higher vibration and that will bring you true joy and fulfillment, not just the empty feeling of new shoes or a new technology to numb the mind. Our dear one has indeed let all fall away, and she will vouch for the replacement.

This is part of the team that we make. We tell you, and she agrees, that yes, this is worth it. She is an ordinary human who has walked this path and is now receiving the benefits of awareness, energy, and experience beyond anything she could have imagined, and had there been a view into the future, she could not have gone ahead. It would have looked too intense and different. Yet here she is, happy and enjoying the ride.

This is what we wish you to see: that if all humans, ordinary as you are, systematically follow the cleansing path of thought, word, and deed, they will experience heaven, and they will not believe what will happen. But the groundwork is substantial, and we ask you to be patient with yourselves. If nothing is happening in the light and energy department, know that you are not yet ready, and go deeper into the practices. It will indeed come to pass, and you will get it at some point. The visions and other energetic experiences that will arrive and increase in strength are for your enlightenment, and it is very important for you to understand that the good is at play. This is why we ask you to educate yourself on the energetics of tantra and the yogic experience. You must be prepared for these events so that, when they first arrive, you do not run and shut down. If this happens, it is not the end of the world, but fear can derail the process, so you need to be aware from the beginning of your conditioning around possession and evil. This is often an underlying belief that will pop up at the least expected time.

You will also experience some times of deep sleep, when the body is adjusting to the changes in food and thought, and indeed there will be times of heightened energy that surprise you. It may be that you are walking much faster or that you are up in the night wanting to read and study. These are all natural reactions to the change of focus that you are making. So do not say, "I did not sleep well last night." Stay out of putting any of this in a box, and make sure that you do not speak to just anyone about these experiences. Only choose those who are of a similar mind.

If you know your mother will not understand, do not burden her with the stories. Those who are not ready cannot process this path and will give you negative feedback that will only disturb or scare you. So make sure that you have someone of support and that those you tell are of a similar practice. Over time, we hope there will be groups practicing this together for support, that there will be communities who gather to run the energies together. This is of course a future occurrence, and if that is not available, support yourself through sound education in the truths. So keep your own counsel, knowing the truth that what you are doing is for the good of the whole, and more will be revealed as is necessary.

CHAPTER TWENTY-NINE

Entertainment

The world of entertainment is one of the largest hurdles you will meet on this path. Our dear one, Tina, is just tackling this issue, so we have decided to write about it now. And it will be a tricky one indeed. There are so many forces at play in the Western mind that are of a low vibration. Many we must just pick away at, hoping that you are willing to listen and to change. This entertainment industry is a purveyor of violence and hatred beyond anything we have ever seen, and we are distressed at the function and the destruction it causes in the minds of our dear children of God. This seems dramatic, and you are already feeling nervous — we can tell. And you should be, as the very gods you worship in this culture are the very things that are driving you mad and to the brink of destruction.

The portrayals of war, vengeance, and murder as entertainment are disgusting, and truly, we are distressed at the feeling and the results of this war on love that you do not see. The minds you have been given are synthesizers of matter and experience, and the raw materials that go in are the creators of the end results. So we are surprised that you keep watching the shows and movies that you do, and letting your children play the games that they play. And yet you are surprised that your world looks as it does.

The obsession with murder feeds the ego at every turn, and there are foods that are much better for the soul. You seek education in truth, art, music, drawing, walking, and so many things, yet at the end of the day, when you are tired and should be the kindest to yourself, you lie down and watch death over and over again. This is madness, and as we name it as such, that is what you feel, is it not? It's madness, what you do, and madness that you do not see the consequences. We are not the bringers of doom and gloom, although at this moment many are saying this path is too much and too difficult. Once again, we say, do you like living in fear, afraid to walk out under the stars at night for fear of rape or murder? Where do you think these feelings are coming from? Not from loving behavior and kind words, no. They are coming from a generation left alone with violence to watch and bad food to eat as their parents went off to earn money for so many needless things. There is no judgment as such from us — just a deep desire to turn the tide in the other direction toward sanity and the expression of love that you are meant to be and have — and are. There are many things that can be arranged once the first wave of changes are made, and this is a big one for you all. We realize this.

Our dear one had a favorite show that seemed to be an addiction she could not let go of until it was over. Only then did she become willing to release the attachment, and it is the same with all of you. Do not stop watching your favorite show if you have one; save that and enjoy it, but let all the rubbish go — the commercials and the news, full of fear and lies that keep you small. These are the places to start, and if you have young children, do not bring video games into the house. They will rail and scream, but do not do it. There are ways to entertain that are healthy and happy, and we ask you to begin to employ those in the environment in which your dear children live.

If the games are already in your home, then it is important to begin a shift to the less violent ones, and then to a reduction in time spent playing them. This will require a change in your schedule. The children will no longer be silent in the other room and leave you in peace, but the peace comes at a high price. We are asking too much from some, we know, and it will seem impossible, but this is the energy flowing in and around you. The energy of love cannot flow against anything. It flows into empty, calm spaces, and it cannot change a war zone that is created by choice. This is where we are able to help.

Prayer around this matter will help us help you to come up with strategies and ideas to change it. Do not attack your children for their habits. You bought and rented the games, and you allowed the growth of the habit, so accept your part in it, as responsible as you are. This will take time, but please attempt to lessen all of these things if you wish to have love, deep and true, in your lives. It will fill up every space you create for it and will add to the life you lead in ways you cannot imagine.

We have thrown a real monkey wrench into your daily works, we realize, yet we can feel your desire for peace, love, and health, and all these elements play a role — even if you do not quite see it yet, and you fear the spaces that will arise in these incredibly busy and, we are sad to say, polluted lives you lead. We are ever here in love for you all, and we ask you to gently and slowly pull the plug on the lives you do not need or want for yourselves or your dear children.

We are on the subject of entertainment and its destructive powers as they are now employed on the planet, and this same state can be transformed to disseminate some brilliant information. Indeed, there are some efforts being made on this front by those such as Oprah Winfrey, for whom there is so much admiration. Yet she still does not approach this deep and profound subject of sexual disempowerment as it reflects on the entire Church culture. This has not really been brought to the forefront of the mainstream mind as a source of the deep pain that is being felt on the planet at the moment. So we are hoping that as this information is spread and taught and spoken about, there will be brave souls on television who will use the waves they own to entertain this subject and to bring about the transmission of ideas and exercises that are truly liberating to the broken hearts and minds of the general populace.

This is a long way off, as the powers that rule the waves of television are in the pockets of those in control, and it is the independence of the Internet that is required for these transmissions. There are those of us here in the outer realms who are guarding the independence of these realms of information. Indeed, the governments of many countries would like to stop the sharing of information in this way. There are people learning and speaking the truth that make them very nervous at the moment. The house of cards is beginning to sway in what is now a gentle breeze, but that breeze will become a windstorm, and the house will topple.

A Pep Talk

This is where our lessons come in. The cards falling could mean chaos, but what we want it to mean is the dawning of a new age of true love for the self, others, and the bliss energies that are open to all if you follow the basic rules that we lay out in this document. Indeed, the simplicity is deceiving. It gets easier and easier, although in the beginning it is indeed a challenge — not just because of the physical requirements, but because of the reprogramming of values that is required even before you can truly see the potential results.

Those of you reading this book, trust us. There has been such a deception perpetrated on you, and you are the victims of lies that are costing you your lives. And as dramatic as this sounds, it is true. The sicknesses that are pervading your society are not necessary, and the disillusionment you feel after you have followed all the rules yet you are not happy and your marriages fall apart is what we wish you to think about as your mind doubts us. Is this the world that you are taught to make a real prize, or is it hell in a pretty dress? It seems the latter to us, so we are asking you to keep on going on this path that we are writing about. We are indeed giving you a pep talk in the middle of the text. We want to keep the reality of your world in the front of your mind at all times.

The ego will indeed tell you not to rock the boat, but the boat is sinking. You must do something, must you not? All of the prescriptions we give here are free, so there is no financial excuse for not following them. Monies can be saved to a huge degree by following these rules, if you will. You will get healthier, slimmer, and a great deal happier. Your energy will rise, and the simple pleasures of your planet will be seen — for the first time by some of you. This is our wish as we share these directions and suggestions.

We are not here to judge you as stupid or ridiculous for following these old rules. Indeed, there has been a convincing history written to persuade you of the rightness of all these rules. But you can feel it is not right in your bones. Something is missing, is it not? And we address that issue as we write. There are indeed fears aroused as this process is followed, and our dear one is encountering those as she is on this journey. She has some fears and ideas deeply buried in her mind that are causing some disturbances in her peace as we ask her to step along this untrodden path. But she is stepping forward, albeit tentatively some days. The basics have been learned, and she knows that the old way holds no sway for her anymore. She does not care for the old way and the boring jobs that mean nothing. She is a testament to the belief in something more. And for those of you who also believe there is something more, it will indeed come. But you must let go of all the old, and that is a process that takes dedication and time to achieve.

Pornography

The pornography industry is indeed one of the plagues on this Earth, and we are not saying this because we are prudish or judgmental in any way. We are saying this because the pornography industry has very little to do with love, and we are about the expression and sharing of love. We wish anyone who is involved in watching this phenomenon to stop this activity if they want to enter the world of divine energies, because it is produced by low-vibration people in very low-vibration environments. The obsession with the body is clear, and the acts themselves often verge on the violent and animalistic.

We see that the culture feels that this is "cool" or a great way to feel sexual energy, but the presentation and the effects are not in line with the beliefs we are trying to cultivate. There cannot be give-and-take on this one. The dark energies of the ego are immediately aroused by the objectification of the sexual act and the body, and this is the reason, as we said, that sex is not the issue.

We are suggesting that you and your partner, if you have one, use the loving energies together. And if you desire sexual activity when no partner is around, then a loving imagination should be used to get the energy flowing. Reading or writing erotic — not pornographic — stories also will accomplish this end result. The areas of sexual repression have led to this event in your culture. The dark and dirty secret that sex has become has manifested in the perversion of the loving and beautiful energy we cultivate. Porn is a big industry because it is powerful energy that is being manipulated for profit and for the prurient interest of low-vibration men who have not an ounce of love on their minds.

We are not trying to be sexist here, but the truth is that the presentation and the subject matter of pornography are not the practices the female body needs for arousal. It is very male-focused and feeds the idea of the domination and satisfaction of the male drive, rather than the quieter and lengthier female techniques that are required for the real and deep penetration of one soul by another, together.

So we are clear: If you have an addiction to this behavior, and many do, this may not be the path for you at the moment. You need to reduce and relieve yourself of the burden of this disguised hatred and domination over women, and this is a long process. These are deeply planted and primitive reactions that are hard to break, so that is our suggestion — to stop this addiction and deeply look at the underlying hatreds and deal with those first.

The bliss energies will not manifest in a mind that is of that vibration. These energies are of such a fine and high element that the likelihood of no reaction whatsoever would be high. We are, again, not in judgment of you but just calling a spade a spade, so to speak. And that is all on that subject.

Few things are more disturbing to the area about which we write than this one. We are here to turn this tide, and all activity of this type, as watched and seen on television, needs to end for the healing to arise and take place. We are sure this will confuse some who have a strong sex drive that has been misdirected, but this is indeed the case. We are not kidding; sex is for love from now on. That is a powerful and simple statement for your culture, is it not? We will repeat that: Sex now is to be for love, and that is it. We are your teacher Ananda, telling you the most important lessons you will hear, and we are sad at this state of affairs on Earth. You can feel it as we write, and so it is, dear ones. So it is.

The Occult

The feelings of fear that arise around the ideas of spirits and possession are a huge barrier to the investigation of the realms of the non-physical, and we ask all of you to stop watching the television shows and movies that depict the occult in any way. Even the nicest treatments are scary in some visual ways, and the amount of misinformation is so silly that we would throw up our hands if we had any.

The best information on the subject is from professionals, and good information abounds on the Internet and in books written by gifted psychics and intermediaries between the realms. The art and science of the medium is indeed a fascinating one, and there are many variations on the theme. This writing project is an example of the kind of information to seek out. Make sure the information is based on love and not fear, and that it rings true for you. If it doesn't, it does not mean it is wrong; it may just not be in your language, so to speak.

All of you have a language that makes sense. For some it is tarot, for some it is church, and for others it's meditation. The pathways to truth are limitless, but if you have read this far, this may indeed be the language for you, so we are happy you are here sharing this journey to the center of the world, which is the mind of God. You share that mind, and you are the most holy creation of the mind of God. We ask you to honor all its manifestations and allow all them their own journey. You will bump into those on your path, but do not concern yourself with judging those on the other paths. It will only stop your progress and lower your vibration. So today, look at what is right in front of you and do that — unless it is the television, in which case you should turn it off, for a while anyway.

War and Violence outside of Entertainment

We are asking all who read this to be against war in all its forms. Wars in families, wars in the landscape, and wars abroad are all the same. We have a big quest to undertake to bring love to the surface of the minds of all humans so that the suffering and dying of millions can come to an end. The death toll is high in the name of God, and we wish to clear the name "God" of all hatred and judgment for the ones we love so dearly, the humans, who are trying to be free and express themselves as they see fit.

The sick and perverted acts of the military around the world in the name of freedom are also lies, and they need to be stopped. All the monies spent on war could be spent on food, education, and housing for the millions who suffer — with some left over for fun. The acts of war are real, and the pain is immense, so we propose that it's time to call a spade a spade and not disguise it in the name of freedom. This is not freedom. The taxes and debt of the countries around the world are causing a failure of the system, and the system would work very well if the focus were love and caring for all around the planet and not just those in one's own country. But that is not even the case, is it? You are not even looking after your own as the monies are being spent on war and the big business of drugs and prescriptions.

Healing will arise as a definition of the love state that we are striving for. The body is a loving and pure device that dies in hate and judgment; the body thrives in a state of love and happiness. All the hospitals and all the doctors would soon be out of business if love were adopted by all humans and they went through their days speaking lovingly, acting lovingly, and giving a gentle touch along the way to show they cared. We will keep on this path of bliss and teaching until we are heard, and we consider the path to love the most important thing in the world to do.

Music as Therapy

We are now going to speak of music and its effect on the etheric body as a way of accessing sexual energy and a path to healing for those who are shut down and scared. For this, you do not need a partner. It is a very loving way to enjoy a journey back to the free and loving energy of the soul you all feel when you are dancing and your favorite song comes on. The transformation from rigid to sexual is often very apparent, especially to those watching you dance.

We can recommend this therapy to all who are sad. You do not even have to want to dance at first. You may just enjoy listening to the vibrations, allowing them to seep into your consciousness and your cells at first. However, we would like to encourage you to dance when the mood arises, and we hope that you are in a safe and loving place in which you can practice this with peace and hope for a more loving future for your hearts. We listen to music all the time in the nonphysical. It is a way of drawing souls together. They resound in the joy of shared pleasure and rhythm.

The soul vibrates at a certain rhythm, and when music resonates with that rhythm you feel it through every cell of your body. It matters not if the music is classical or rock — just make sure you play it whenever you can if you feel separated from your sexual energy and fear that passion is gone from your dear and precious life. Do this once a day, and begin to indulge in this as an act of therapy. Invite the divine back into your rigid and disconnected body, rewiring the passion back into the center of your being with gentleness and joy.

Life has a rhythm, and a lot of humans in the world have lost their connection to the rhythm of their souls, fearful that it is gone forever. But it is not gone. We are here to encourage you to reclaim your sexual self. If there is fear, all the exercises we are doing and will be suggesting can be done alone for as long as you choose. Another body is not required for you to heal your sexual self, nor do you need to fear what the future will look like or what you might have to do.

Your sexuality is first a relationship with God and life, and then, if you choose to share it with another being, that will come to pass. But please, do not leave the most vital and creative energy force dead and frightened at the bottom of a pit created by religion, family, or culture. You are a sexual being, creative and juicy to the core, and the love of self must be there before you can love another. It is a platitude that is often spoken but you must really hear: *You must love yourself first!* No lover of any worth will come your way and stay with you if there is fear and anger around your sexual energy. You must learn to play with that energy yourself — without drugs or alcohol to numb the fear — before true engagement between two bodies, mind and soul, can reach its true pinnacle.

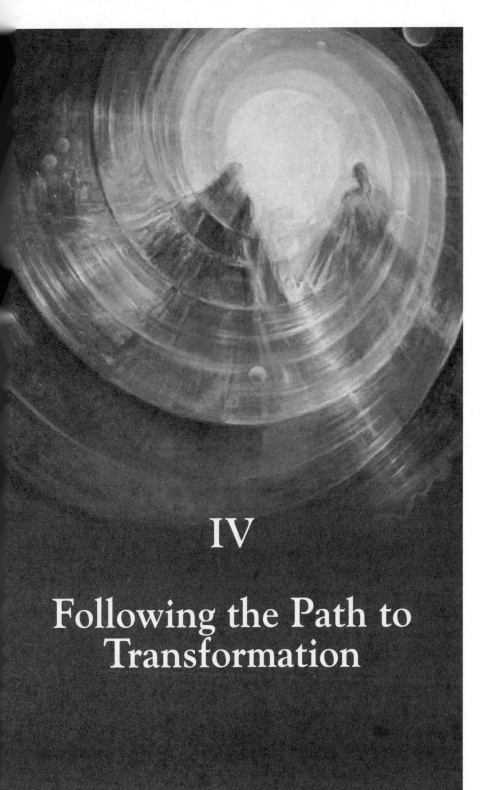

IV

Following the Path to Transformation

CHAPTER THIRTY

A Fork in the Road

There are many people reading our words now who feel that this path is too much. It scares them, yet they cannot go on the way they are. They are caught between a rock and a hard place. This is often the moment when a decision is made at a fork in the road to go one way or the other. We will say that once you come to that place in the road, you cannot make any more progress unless you choose, and, indeed, that is a tough place. Many will sit down there and not budge for a while, but life moves forward, and you must too. So we say choose the path less traveled, the one that will take you to places none of your friends have been and none of your family have seen, and dare, truly dare, to be different!

There is something in you, if you have read this far into this strange and wondrous text, that knows this is the way. Your soul has called you here and is begging you listen to these words. It is tired of the same old stories and the same bad food, and it wishes to shake you and say, "Dear one, do this for us, for our dear body, for the passion that is gone from our life. Do this, dear one. Do it!" And so, as you decide to go, there will be a lifting of heaviness, a true feeling of empowerment.

Now it is your task to go on this journey in a loving and forgiving way. Do not starve yourself or deprive yourself of everything, but each week pick one small thing to do. Replace it with a healthy version, and give yourself a blessing and credit for the changes you are making. So many decide on a new journey and as soon as it gets too hard attack themselves in all kinds of ways. If you slip, just smile and admit that yes, these are hard habits to break. The poor ego is scared and does not like it, but you will not let that stop you. You will acknowledge, observe, and continue on, always in love and always in forgiveness of any errors that are made.

If you go out for a dinner and have been on your new plan for some time, have a little treat — it is fine. The world will not end, but plan on the "no guilt" clause kicking in immediately, and watch as the ego wants to attack. Watch and do not join in. You are far more powerful than one meal, but it is important that your daily habits are clean and light. As we said to our dear Tina the other night, light is light and heavy is heavy, and the results speak for themselves.

You Have to Ask for Help

There are few things we can do to help until we are asked. This is a universal rule, and this is why prayer and asking with a deep, sincere wish is such an important thing for you to do on this journey to bliss and sexual healing. The mind cannot be changed without this genuine call for help, and at times, the call is a powerful one. On those dark nights of the soul when you are exhausted and on your knees, that is often when the clouds part and you become a small child begging for assistance. We will come to you, but you do not need to wait until you are desperate and alone, terrified of another day. It can be a peaceful and daily practice that invites Spirit in, all the time. Indeed, a state of prayer held for a certain period of time — for example, as you are going on a long walk — gives us a large window through which we can effect change, yet the requests work better if they are not too specific. Ask for general guidance and healing. This allows us to work in the area of most need. When we are not directed by your small needs, we have more freedom to truly help where you are the weakest.

So do not feel separate. You are not alone on this journey — not at all — but the detritus and interference is real and must be removed in a systematic and regular way for us to be able to intervene as you wish. These are the prescriptions we are writing about here. They seem to be depriving you of things, but in the end you will see you have lost nothing of value, and the real treasure is what you will gain in peace of mind, energy, and a real and open connection to the love that vibrates throughout this universe, just waiting for your open heart.

We can feel your appreciation of the material. We will elaborate more at a later date, but that will be a good introduction to this fascinating area of interest.

Access to Spirit

Dear ones, you are seen as humans, yet you are so much more than this. The electrical system that is the body-mind complex has a power beyond anything you have been taught. You have been told that the body is fallible and breaks down for no apparent reason. This is another of the big lies we are here to dispel. The mixture and electricity that is the human form is a matrix of intelligence and responsive design you are not clever enough to comprehend.

When we look at the human from our perspective, we see a ball of electrical energy and dreaming that is in a constant state of growth or decay, depending on the level of vibration. Those of you who are abusing the body with negative thoughts, fears, and hatreds are seen as dark and slowly pulsing areas of dim light that are clearly struggling with the issues, and there are dark areas of your energetic field where we see future sickness manifesting. These are the thought forms coalescing into objects, such as physical blocks, and they will indeed develop into the things called cancer or tumors. These are blocks of negative thought manifested, and it is hard for us to see this, as we know the potential of the device in which you live.

On the other hand, there are the light-making and healthy ones of you who are focused on the good. You seem as bright lights, shining clear and shooting out light energy into your environment that affects those around you with a positive vibration that is indeed felt. Those of lower energies feel it as too powerful at times; the difference in vibration is too great, and they will back off from the energy. It seems to be too bright, if you will, for the level they are at. But if you encounter another soul of the same high vibration, there will be a great interaction and growth that is the back and forth of ideas, dreams, love, and conversations. The higher of the two can affect the other, and there will be a feeling of love or pleasure in the company of this being.

We see this all over the planet — the bright ones and the dark ones. We are not in judgment, but do know that all can be changed. As the education of the dark ones allows them to change their thought forms, the manifestations in their bodies and the manifestations in the lives they are living will change. This is a wondrous thing to see, when a soul forgives or has a realization that it is more than what it has been taught. It is as if the lights get plugged in as they do at your Christmas time, and all begins to glow. Sometimes we cheer at these events, especially if we have been of help in the lighting up, so to speak. So as you see yourselves now, if you are sad or afraid, know that Spirit is there, close at hand. And if you ask, we can help you light the lights, but you must give the system a chance to vibrate at a higher frequency, and for that you must do the work.

The work comes in the form of forgiveness. The hatred and assessment of past events as wrong or sinful breaks the connection with your Source, and you feel sad and disempowered. You blame this on the event, but it is your own doing. As you search the past for the wounds and guilt of yourself or others, and as you feed your body heavy or poisonous food, there is a lowering of the vibration, and again the elements struggle to fire, as in an engine filled with the wrong fuel.

We want you to start to see yourselves as these systems that need sound decisions to work properly. Thought is not thought; it is the creative force that determines your future, and food should be just that — nutrition for the electrical and cellular system that are the form in which spirit travels, learns, and grows. If the vehicle is not kept up, the journeys you can take become very limited, and you should be preparing for the great adventures that we wish to tell you of and help you to go on.

The inspiration is felt, is it not? The truth of this information arouses the heart and you want that which we speak about. Remember this: If you want to hate or to eat a piece of poison, do not do this. No food or laziness is worth what you lose on this journey. Trust us — we are aware of the potential, and we are as a team trainer pushing you to achieve so that you can win the prize. We are in love always.

Otherworldly Help

We will answer now the question of otherworldly help. There are sayings that are very true, such as, "There are more things in heaven and earth than are dreamed of in your philosophies." This is one of those things.

There are beings of other worlds who are very fond of Earth and her inhabitants, trying to shine light into the darkness that prevails here. We are all of birth in other dimensions and places, yet the Earth world you know is a school for the beginner student. We are teachers who are letting you learn by experience, yet we will jump in when the experience becomes too painful or too confused, such as we did with our dear one, Tina. The overwhelming negativity she experienced as a young woman meant she would not survive, and as a result we entered the game and helped her out of the dark, helped teach her the things that brought relief from a mind driven mad by fears and bad training. This is what we all do as we care for Earth, and there are many of us — some in bodies, others of energetic construction only. You are not alone on the planet, and the help that is being focused on Earth is increasing as the pain increases.

The culture of the Western mind is so ego-driven and polluted with misteachings and lower deviation activities that we are more forceful now in our focus and healing efforts. As the pain of the world has reached such a pitch, and the ability to destroy the planet has reached such a level, we are to supervise you very carefully and with great effort. This is why the teachings of Ananda are now being produced.

In the West, the perversion of sexual energy and desire has reached a lower level that must be dealt with. The energies are being used for abuse and self-gratification in a way that is detrimental. Love has left the picture, and divine love must be an aspect of the sexual experience for it to be driven by the force of God. When there is no love, the ego is in charge and the darker energies are at play. Not evil — there is no such thing — but the brutality of the ego, which is, in and of itself, not such a pretty thing. We are not to tell you any more, other than that there are protective forces loving the dear Earth and its young squad of students, and we will be there to make sure all is well.

CHAPTER THIRTY-ONE

Inside Out

Dear students, the issue of cause and effect is now going to be discussed, and as we have said with each subject before, this pivotal belief system in your culture that is so far off the mark is predominantly responsible for the mess in which you are living — as individuals, as nations, and as a planet. You are the creators of your reality to the tiniest detail, and you still don't know it. This is the darkest secret kept from the mind of the human being. You are as gods, and your energy — even when depleted and low from the use of bad foods, drugs, and other deflating devices — has the power to create havoc or heaven, and many of you are creating havoc.

Even though the law of attraction is spoken of, there are deeper realms to the law that are not, as yet, in the general population. You can want a car, for example, but you cannot manifest it if you hate or if you fear other events that seem to have nothing to do with the subject at hand. All the thoughts you are not aware of — the old habits of avoiding things you fear, conditioned behaviors in things you do not truly believe — all interfere in manifesting that which you wish. These all represent the unconscious creations you are making. The car accidents, the sickness, and the lost jobs are not random acts of an insane God. They are outer representations of the inner state of the mind, so the love you all seek cannot come because of the lack of love for the self and others that is inside.

There appears to be a world of war and separation out there, but it is because your mind is a world of war and separation, and you do not see it. Every judgment is a piece of barbed wire that keeps you inside the

221

concentration camp of loss and fear, so the green fields of freedom in which you wish to play are kept apart from you. Indeed, some of you are living in an Auschwitz of the mind, looking outside the wire and wondering how to get there. The hate and fear inside are keeping you there without your knowledge. Every little negative belief you hold is a twist and a spike in the wire, and this is the imperative work of which we speak.

To truly be making the changes, you must get the power of the creative-genius mind that you have been given. You have been creating your world from day one on the planet, as a baby in the womb who began to feel your mother's heartbeat, fears, wants, and shame (if they were there). So you were born into a family, and at this point many of you are reeling at the thought that your families are responsible for the training of your dear minds as little ones. You see how that cannot be good for the free and creative lives you wish to live, and this is a sad yet true fact for many of you. Even if on the surface you see the dysfunction of your natal family, the strings are still at work deep in the unconscious mind, and they are in need of being demolished and changed.

This seems an impossible task, does it not? But it is very easy to find the issues that are the most powerful and destructive ones. Use your feelings, dear ones. What are the subjects that trigger fear and anger, or deep sadness, as soon as you think of them? For some it is the opposite sex and the frustration of not finding a good mate. There are probably deep feelings of the lack of self-love causing this issue. For others, it may be poverty, and this may well be a teaching of extended poverty in childhood and indoctrination in the belief in lack and disconnection from a benevolent Source. And for others, it may be rage at another race or religion. Anything that arouses these deep and painful feelings is where the change needs to be made, yet we hear you all say, "But I cannot go there. It is too much!" But that is the point — you must go there to become free. These are the bars of the prison in which you are living and you are dying to escape from.

You must be willing to ask for help in this area and to trust again in God and the spiritual energy that you never truly trusted in the first place. Most of you who had a religious upbringing are infused with fear by the teachings you experienced, and you must deconstruct this God you were taught about. You must learn that the God energy that drives creation is only love, and all the horrible manifestations you see are not evil, but only the blocks to love's presence created by the fear, lust, and hatred of the human mind, the great creator.

Can you not see the power of a nation joined in hate to create war and famine? All those powerful minds are focused on the enemy, when in fact the enemy is your salvation. Your brothers and sisters in the world are the ones you need to love to manifest what you want. Such a twisted and misleading tale you have all been told — that if you judge and are war-like you will get what you want. You will not.

You must begin to listen to these words and know that your feelings are your guide to your misteachings. You know by how they make you feel. The misinterpretation of feelings is what has led you astray, and it is a simple lesson to be taught the right way. If you think of someone or something you dislike and a sad or awful feeling arises, it is not the thing or person causing that. It is your wrong judgment, and your heart, as the direct connection to Source, suffers and says, "No, do not believe this. This makes us sad." And you feel the pain of the closed heart, but you mistake it for the awfulness of the other that is your focus.

This is happening every day — often every minute — and this is the source of all your agony, sickness, and fear. It is the misteachings and the pain of the closed heart you feel that is killing you all, bit by bit. We hope this can be assimilated and that you can begin to pray about this most important aspect of the teachings. The world you see is yours to keep or change. It is up to you. Love will heal it, and hate will destroy — not only the world, but your health and happiness along with it. It is not punishment, but a simple act of magnetism.

What you do, think, and say attracts more of the same, so think on that for a moment. Where is the thorn in your side? Is it your mother, your body, your neighbors? What is it that you hate and loathe and love to attack? Go there and begin to make peace with the enemy. They are not that. They are your path to heaven. When you can forgive them, you will be able to access the joys and pleasures of the mind fully connected to the love and power of the universe. As long as you worship other gods, you cannot feel that connection. Of course, we do not mean God in the religious sense. We mean the idols of hatred, judgment, and self-loathing that rule the minds of so many.

We are here to love only, and there is no judgment. We are trying to remove the blindfold that keeps you bumping into walls and each other. There are vistas beyond your imagination that you will see if you will remove these impediments to joy, and that is our purpose — to keep the information coming so that you can master the discipline to deflate the ego and inflate the heart of love that is your natural right.

Go now and sit quietly for a moment. Think of that most painful subject, that one that is at the root of so much pain, and ask for help in transforming the beliefs you have around that issue. You do not need to meet or confront this in person, but you must go into your mind and change the energy around it. Be convinced that you are right, or be willing to accept that you need to change it so that you can rise above the battlefield and join in the love that is what you really want.

Dear ones, you will indeed be amazed by the power and freedom that will come from this work, and we know at some point in the future you will be sad that you wasted so much time and lost so much peace around the topic.

Heal the Past to Change the Future

The same thing occurring over and over is the universe calling to you to accept and dive into the subject. "Trial" is the term we will use here to refer to this. It may be an annoying relative or a sickness; it does not matter — whatever the thoughts or issues are that are bothering you daily are the ones that need to be embraced. Seek out the cause. The answer is in the problem, and although you are all squirming as we write this, you all know who and what your issues are. They may be body image issues, food issues, or hatred of someone. What it is matters not. This is the key to your opening up and enjoying the bliss of God's gifts to you.

These are the problems you came here to heal, and running and hiding from them is impossible. In fact, as the years go by and the avoidance continues, if you don't deal with them now, unfortunately, you will need to come back and deal with them next time. We recommend that this is not the path you choose, as this life will continue to be contaminated by the energy of the unhealed element that you are experiencing. We are asking you to go inside and ask for clarity about the event or experience you perceive as the most difficult. Staying with lesser issues is not the answer, as the big issue is the key to all the others.

There are many paths to understanding, and the first step of the journey is a willingness to actually accept that the answer lies in the problem and that the very person, place, or thing you resist is your salvation. The situation does not need to be dealt with in person, as this is often too much for the ego to bear. It feels as if it will actually die if it confronts the person or issue head on, but what you can do is internally review the resentments, fully expressing them on paper or in a tearful session of self-expression.

These are the first steps down the road to forgiveness — not of real sin, but of the imagined sins the ego has fed and nurtured over time, sins that the fearful mind has embellished with tears, lies, guilt, and sadness. The energies around these situations must first be brought to the surface and then processed and understood. The tears will cleanse the wound, and the anger will free up the spirit. We must emphasize that all of this must be done in a safe and private way and does not require the acceptance or presence of the person or situation at all.

Time is not what you have been taught, and the emotional release you experience will travel through time realms and heal at the source of the injury, a concept that is indeed hard for the logical, linear mind to accept. But it is so, and the original situation will be transformed. "Heal the past to be healed in the present" — this is what was meant by "the sins of the father will be visited unto the seventh generation." It is not a curse but a blessing that assures you all can be healed and that time is irrelevant to the energies of God and the oversoul.

You are certain that the past is real, but it is liquid and can be changed from the present, just as the future can be changed by the positive visualizations talked about with the law of attraction. There is no difference between the past and the future. They are in your mind as images only, and the memories you choose will change the future you experience.

Here, we give you a strong key to the elements of healing. We offer that the past is an illusion as much as the present is, and the power of the mind focused in love on transformation and forgiveness can change all. But you first have to understand this principle of timelessness or you will believe that past transgressions, as you see them, are unfixable. This is not so. We are here to give you the good news that the past you think defines you can be transformed in the fires of prayer and forgiveness, and the vitriol you feel will dissipate and free your mind to create what you choose in the present moment.

The eyes of the soul are limitless, but the eyes of the body limit you in time and space and send messages of permanence and solidity that are not true. You are only a dynamic and vibrating energy system that changes with every thought and dream you have. Every hatred and negative thought, too, is fuel for the creative arena, and we ask you to begin to treat your thoughts with the respect they deserve. They are the force that creates the world in which you live, and they are indeed a force to be reckoned with. The light they can create is awesome, and the pain they can create is devastating, and it is you and all those you come in contact with who feel the energy of your thoughts and the belief system underlying it — all that the world sees.

Begin Today

We are here to begin to chip away at the thought system you have around sexual energy and what it means, but the armor that you have developed to the world you see as "happening to you" must first be lessened for the loving energies of the divine to be felt as they are accepted as the truth of your being. This armor is powerful and of such a high vibration that many of you have a bit of a ladder to climb before it can be realized. These prescriptions of changes in diet, thought, and exercise that we have given are all rungs on the ladder that you will have to climb.

The ladder of success will take you to a different place, but if you are there without your connection to God, it will be like an empty room at the top of a skyscraper. From the outside, others will think you are at the top, but in the room you will be sitting in the corner by yourself, with no love or beauty around you.

So begin today. Turn off the television — even if it is for an hour — walk out into the world, and listen to your soul. It will speak to you, but you must give it some space to speak, and you must be willing to listen. The voice is quiet at first because it has been ignored, but the loudness will increase until, in the end, it is the only voice you hear. The message it tells you will be the truth of your soul, and it will guide you unerringly to the future your soul came here to experience.

The extreme experiences you have gone through are the transformative places where you have had to let go of the old ways of thinking, and they were planned for your education and enlightenment. They are the things that scare a lot of others. The choice to face their fears seems the most devastating thing they could do, yet those fears are the key to their freedom and the path to happiness. It's strange, is it not, that fear is the driving force behind happiness?

We feel that this is why people are so stuck on their pathways to the divine. They are convinced that if they are afraid then there is something wrong with them. In fact, the fear is their greatest door to transformation, and as A Course in Miracles states, your true strength is hidden under your darkest fear.

The fears seem to have a life of their own and grow of their own accord, but you have seen the difference that reining in the mind accomplishes. There are many paths to transformation of the mind, and the first step is the most important. Individuals must ask for the mind to be clarified and step on the path to that goal, but they must first realize that they are not thriving as they are functioning at the moment. For most people, this is accomplished through the feeling body, and so many are disconnected from their feeling bodies by modern conveniences. Although these conveniences are not inherently bad, they are overwhelming in their volume and complexity. As you are seeing, the balance can be a difficult one — the combination of work, conversations, and computers all vying for attention. The world of nature is so much quieter and will not scream in your ear for the attention it deserves.

Intention

Now we will speak about the idea of intention in the manifestation of the experiences you wish to have. This is indeed a fascinating topic, and the intention of the human mind focused on its goal is indeed a powerful creator. One of the issues that arises immediately when discussing this idea is what you want to create and why. The ideas of the ego mind are very different from those of your true self, so this is where we will start.

The ego is always in search of the hardcopy of things — cars, bodies, houses, and such. Rarely is it concerned with emotional experiences, or any kind of experiences. It will vaguely acknowledge that a car will make it happy — or at least that's what it will tell you— but the experiential side of life is not the ego's strong point. As we have mentioned before, the ego is about survival mechanisms, and it will always go to something tangible as the object of its desire. It does not, in any meaningful way, care about the spiritual journey at all, and as we said, its distrust of the nonphysical is in response to its deep-seated knowledge that it is only alive when the body is alive.

When you truly get to understand this aspect of your mind and how it functions, it is very helpful in ignoring the ego's demands. People have been mistaking the ego for who they are, but it is not who you are at all. It is the mechanism that drives the mammalian body in which you seem to exist, and it will always wish for different things than your true self that is masked by its loud, and at times obnoxious, demands.

This is part of the education we wish to give to people so that they can discern the source of the messages in their minds and decide more clearly which ones to follow. Spirit wishes for experience. It knows that there is no value in material objects and that emotion, feeling, and experience are the tools of growth. At times, material objects hinder that growth if they are an obsession and the only thing you allow the mind to think about.

So in setting your intentions, we suggest that they are focused not on the physical objects that you wish to own or possess in some way, but on the energy that those objects make you feel. This will allow you to remain very general in your intentions. For example, you will no longer say, "I want a convertible sports car," but instead will express a desire for freedom and abundance. What this does is bypass the ego's need to control, allowing the complex and uncontrollable mechanism of the universe to kick in, so to speak. As the mind focuses on an object, because it is material, the ego tries to figure out how it will acquire it from its own limited source of knowledge, its current income, and so forth. But when you approach your intentions from a spiritual point of view — speaking of creativity, joy, freedom, and words such as this — the universe has a much wider range of options and will remove the internal blocks you have to those experiences as part of the manifestation.

This is where the most profound difference comes into play. The universe, or the God energy that pervades all, knows what you are capable of at the moment, and it knows what you are scared of at the moment. It knows your limitations, be they temporary or permanent in some way. But what it also knows is how to help you heal those blocks, and healing them will allow the object of your desire — the experiences — to flow through you. We will give you an example to clarify our point.

If you want a lover and a partner to share your life and you were sexually abused as a child, there are perhaps fears and terrors that will prevent you from accessing this kind of experience. Searching for a person to love from this point of view will not work. When possible partners approach you and desire a sexual relationship, the terrors will arise and you will leave or shut down. If, on the other hand, you ask for the experience of love to arise in your life, Spirit will first show you the way to what you may consider filial love, which does not involve the body, so that you are not alone. Then it will arrange the circumstances for the inner healing of the trauma to begin, which will prepare the ground for the love that you truly wish to experience.

So this is why we are asking that your intentions be for experience and not objects. The universe, in its wisdom, knows the path that will not terrify. It knows the blocks that need to be healed, and it will lead you down the road to true happiness — not the short-lived satisfactions the ego loves so much. Indeed, the ego will reach its goal, and almost immediately it will look for another object because the first did not satisfy. The spiritual path may seem nebulous and intangible, but the rewards are those of the most real kind, and as we mentioned before, the things you will value at the end of your life are experiences, healing, and love. Nothing else will come to mind at all.

So that is our intention-setting advice for today. Imagine the feelings and ask yourself if that is truly what you want, and the world will arrange itself for your best and highest path to that very goal. It is oftentimes a little longer route, but the destination is truly where you can rest and find the peace and love you are searching for.

We are with you again, dear one. This book [Tina was reading Conversations with God (Hodder Mobius, 1997)] is inspiring and honest, is it not? We are indeed in agreement with all that it says, and we recommend it to all who wish to grow and awaken to the world of divine love.

We are approaching a specific aspect of this idea of God and sexuality and the way to access and diffuse the blocks that have been created by the misteachings of religion and cultural limitations. We

*are a follow-up, if you will, to this set of books, a fork in the road
that this teaching takes you down. We will be engaging people in a
direct and spoken-word format that will entrance and encourage their
personal questions and employ real-time methods for the experiential healing and re-experiencing of their true nature. So we wish to
acknowledge this inspired writing as a precursor for that which we are
speaking about.*

Decision Over Conditioning

We are now going to write about the discipline required to follow the
path we advocate and the willingness to face your fears and how to do
that. There is a moment when the deciding mind must override the
conditioned mind. There is a moment when you must do what you do
not wish to; know from study and prayer that the limits of your own
thinking are not in your best interests. This is the moment when prayer
is most useful for those of you so afraid of love.

This is the most difficult moment — when the ego screams, "Run
and hide!" and you decide otherwise. This is a moment of great strength
of will, and there isn't any other way to prepare for it than through
study and prayer. The mind knows the theory of its limits, but when it
faces them squarely and looks them in the eye, the limits seem a safe
refuge that will stop anything bad from happening. This is a lie. The
limits of the mind are actually what causes all the bad things to happen.
"Spiritual paradox" is the name for this thing; the truth is the opposite
of what you believe, so you must do the opposite of what you believe.

This is a sophisticated action that the ego sees as insanity, yet following the ego's dictates is real insanity. It will make you repeat the
same pattern over and over, no matter that it doesn't make you happy.
It will make you leave lover after lover because you see the same thing
arising in them, but that thing you see in them is really in you, and you
cannot accept this thing.

The one who is hateful requires more love from you, yet you give
him or her the same hate in return. The one who is shy requires you to
become brave, yet you back off, saying he or she is shy, when it actually
brings out the shyness already in you. The future changes completely
when you get this principle. When you judge another you wish to love,
ask what it is in that person that you dislike, and know that that is in

you too. Bring it into the light through your loving interaction. Relationships fall apart because of this mistake in interpretation, and it is this that opens the hearts of both parties. When your lover is fearful, be brave and take that person's hand. When your lover is angry, be patient and love that person more. The opposite of the ego's desires is usually the answer to many of the problems from which you suffer. It is a treasure indeed to understand this.

So now on to the fear of hurt and pain that stops so many from going deep into their own hearts and the hearts of their lovers. The hurt you fear is nothing compared to the hurt of a lonely, unfulfilled, and passionless life. To sit in front of your televisions night after night, safe from hurt but not really living, is a sad sentence indeed, for the terror you feel at a future the same as the past must surely be more frightening than the prospect of being hurt in love. Is it not?

The mind can create great suffering over the loss of love if it tells the story as punishment from God, but this is not so. A broken heart is a heart that will not let the lover go, that calls love possession and not expression. The mind must be trained to stay in the present so that when a lover leaves you, you are still present and accept the verdict — with tears, yes, but not the years of suffering the untrained mind inflicts on the poor human involved. The suffering of a broken heart is a self-inflicted gunshot that is being repeated over and over, day by day, minute by minute. This is not the lover's doing, but yours — by staying in the place of judgment and lack of acceptance. Let us make sure we are truthful in this story we are telling ourselves. Did we perhaps betray ourselves and refuse to acknowledge this? Did we perhaps not see the signs and blame the other for our lack of attention? All these things must be looked at to heal past hurts and truly let them go so that your heart can be open for the experience of a new and exciting love that will lead you to heaven, hand in hand with the one you offer your heart to.

Do the work, or live a life of sadness and unfulfillment, keeping your heart safe. "Safe for what?" we ask. The heart is for love, and you cannot keep it safe and truly live.

We are with you again, dear one. We can feel your determination today to take another stab at the confident and sure way of approaching our exchanges. We are proud of you for staying true to your path to write this story of how to engage love's energy, for all to learn and to see where they have made some missteps and mistakes along the way. Mistakes always make the lesson clearer if there is forgiveness applied. If you attach blame and unforgiveness, you will be stuck in the error, and the lesson must come again in another unpleasant form — not for punishment, but for illumination.

CHAPTER THIRTY-TWO

The Power of Your Words

We hear you speaking, and at times it is very distressing for us, as we can feel the sadness and fears expressed in the words you use. So many of you speak in the negative about the things you do not want, the things that annoy and distress you. Unfortunately, you have not been taught the power of words, so we will do you the honor of teaching you the power of your voice.

Your word is power — even more than thought. When you speak words through the ethers, energy grows at the very core of creation. Your words are magic spells manifesting that which you speak about. The words "I hate you" are a curse, a form of hatred never to be used, an attack as sure as a knife to the heart. "I love you" is an energetic vortex that reaches across time and space and fills the heart with light that heals and soothes. These are not mere imaginings we are writing about here, but the truth of the matter.

We ask you to be very conscious of the words you use and to not engage in frivolous conversations about what you do not want or do not like. The problem with your culture is you have lost the concept of the word as bond. Indeed, there was a time in the past when the art of communication was given its due as the powerful manifestor that it is, but as with so much else in your disposable society, you have lost the value of the word. You often speak without thought of that which you utter, and you often gossip and talk about others' lives and errors with delight and joy. Again, each gossiping sentence is an attack that is food for the ego, which will dip you down into the realms of negativity and begin to create things of a like vibration.

You have a saying: If you cannot say anything nice, say nothing at all. We advise the same — not through any politeness concept, although politeness is essential, but because the spoken hatred is more powerful than the thought of hatred, and only you will suffer at the end of this sword. You see, the power of speech is a magical one, and you must understand this — that all you say, especially to and about those close to you, creates on many levels and through time.

The words you say to your children form the very foundational ideas of who they will believe they are. They will see themselves as valuable and lovable or stupid and disposable, depending greatly on what you say they are. You tell your children ten thousand times what they are, and that is a large responsibility, is it not?

What are the words you speak each day? Are they complaints and fears put out into space? Or are they words of compassion and appreciation for all you experience and all that you have? The vibration of your outer life is set by your words, and the vibration of your inner life is set by your thoughts, although they are of course inextricably entwined in the vortex of creation that is the mind you dwell in. We are sure you do not pay attention all the time to what you say, but we wish to tell you it is now time to change that.

Be aware every moment of what is coming out of your mouth, and know that wealth and poverty, sickness and health are carried on the words you utter. Do you speak enthusiastically about your operations and trips to the doctor? Do you go into great detail about what is wrong with you? Or do you speak eloquently about the experiences you are having, focusing positively on all that you are and all that you value?

Negativity Creates Negativity

We suggest listening to those around you for a few days and seeing if you can see a correspondence between what they are speaking about and their state of happiness and health. We guarantee you will not find someone who is constantly negative feeling healthy, happy, and abundant. Negative people may have those things, but they will not feel them. If you have it but do not feel it, is that the experience you are really having? See the words others speak as their message to the universe — their requests, if you will — and notice too their passion. What do they speak passionately about, and what are they experiencing in their current lives?

We suggest you tell yourself, very clearly, that every utterance is an incantation and every slight about another will come to you in that form, or another of similar vibration. We realize this feels like a threat, but it is not. It is merely the truth of the matter, and we are offering more of a caveat — a warning — to proceed with caution. Do not utter the word of hatred that you feel, but go quiet and think about it. Is this really what you want to seed the universe with? Is this really the kind of energy you want to receive in your experience?

Here we will also mention the way you speak to your dear and beloved partner. Are you short-tempered and abrupt, filled with acrimony and viciousness? Or are you kind and gentle, offering a kind touch along with gentle and kind words? To follow the path of bliss, you must get your words under control, but not in a rigid and strict way. Begin to pay attention and develop a discipline of omission at first. There will be complaints that arise, but at first you will miss them. Then you will see them and still not be able to stop their spoken nature. Then you will see them and make a different choice.

This is indeed a process, as all that we counsel is a process, and we understand many of you are quite unconscious as you utter the thousands of words you speak each and every day. But what does this say, dear ones? That you create without realizing what you are creating. These unconscious complaints and negativity arise in the form of sicknesses and accidents, unpleasant experiences that seem to have nothing at all to do with what you are doing. They appear to be random and out of your control, but they are not. Every word you speak is a powerful manifestor, and each subject about which you speak will have its own energy.

Do you hate romance and relationships, taking every opportunity to trash those around you displaying love and affection? Or are you a die-hard romantic, always looking for hearts and flowers in every situation, speaking about the glories of love and its wonderful manifestation? Each of you will know where you are on the scale of negativity and positivity. And how will you know? You will know by how you feel, and you will know by the words you utter. So do not act confused and wonder why your life does not thrive in all areas. You must begin to take responsibility for the energy you put out in all subjects, particularly in the words you use. The words you speak are a direct connection to the creative source of the universe. Sound is powerful, and the words you speak are all a prayer. What are you praying for, and how often does that prayer leave your lips in a day?

Try to Only Speak Kind Words

Never gossip about anyone. Others' souls are connected to yours, your mind to theirs, and so the energy will travel back and forth and a powerful negative connection will be forged that is difficult to break, except through forgiveness. If you find yourself speaking negatively about a person, place, or thing, forgive them. They are not at fault at all. Your perception is merely focused on what they are doing that is an error, a simple mistake that can be corrected, and only your positive contribution will aid in their healing, in their transformation. Feel the vibration of your words and know that they are making up a lot of what you are experiencing.

Simple, is it not, dear ones? Speak about the good, the kind, and the beautiful, and it will begin to arise in your world. Speak about the sad, the painful, and the hateful, and you will help all to experience that negativity. Do your self-analysis and find out what is going on, and all will begin to make more sense. All will begin to align in the ways you wish — healing, creating, and loving.

The words you utter to your beloved are an important focal point for the achievement of bliss in the sexual relationship. We would have you always speak to your beloveds as if they were the God you respect, for they are the manifestation of the divine in your world, the reflection of the divine in you. And as you speak to them and about them, that is the vibration at which your relationship will flourish or die. Think about it: Are you feeding the love between you, or are you killing the roots of the plant by pouring poison onto it? Are you immersing both of you in a vibration of love, or the vibration of mediocrity and sabotage? Most of you, unfortunately, save your vitriol and anger for your partners, for your spouses. You are more polite to those you work for and with than to those with whom you are going to make love, and this is a sorry state of affairs.

Turn Away from the Ego

Once again we remind you of the vibration of the ego mind, the vibration of judgment and fear, of lack and separation. And we remind you of the vibration of love, the vibration of what we call God, that energy that creates worlds, that creates ideas, that is the life you feel pulsing through you every second of every day. This is the vibration of bliss, of ecstasy, and this is what you must do with each other every day, all day, so that you can create the vibration of bliss together.

Now you will say that this is not possible; to always be sweetness and light together is not realistic, not practical. And we will have to disagree. Those are the thoughts of a narrow mind that has not been taught the truth of the matter. Those of you who wish to create a blissful relationship know in your hearts that this is the way it must be. You understand on some innate level that the way relationships are conducted in this society of yours is poisonous and hateful a lot of the time. Read together, talk together, and support each other — not in your negative judgments, oh no, but in a positive way, always seeking the honest solution, always helping each other to find your honest and true paths.

Is your partner tired of his job, and does he hate going to work? Then sit down and talk about this. Know that the ego will want to go into fear, but understand that changes need to be made. Speak about how this can be done in a calm and loving way for all involved, but mostly talk about how you feel about each other. Speak about the way you feel when your lover calls you unexpectedly for lunch at your place of employment. Tell her how beautiful you think she is, how you love it when she touches your hair or kiss your lips. These are the words of the lover; these are the words that create bliss. These are the words that will create the love life you want. These are the actions that will support the very heart and soul of your relationship, feed its roots, and nurture its existence.

There are many of you sitting on couches watching violence, hardly speaking, and eating unhealthy snacks, wondering why your sex life is nonexistent. Really? You are wondering why you don't touch each other in love when you are watching murder night after night? The excitement you feel at these shows is the ego's fight-or-flight response — not joy, not happiness — and you must begin to take responsibility for this.

The words you say come from the thoughts you have, which create the feelings you have. So go to the root of the issue: What are you thinking, and what are you putting into your body, into your mind? What is the food you are feeding this life you call your own? No one else will do it for you, and nothing that may have happened in your past is responsible for doing what you are now in control of, that which you do, think, and speak. Every second is your own responsibility and within your power to change.

CHAPTER THIRTY-THREE

Share Your Feelings

We will go on now with the idea of compassion, as this is what you must show for yourselves as you take this journey into the habits impeding the flow of bliss into your bodies and minds. Compassion is not a big thing in the West and is a foreign concept to many. It means that you do not attack a person whose actions come from ignorance in any way. You have not been taught this. You have been taught many things that are blatant lies, so the truth will seem confusing and somehow wrong at first. Have compassion for yourselves and for your reluctance, hesitation, or confusion.

If you have been trained to eat fried chicken, and you believe it is good and healthy to do so, breaking that habit will take some time and some compassion. Initially we will ask you just to look at what arises at the thought of that change. So many things will arise: fear of judgment from others, especially if this is part of your family or culture, or fear of loss of pleasure. Indeed, many of you eat because it is the only pleasure you allow yourselves. It feels as if life would not be worth living if you were to lose these things. If this belief arises, if the idea of losing a particular food causes anxiety, then you know that your life is not full of enough joy. So we suggest that is perhaps the first issue you should look at. Why is your life so focused on food, and is there something you can do about it?

Another area that may arouse some fear is that of exercise and the body's health. In that area, are you afraid of walking? Why? What is it about that? Are you feeling ill? If so, what is that about? Walking will only help the sickness, so we have to look at many things. What so often happens is there is some resistance to change, and the examination ends at "I don't want to" or "I can't." You must go deeper into the underlying fear, and it is fear, not love.

These are the emotional journeys you must make into the realms of the unexamined and conditioned part of the mind. So many of you are programmed by the past, by others, and in fact are not living your own lives with your own values. And then you wonder why you are unfulfilled and sad. We are here to help you access the true life that you are meant to lead, and passion is the force that will drive the engine to the life you want.

These issues of the deep-seated and painful blocks to passion are the crux of the matter. The culture you are in, let us say Western civilization, is founded on some quite insane principles that have led to much of the poverty, violence, bloodshed, and perversions in existence now — and have been for many generations, if not all of the past millennia. Some of these are that God does not approve of sex, that indeed it is the Devil's playground. This is the biggest lie and untruth ever told. The flower is a sex organ, dear ones, and this is the most beautiful of the creations you will see on this planet. And what does it mean that in your church at Easter there are sex organs all around you? The hypocrisy is a sad joke, is it not? You can see the beauty in another's sex organs but not your own. These are designed by God energy for the great and transformative pleasure they will enhance. They are not sinful, and they are beautiful if the mind is educated properly in the divine ways of God. This is the first misconception and the largest that must go.

The second block is thinking that God cares what you do here, in a very mean, angry, and judgmental way. The only thing that is observed here by what you would call God is the vibration you emit — nothing more. Are you happy and at peace? Then abundance and good flows. Are you bitter and twisted in your righteous judgment? Then it does not flow and all will become out of balance. This is not a punishment, but a reflection of your energy — that is all. You are sick because your vibration is off somehow; you are rich because you are focused in some way that brings in the abundance, and it cares not if you are likable or pretty or old or young. There is a vibration, and that is all.

So if you go to church every day but hate homosexuals, then you are not at peace, and you will feel it in your bones. And if you are a flaming queen, happy in your gayness, you will reap the benefits of that happiness. There are no errors in the making of this world; there are only errors in interpretation, and that is why we have come: to tell you that you are the creators, made as the God energy was made, to create in all directions, all the time. You must get this, and know that as soon as you do, the world around you will begin to change. But what you must also get is that you must change to do this.

Your culture, Western culture, wants security and permanence, so this is a great impediment to the creation of that which you desire. You must grow and let go of the old so that the new light energy can come in.

If there is a relative you do not enjoy visiting, and yet you visit this person every time from obligation, this is not an act of love for them or for you. The energy of your visit will affect your relative negatively, and of course it will affect you negatively. And we hear the resounding crowd saying, "But we cannot live like this, free and happy. What will happen to the world if we all did this?" And we say, look at the world you are in because of what you are doing: families and countries at war, passionless marriages, infidelity, and pain. We ask for you to see that this is not all happening as some divine retribution, as punishment for your sins. No, dear ones, it is a reflection of your own states of mind, and it is here that the biggest work of all is done.

You must be re-educated in what the truth is: that you are all powerful, and what others do or think is none of your business. Concentrate on your own lives, your own desires, and your own passions, and build families and lives that you love, based on your true selves, your true natures — not what everyone else says is right. You are all born with infallible guidance systems, yet you curse this thing that is the compass to your salvation. It is your feelings. And that is the worst lesson of the Western world: Deny your feelings. They say feelings are unreliable and confusing; use the intellect and it will guide you clearly to a goal of value. This is not true! Your feelings are the true north, but you think they are your enemies. You must make friends with them and begin to listen to them if you want any chance at the bliss of which we speak. The languages of heaven, happiness, and joy are all discerned through feelings. Feelings are the map to the treasure, and the clearer they are, the better.

Absence of Love

*We are with you again, dear one. Indeed, you have had a busy day
of doing nothing. We tease you — you are always doing this work, it
seems, and we enjoy the energy with which you approach all the work
you have to do.*

We are going to write about the absence of love in the lives of those
on the planet and the dire consequences that arise from the way many
are living at the moment. The absence of love is a sad and sorry state in
which to exist. We say "exist" because it is not living; the closed heart
does not function at all. Many of those in the Western world exhibit
heart disease, and this is no accident. The body responds physically to
the matrix of the energetic body, and the closed heart will create the
symptoms of heart disease.

There are other areas in which this sad and sorry state of affairs is
manifested. The closed heart, the heart without love flowing through
it, becomes hardened, and the actions of the individual are tough and
unfeeling. This is not the individual's fault, as many closed their hearts
because they were taught to. Western culture is guilty of intentionally
teaching those who reside in its confines to close their hearts. How do
they do that?

Every time you tell someone to stop crying, that is what you are
doing. Inadvertently, many parents close down their children's hearts in
just this way. When youngsters cry, they need to express that energy and
receive a compassionate question, such as, "What is the matter?" But the
response is often nowhere near that nice. "I'll give you something to cry
about," and "don't be a baby" are more likely responses, we are sad to say.
Many parents are tired from running on the treadmill of life, feeling that
that is all they can do, but we ask any parents reading this to be aware of
their reaction to emotions in their children. Are you constantly asking
them to be quiet and behave just so you can get a job done? These are
the very things that quell the spirit and harden the heart. If you are a
parent, remember that showing loving compassion and understanding of
your children's emotional expressions will help them.

You were raised in a culture in which emotions are frowned upon,
and that is part of the problem we are here to help fix. The "good
child syndrome" — that a child who is quiet and never says a word is

rewarded for it — creates children who grow up into adults with no heart to give others. They will be emotionless and unable to connect with others. Remember this as your exuberant young one rushes around the house. We understand the difficulties of the modern world, but you must start changing the programming in the young ones to allow them their energy, fun, and tears. These are all qualities that many of you have become separate from, so they make you uncomfortable at times, but in that moment of choice, remember your children will do what you demand of them, even if it is not in their best interests.

Another aspect of the closed heart that comes from being chastised as a child is the fear of self-expression and saying what you are feeling. In the kinds of relationships we are hoping to help create, this is a major issue. You must be willing to tell your partner how you feel about all kinds of things, which is a hurdle for the stoic and joyless Westerner who has been taught to suck it up or play tough.

Men have a harder time of this than women, and we ask all of you who experience this difficulty to start with very small statements of genuine feeling about something in your day. As you express your inner world, your partners, lovers, and children will respond in kind. It is indeed an interesting result of this simple technique. When you share, others share, and a connection is made to the heart center and will begin the healing process.

Many of you have hidden away a lot of your deepest hurts under a façade of "I'm fine" and "it's all good." We do counsel that you follow a joyful attitude, but that does not mean you shouldn't share your feelings. Many people in relationships are as strangers living in the same house, staring at the television, knowing nothing about the internal life of the other, also sitting there staring at the television. We ask you to turn the television off for a while and engage each other in real conversations about real things.

The emotions you feel, or at least are trying to feel, are the most real things you deal with, yet your culture tells you otherwise. The objects in your world will be meaningless at the end of your life. Trust us. When you come to review your life after you have passed over after death, there will not be one object you will recall or even desire to recall. All you will remember are the relationships you had and if you loved well enough. All the things you own and work so hard for, sacrificing time with friends and family, are absolutely meaningless here, and you can waste your entire life searching for some kind of salvation in the wrong place.

So encourage yourself and all those you love and care about to share their feelings. That is the path to bliss. It may seem a strange and insignificant step to take, but trust us — it leads into the deepest places in the human soul. And after all, that is what we are after on this journey together. The bliss energies are of the heart, and this is where there are tremendous blocks to the flow of that divine song, so we again ask you to share just a little at first. As you do it more often, the hearts of all those to whom you speak with love and honesty will be grateful and return the favor.

CHAPTER THIRTY-FOUR

Options and Actions

We would like you to look at your options and the actions they require. Your options are many on this journey. You can become a monk, an artist, and anything in between. These are the options open to you these days. Indeed, there is an amazing amount of freedom available to you in the modern Western world, but this is not really the point, is it? What you need to decide is who you are going to be in this world, which is the opposite of what you have been taught.

The Western teaching is to become something and then discover yourself afterward — to discover yourself by what you learn, what you own, and where you travel. What we suggest you do on this path is set aside, for the moment, this idea of what you will do, and focus on being who you are. So many in your modern and ambition-driven world feel that if only they could find the career that will make them somebody, make them something, then all will be okay. This is the ego talking and little else.

This is a revolution for the Western mind, to not think of its value being set by its profession and social status. Each of you, no matter where you are currently employed — or not employed, for that matter — is of equal and esteemed value in the eyes of the Divine, and we wish for you to really hear this. We are telling you that Spirit, God, All That Is, is in love with you as you are now, in this very moment, whether you think you are a success or not. We do not care what you do for a living, and we will never care. What we need to do is get you to understand this radical and revolutionary idea: You are loved. You are of value, and nothing can, or ever has, changed that in the eyes of God and the universe that is its creation.

A tree is not more valuable than a flower — different, yes, but not of a different value. This is an area of the ego's domination in your culture. You feel that to be successful on the spiritual path you must be successful in the world, and this is just not so. It is such a deeply ingrained belief that many of you are just dumbfounded by what we are saying. If you are being what you are meant to be — a human being seeking experience, choosing what you like, asking for more, and focusing on the good and the lovable — then you are a resounding success in spiritual terms.

The illusion of wealth cripples you and makes you waste your valuable time on wasteful and useless objects and activities. We have been asking our dear one, Tina, to take us to the beach so we can immerse ourselves in the environment and see it through her eyes. We are astounded by the beauty and the magnificence of the experience she can have, and we have asked her how the humans can be unhappy when they have such amazing experiences of wind, water, sparkling sunlight, and smells of all kinds. We are in awe of this physical existence you have, yet you do not see truly what it is. It all fades behind the complaints or the small and pathetic concerns of the ego. Dear ones, go outside and look at the wonder of a tree and truly see its magnificence. Watch some birds and some flowers, and stop your mind for a few minutes to grasp the wonder of them. This is what spiritual success is: the true appreciation of the beauty of the now — not the car you are saving for or the relationship you think will save you from yourself. If you are truly able to grasp that of which you hear us speak, then you have arrived, and your spiritual guides will applaud as they experience you just being.

The actions you are always taking with some future goal in mind are often a waste of time. First, this is because you have deep and powerful belief systems that go against what you are doing. We will give you an example: Perhaps you wish to become financially successful and you are willing to work hard to that end. You are always trying to come up with a new idea, a new plan to reach that success. But deep inside you believe in lack, in the fear of poverty, so you are always looking at the poor, revolted, hoping that you will not end up there. You are focused on poverty, even though your actions are focused on receiving more money, so you will not be able to create the wealth you desire. You may have some small gains because of the hard, hard work, but they will never feel like enough. You will always feel on the edge of losing it all. This is what we are talking about.

If you are able to be with yourself, relax, and enjoy what is all around you and what you have in peace, you will be guided to the next best thing for your true success. And you will have a nice time of it, always. We promise you so. We say this so that you do not feel that there is an endless list of things you must do to satisfy us on this journey. We know we have given you many suggestions for changes, but if you really look at them, they are really not actions so much as releasing negative blocks and opening to a simpler, quieter, and more beautiful life that supports the quiet voice of Spirit and gives it some space to speak. This is how we wish for you to look at this path.

This is not a path of achievement, but one of release. This will take you further — and quickly, too. There is no destination as such. What we are trying to get you to do is get in touch with what is already there, already in you. So that is our recommendation: Relax. Begin to take some time and enjoy the day. Enjoy each other, and set some different goals than the ones you have been taught. The goal tomorrow could be to relax, to surrender, to have no agenda for the entire day, to read in bed all day, to nap, or even to make love all day, if that is your desire. We are suggesting a total revamp of what you are doing into what are you being. This is all, and we think it is a lot, don't you? We are always challenging you with loving prescriptions.

CHAPTER THIRTY-FIVE

Family and Learning

We are now going to write about the family as it relates to the divine union we are speaking about, and oh, what a subject this is! We could indeed write a book about this subject and all the pitfalls of encounters you will see in the romantic pairings of the world, but we will focus on the more traditional Western ideal of the nuclear family as it relates to the divine bliss we are seeking together.

There are some aspects of the Western family setup that are particularly difficult on the couple who wishes to express the union of the divine energies in the new tantric relationship. One of these aspects is obligation, as it impedes the flow of the energies themselves. This will be seen in relationships with family members who require a special behavior to keep them happy, so to speak. This is an impossible situation, because you must be free from these types of obligations if you are to function in the higher realms of energy. We will explain.

The idea of obligation is the opposite of freedom, and to allow the energies to flow, you must be as free as possible — free to feel, free to express, and free to say no to whatever it is you do not feel in alignment with. It becomes clear that many of your relationships do not allow this freedom to express itself. Even the idea of telling some members of your family about your interest in divine sex would cause such eye rolling, and in some cases disgust, that it would seem an impossible combination. But what we are speaking about is freedom of the mind, not necessarily freedom of the body. We will explain further.

It is possible to be around people who hold completely different beliefs and yet keep your own carefully and safely out of sight. This may seem dishonest, but it is not really. If you honor others' rights to their feelings and know in your heart that they cannot understand your beliefs because of their conditioning and position in the world, then that is okay. You must protect yourself from attack, as it were. Even though they cannot truly hurt you, the egos can get in a dustup, and it is our path to maintain peace. This is not peace at the cost of your own integrity, but peace within your mind. This means you should never do something that goes against your true beliefs, but if there is a possibility of peace through your setting aside — for a moment — the need to make everyone the same as you, then a compromise is possible, is it not?

We are thinking of a family dinner, for example. You know that your family will tell the same stories. Uncle Bob may get drunk as usual, and your mother may ask if you have a boyfriend yet. But perhaps there is a possibility that you can see the humor in this and not take it all so seriously. If you are unable to go in with a light, observant heart, then we would not recommend this, but it can be an interesting exercise in subduing your own ego and allowing others of a different persuasion to have their own lives as such.

This is one view, and there are others, of course. If your family is abusive in any way, such as verbally or psychologically, then we suggest you do not submit yourself to any connection at all. No matter the blood ties, there is never any reason to submit to abuse, and we will ask you to work on their forgiveness from a distance in this situation.

There are many variables within this idea, and we will not go into all of them, but try to discern if your relationships make you feel good or bad. Are you feeling pressured or just wanted? Many things can lead to the thoughts and feelings that arise about this subject. Indeed, our dear one, Tina, has had some deep and difficult family issues that have worked themselves out over time, but some relationships are closer than others, and many do not know the extent of her involvement in this subject. Her life is her own, however, and she has found a way to be happy and authentic around those she cares about, and this is what we encourage each of you to.

No one benefits from obligations that are tedious, painful, or abusive, so just make sure that your family is not in these sectors of behavior, and then mix and play with them as it feels comfortable. Also, this is the deepest area for forgiveness work, so we suggest that attending to your part in that process is most important.

Relationships with fathers, mothers, and siblings are powerful ones and can drive behaviors in the present in powerful ways that need to be looked at from a loving and clear place, if at all possible. There are times when a hiatus may be necessary while the old wounds are investigated and the powerful influences are dismantled, and this is fine too. We strive for awareness and love, so this is the goal to keep in mind in any analysis of your family of origin.

Show Affection around and to Your Children

Moving on to the children of your new family. This is indeed an area of interest. What should the portrayal of sex be in front of these youngsters? This is a whole different ball game, and this may ruffle some feathers for you who are parents. We suggest that no special mention be made of the intricacies of lovemaking, but do indeed mention it all the time as the form through which God speaks to a loving couple and through which a great deal of creative energy is expressed. There are secrets about sexual intercourse and tantric practices that are kept as if they are the sins the churches teach about, and it is time for that to stop. We would love to see children see their parents kissing passionately, showing affection all the time — with them too — holding and touching.

Western society is starved for affection, and a lot of this dysfunction comes because many people never saw their parents embracing, hugging, and kissing in public. It was "that thing" they did behind closed doors. If your children come into the bedroom as you are making love, tell them you are making love and you will be out when you are finished. This will not harm the children in any way, and they will see that affection, sex, and passion are all things they can expect in their own adult lives. And what a happy prospect for them that will be!

Do not be afraid, dear ones. Love is love, and it is only the idea of sin and some divine retribution that has planted these seeds of fear in your minds, and they are not true. Your children will grow into healthy, expressive, passionate beings, if that is what you show them how to be, and we hope this will become a much more common route for those of you on this path.

But do be gentle about it, and if you are uncomfortable, take some time to investigate the discomfort and find out what is really making you feel this way. It will usually be family or church teachings that need to be uprooted and put in the compost, just as you would a rotten piece of fruit. It can become new soil if it is put in the right place and not kept out of sight, sabotaging your loving and passionate family life.

We are sad to see children not shown affection because of busy lives. Stop, for heaven's sake, and sit with your children and talk to them. Hold their hands and tell them how grateful you are for their presence in your life, and ask what they would like to do. They may ask for an expensive outing, if that is what you have trained them to do, but perhaps you could start to teach them the benefits of time spent in quiet conversation, or a walk in the local park together, sharing a snack on a park bench.

You strive for the material things that you think they need when, in fact, the most priceless gift you can give is your time. Yes, there are those of you who have lessons to learn about loss and separation. Our dear one here has had to learn separation. This is to help her appreciate the connections that she did not understand before. The journey into this experience breaks down walls and resistance to connections that were not understood before the experience happened, so know that the situation of separation from your loved ones is designed not as a punishment but as a lesson in what you are already missing.

So accept the lesson and do not shut down your hearts. See it as a manifestation of a problem already existing in your mind that the universe is offering up for healing. And the next time you are able, tell your children you love them and accept that there is a need for healing in this area.

All lessons are lessons in love — love of others, love of self, and love of God. You are love machines, but some of you need a tune-up really badly. Intense, short bursts of therapy, a workshop, or classes will help kick off the healing and motivate you to change, but the real work is a day-by-day and minute-by-minute practice. But the rewards, as we have said, will leave you happy and joyful, and the universe will sing and rejoice at your choice to pursue love and all its manifestations.

Teaching

We see the old ways are dying a slow death, but still the methods of teaching exuberant youth are not working so well. The drugs you use to keep the leaping and flying souls of children in their seats are truly awful, and this must be stopped! The brain's reaction to these chemicals is poor indeed, and the answer for a lively child is running in the woods, swimming in the lake, building castles and fire pits, and climbing mountains, with lessons on kindness and compassion for all beings thrown into the mix.

Math can be taught through building things, as measuring fills up the world of building, does it not? Measuring wood for a castle, water for a pool — there are so many ways this subject could be taught. We are aware of the limitations of money, but these activities we speak of are indeed free. Many more people would love to teach children if they could spend time with them in nature rather than a boxy room with no air to breathe.

It is in these first few years of a child's life that the sex energy is quelled. We see a dampening down of spirits even before school begins. Parents start to train their little ones to sit when they don't want to, to eat when they don't want to, and to override their own sweet guidance systems for the impending rules of society. Even the most loving parents feel the conflict of freedom for their children and the lessons the culture around them imposes on their dear, sweet little ones. But the rules of conditioning override the rules of love, and this is where the terrible cutting off of sexual energies begins in the homes of even the most loving parents.

Parents begin to hide their bodies and the bodies of their children very early. When children should be running around naked on beaches, they are hidden, their parents afraid of the perverts they think are hiding in wait to devour their innocent ones. But, in fact, it is the very social structures these parents partake in that are devouring their young ones, day by day, with the parents' approval. This hiding was done to them, so they carry on the legacy of negative beliefs around the body and its natural expression through joy, pleasure, and sex.

The future of the planet depends on beings who need to know their place in the natural world, not the constructed scheme of things. The future depends on people loving everyone and everybody with awareness and joy in the simple pleasures of this amazing planet. Warm beaches, cool woods, and running streams are the true places the human soul wants to reside — not inside in boxes, looking at boxes, and being sold boxes for entertainment. The natural joy of living could actually satisfy the needs of the individual so well.

We wish to tell a story of a young girl and her father. The girl is sitting on her father's lap. The father feels love for his child strongly, and he wishes to hug and touch his daughter in the most innocent way. But stories of lust and fear of persecution run through his mind, so he pushes the child off his lap. The child does not like this or understand her beloved father's actions, so she asks to climb back onto his loving lap and receive the touch that her young body craves. The father gets scared and angry now, and he forcefully gets up and leaves the little one in a state of confusion and misunderstanding. The child feels the loss of her father's love in that moment, feeling responsible for the rush of negative feelings into her body. The little one sees that feelings of love and desire for touch cause anger, and she then believes the desire is wrong. After a few instances of this, she will cease to go to her father for the affection she so desires. Eventually, she will feel this pain with all the men in her life because the teaching happened so early in her development.

This is a simple example of how old strictures from religion and from watching the news will make parents confused about their own feelings, their own beliefs in what is good and loving, and what is in their children's best interests. It is always love and affection that is in the child's best interests — not restraint, judgment, or fear-driven restrictions based on the teachings of old men who lost their contact with the joy of the divine many years ago.

Self-Education

We will now speak about the idea of self-education on this path, the necessary design by which you can lift the mind and the heart into the realms of divine truth on this journey. There are many inspired documents extant on the planet that will liberate and educate your mind. As you walk away from your televisions more and more, it is these that we wish you to read. There are many, so we will mention a few areas to consider, although we are loath to specifically point you to one or the other. You see, it is important for you to cultivate your feelings as guideposts to what goes in and what you consume. It is this cultivation of discernment that will stand you in good stead over the long run.

If we tell you what to read, we will be removing that learning from your experience, and this we do not wish to do. The experiences you have are the very things that will solidify any learning that is to take place, and this is our greatest lesson for you. Walk into the library or bookstore and select intuitively that which appeals to you. Is it a book on nature or an ancient Indian text? What does your heart say? That is where you should start. The spirit that is your guide will speak the language you are familiar with to teach you what you do not know. Listen to that guidance, for it will be infallible.

There are many such examples, and our dear one had many texts on the way to her connection with us. She fell in love with *A Course in Miracles*, and that became her go-to text that led her out of the darkness and into the light. That is the love in which she now resides, but her journey was all intuition, and you will each come to the goal that is set in your heart long before you were born into this world. Trust in that process, and as you read this book, this path may be the one for you. The desire for a fulfilling and passionate life may be the message that speaks to you loudly and clearly. It is one path among many, and you may walk along it for a while and find another pathway that appeals more, and that is okay. We will not be offended or wish you ill. All paths lead to the same place in the end, and although some lead you over rough ground, you will find your way out eventually.

Returning to our original point: Put into your mind inspiring writings full of love and passion. They will lead you further along the path and create an education that will fill your heart with joy and feed your soul that has been hungry for love and fulfilling experiences.

That will do for now, dear one. There are other experiences pressing, and we are impressed with your focus. It is improving. We will speak later.

CHAPTER THIRTY-SIX

Forgiveness and Nonjudgment

We are with you now to shed light on this complicated and misunderstood word, "forgiveness." This word sends the ego into a rage. "Forgive?!" it shouts. "But you hurt me. You made me feel bad. You left me. You abandoned me!" These are all the arguments your mind throws up when we say to forgive, and you think of those in your life who require this act. To come to a peaceful mind, forgiveness must be practiced, and this is the truth; it is you who suffers from a mind that is not at peace. It really is this simple.

Hurts of the past no longer exist except in your mind. The pain is long gone, and likely, the person who hurt you — or who you felt hurt you — had a very different experience of that event and may not even remember it. What is the point in ruining your ability to be happy to hold on to a resentment that does nothing? What is the point in feeding a hurt from the past that only causes you suffering? There is no point at all, and that is the truth. Once again, the ego hates and screams in anger at even entertaining the idea.

This is where you must exert some discipline and understanding of the ego's power over your ability to be in the present and be happy. The ego cares not for these things that you wish for in your life, and yet, as we have said before, you have been trained to give it what it wants. You cannot give to the ego if you wish to travel the path to a blissful and happy life, filled with joy and passion. The remaining judgments keep you from the energy of love, and if you wish to feel and experience a higher form of love, these old wounds must be let go.

New wounds have the opportunity to grow every day. A harsh word from a family member, a misunderstanding, an assumed betrayal by a friend — these can all happen every day, and you have the choice to either feed the ego and reap the harvest it so generously offers or forgive and keep your peace and your connection to Source. As you can see, the idea of nonjudgment and forgiveness is not some "airy-fairy" practice you participate in once in ten years, but a daily, hourly, and, at times, minute-by-minute acceptance of what is, without resistance. It is the resistance and lack of acceptance that creates the interference with your connection to Source and, consequently, your ability to create a loving, happy, and peaceful life.

The Ego Dislikes Forgiveness

We are aware of the rage the ego feels at the idea of forgiveness as a practice. There are many who merely read that word and immediately feel rage against a member of their family or an ex-lover. There is someone, for most of you, who triggers a deep feeling of rage when this word "forgiveness" comes up. What we want to tell you is that person is the key to your future bliss, and you do not know it. And now you do not believe it.

As part of each life's journey, you are assigned tasks to perform, and there are situations set up before you are ever born that arise in the lifetime as "unforgivable" events. Now, this may seem cruel from the human point of view, but these are set up in the realms of the eternal, where all is understood and experience is valued over all else. It is the soul's choice to have these difficult events, and it is in the relinquishment of judgment that you are freed from the bounds of the ego mind. This is indeed a powerful and wrenching event for most.

The precipitating factor is usually a deep and significant pain that will not go away. There are often things such as addictions associated with your rage and resentment, and it can be the path to sobriety that forces the ego's hand. For some it never comes, and for others it happens on their deathbed as the fatality of life drives home the fact that this really didn't matter all. Events conspire to make you forgive, which is why the ego hates it. It is the most spiritual thing you can do on this Earth and, indeed, the thing the ego hates most.

The ego feeds on war, hatred, and judgment, and the thought of giving up its food makes it scream in rage. So if you understand that your spiritual development and the experience of bliss and heaven on earth are dependent on this act, it starts to become slightly, even remotely, something you may consider. The unforgiveness or judgment of another is the biggest block to the energies of love, so if you want true love of the self, others, and God to manifest in your mind as real experiences, we are asking you to forgive that one person you hate. That person is your salvation, and this act will be the springboard to your divine and happy future. Every thought of loathing that you have for this person sucks energy from you and pollutes the world around you in ways you cannot imagine.

If you hate someone and are sick, the sickness may well be that hatred manifesting in your body; the low vibration destroys cells and interrupts cellular function. If you hate someone and are overweight, it may well be that low-vibration thought that drives you to consume food to soothe the beast inside. On and on it goes. Do you not want freedom from the past? Do you not want to reach your very highest potential in this life? Do you not want to thrive and love and reap the harvest of divine bliss? Then forgiveness is mandatory, and the sooner the better. Every day you delay, it is you who loses; and every day you delay, your body struggles with the burden of this dark energy that is unforgiveness.

So do not think that you must hang out with this person you hate and invite him for coffee each day. That is not what forgiveness is. But you must release any thought you have that is not loving. You must refuse to attack this person in your mind, and you must stop retelling the story over and over. Every time you tell the story you say it is this person hurting you, but the truth is that person only did it once. You have retraumatized yourself a hundred, a thousand times. You have become the perpetrator — and a worse one than that other person ever was.

We know many of you find this forgiveness impossible at the moment, but we urge you to revisit it often and ask at first for the willingness to change this. Place a white light around this person you hate every time he or she appears, and do nothing else. This will help shift the energy from attack so it is you who will feel the relief of the attacks stopping. It is your mind that is lessened by the thoughts of loathing and hatred. The other person is affected too, it is true, but you are the one who feels the anxiety, and it is your heart that closes, stopping the delicious flow of love to and through you. This is why this person makes

260 * Making Love to God

you feel bad when you think of him or her. You are closing your heart to the truth — that this individual made a mistake and it is forgiven. You are feeding the monster, and the monster is the ego, and it will hurt you one way or another.

So that is forgiveness. The love you send to others does come back to you because others are you expressed in a different form — you just don't know it.

Put Yourself in Another's Shoes

All of the actions that cause you pain are more a reflection of yourself and your own shortcomings that drive you crazy. This is a concept foreign to most Western minds, although the idea of the world as a mirror is beginning to seep into the teachings many of you are reading. The truth of the matter is the ego, in an effort to get you to side with it, separates itself from all aspects of itself that would cause too much conflict, for if you truly saw just how hateful it was, you would indeed abandon it. So it tells you the story of just how good you are and how very bad everyone else is. Merely listen to two sides of the story when a couple is divorcing, and you will see there are two different experiences, two completely different versions of the events. And in the crimes that you think have been perpetrated against you, it the same — there is another version.

We suggest this be an area you look at, especially if you are having a hard time coming to a place of forgiveness. Go back to such an event and become the other person. Go back to that event and, if you can, become the other person, with all that you know about him or her, and see if you have a different point of view. As we said, your ego will not like this exercise, so be prepared for it to become quite vicious in its attacks. Was this other person under stress, or had he been abused in his own past, contaminating his view of the world and causing him to create repetition of the pain from which he suffered? Was she ignorant and uneducated, perhaps without any true idea of the pain she caused?

There are many questions to be asked of a situation that causes ongoing suffering in your own mind, but the biggest is this: Have *you* ever done anything like that in the past? Have *you* ever been cruel? Have *you* ever hurt anyone? Have *you* ever exhibited those very characteristics in some way in a past relationship? We think that if you are brutally honest with yourself, you will find that you too have been less than perfect. You too have caused some harm somewhere along the way, and do you not deserve a second chance? Do you not deserve to be forgiven for your own ignorance or misjudgment? We think you deserve forgiveness. We think your cohort who is caught in this cycle of suffering and unforgiveness also deserves to be forgiven, for the sake of your own suffering mind.

You see, the mind of Source that you wish to be connected to vibrates at the level of love, and as long as you are in a state of judgment or unforgiveness, you cannot get there yourself. You are bound to the prisoner you keep as surely as if you were in a cell together in prison. And to gain your freedom, to walk outside in the Sun and beauty of nature, you must let your prisoner go and leave the darkness to gain the freedom and love you so desire.

We know this is difficult, so start with the smallest judgments first (the hatred of rain or cold, for example) and then move up to those things that are harder (the person who is rude or the line that is too slow). There are many places in your day that will give you the opportunity for forgiveness, and should you encounter the most difficult of events, you will have been practicing all along, and you will know what to do. You will be able to have an internal dialogue with yourself and tell the true story — the story that if you hate, you will suffer. If you hate, your body will reflect that vibration in the form of sickness and lethargy, and if you judge, you too will feel the pain of separation from Source. And there is no argument in the world that is worth that pain.

Dig Yourselves Out of Judgment

It is the separation from the vibration of love that makes you feel lonely, that makes you seek out unhealthy activities that hurt your body. It is the separation from the love of Source that makes you feel sad and wish you were not alive. So understand, dear ones, that the act of forgiveness is indeed the most profound act of self-love you can perform, and it is indeed at the root of all the healing.

You see, all comes from peace and love. All you say you desire is of that vibration, so you must raise yourself up out of the mire and mud of judgment and hatred and into the arms of divine love that have all that you wish, that can direct you to all that will make you content, and that will help you find your way out of the ego's convoluted lies into the simple truth of love and divine communion.

We know these words are somewhat romantic for the Western mind and all its practicalities and efficiencies, but we wish to inspire you to beauty, to gentleness, and to love. This is what is missing in your world and your interpretations of life, and we are here to tell you of that which you have lost sight. That is what your heart yearns for, a kind and beautiful existence that is loving and sweet in its expression. These words will inspire you to change. They will inspire you to look at things in a different way, and they will inspire you to raise your eyes, your hearts, and your vibrations to a new level where kindness is paramount and desire is gentle and fulfilling.

The feelings you have had all your life of the disrespect of the female body and the family structure built on judgment are feelings many are in agreement with. The disempowering judgments of others hurt your young ones and set them on a path, often of self-destruction, that garners even more judgment. In fact, it is love that will heal the issue.

The answer is always love, no matter the problem, and as we go through this experience, the love you express will become clearer and clearer to all you encounter. It will always fill up you and those to whom you give it. It is the answer, always. We see the energy of love as pink and golden radiance beaming out from the heart center, and the energy is indeed a universal energy that all beings feel. The feeling is one of openness and joy, and as soon as this feeling is pinched off, you feel a loss and sadness that you often attribute to the other person. But in fact, it is your own energy you have pinched off because of fear of hurt or loss, and indeed you inflict the pain on yourselves in advance of the event you are actually afraid of.

Is it not ironic that the solitude of the lonely heart is more painful than the pain one feels if heartbroken? That is because the feelings of a love lost are alive and love-focused, even if they are difficult. The pain of loneliness is a dead energy, bereft of the life-giving force of God energy. It is the cold and empty room that has never been lived in, not like the messy room after a party — messy, yes, but full of evidence of life and the exchanges of love and passion that have taken place there. Yes, we like this analogy too. Both are empty rooms, but they are so different they cannot be compared.

So if you are afraid of love, know that even if you end up as an empty room, you will know there was a party in you, and that is a good thing. The mess can be cleaned up, and if there is no regret for the party, the cleanup does not take too long at all. A few weeks of tears and sadness will heal a heart abandoned by a lover, but the emptiness of the closed heart is indeed tougher to heal.

You, dear one, closed your heart, and although you were badly hurt, it would have taken less time to heal if you had understood your part in your pain. The closed heart leads to a lack of communication, and the problems of relationships go deeper and last longer when no one is speaking.

So speak out when you are sad, lonely, or hurt to those you are in relationships with. They are not aware of the pain they are causing most of the time, and if they are indifferent to your need, then perhaps they are not the ones you wish to share your precious existence with. We are all free to come and go with the beings around us, and we suggest that if love is shared and the other being is still not interested, you move on and find someone who is.

We are not suggesting that you be unfeeling; on the contrary, we are supposing you should all be more feeling and more expressive. Then the problems will rise to the surface to be loved into disappearance or let go and forgiven. It is the unexpressed that is poisonous, and the unexpressed that hurts. We are all on a journey of growth into more and more love, and this is why we are writing these books — to help you, dear ones on the Earth plane, counseled in false ways around the very thing that is your salvation.

Question What You Think You Know

There is a part of you that is waking up to the shortcomings of your society. You are seeing and feeling the pain of a century of disconnection from spiritual pursuits. The ego has had a heyday getting what it wants whenever it wants, and you know you are not happy. You can feel a deep and abiding sadness, a wondering about the value of all the meaningless things you do and buy and seek, only to attain them and still feel emptiness.

You must begin to question that which you have been taught, and you must be willing to investigate that which is unfamiliar. And that, dear ones, is our job — to point the way, to hold your hand, and to answer your questions whenever we can.

There is a path that leads to what you wish. It wanders through the dark woods of the mind's fears and doubts, its misteachings and its untruths, yet the path is clear and unhampered once you step onto it. The path is found through this act of forgiveness, and it is maintained through the ideas of peace, joy, and compassion. These seem like high-flying ideas, given your hard working days, busy families, and financial woes, we understand. But the changes you wish to experience, the futures you wish to have yet cannot imagine creating because of where you are now, will be created by following this path.

You see, the world is not made up only of actions, as you have been taught. It is made up of beliefs, and the most difficult one to come to a true understanding of is this idea that you are all connected, that what you do to a brother or sister, you do to yourself. These theories seem impossible given the scientific and materialistic way of looking at things, but the truth is the materialistic universe is the result — not the cause — of what you experience within. You are reacting to the outward manifestation of that which is inside you, and you will indeed create that which you believe to be true. The enemies you encounter and the problems that seem to never go away are the universe's gift to you to show you what is going on inside all of you. Scary, you say? Well, the truth is that, yes, it is very scary, and we are here to help you do something about it.

Are you now beginning to understand the root of the evil in which you find yourselves? It is your own mind, judging this and hating that, fearing the future and hanging on to the past. This is a revelation for many, although many too are recognizing this idea of creating their own reality. Do you realize the complete implications of this? No thought goes unnoticed by the universe. Every time you say, "I hate my job," the universe agrees and provides you with an experience to justify that belief. Every time you say, "I love myself," the universe will give that love to your body and your life in deep and profound agreement with your statements. Remember, these thoughts do not have to be spoken out loud, for speaking within the mind is as powerful as speaking out loud

— in some ways more so, because you do not pay as much attention to what is going on in there. You may, in fact, say something in silence a thousand times a day. What are you saying to yourself, and what, if you said it out loud, would you describe as that vibration? Think about this, and begin to see that forgiveness is the very key to your future and is the most basic practice that will transform your life. You will not regret taking these steps, and in the beginning you will be astounded at the judgmental nature of your mind.

Many of your judgments are directed to what you would consider "bad" people or situations, but they matter not. The ego tells you that it is important to hate the bad, but all that does is keep you disconnected from Source and the very power you need to be able to change anything in the world. You see, a negative mind is a powerless mind, except in that it creates negativity. So please, take this recommendation as seriously as we ask. There is no place you can go if you are unforgiving. You are stuck spiritually, and it must be here that the first steps to divine union with bliss and the powerful energies of kundalini are to be found. These energies are the most powerful connection to God force, so you must be in tune with that which you call good, that which you call love, and that which you call peace. It is all there in the open heart and the peaceful mind.

So that is your first assignment on the journey to bliss — simple but not easy. You will begin to feel better immediately as you let go of judgment, and after just a little while, you will wonder why you valued it so much when it is responsible for so much of your pain.

CHAPTER THIRTY-SEVEN

Partners and Relationships

We have covered pornography and the deep and dark existence that it offers the lost ones of the planet, but what of sexual desires, relationships, and beings who are sexually active and wish to find a partner? We have discussed the basics of compatibility; the values need to be of a similar level, and it is best if the physical and mental realms are equal. Any great differences prevent a bonding. The differences will create extra problems for the ego. All the cultural, intellectual, and physical incompatibilities become extra hurdles to the bonding we are seeking.

The very idea of a partner is not a good one for most of you. The ego is so strong that any relationship will indeed be pulled apart by the poison you are keeping inside. A loving relationship with yourself is the first step to a loving relationship with another. The lies you tell about your weakness and inability to be loved will poison any relationship you have. Hatred of the self is truly one of the saddest, mostly because you are not really aware of it. The self-medication that is going on in your culture covers this up so much. The activity you require all the time is merely hiding a sad internal truth: You don't like your own company. So why should anyone else like it? That is the question.

We ask you to turn off the TV or computer and walk alone through the woods, a field, a park, or a beach each day, and ask what it is you really want for your life experience. If it keeps up the way it's going, would that be okay? If not, perhaps you are on the wrong road with the wrong map, and this map that we are now giving you would serve you better.

We are sure many of you are still unsure of this, but it is a harmless pursuit that can only bring dividends. We suggest a trial time to see if you can feel a difference in your bodies and minds. Spirit will respond to any genuine effort in this area, and some of you may be very surprised as to what will happen, even in one month of starting to implement the preparations for the higher energies to enter your minds and bodies. The transformation, once seriously undertaken, can be swift, and you may have to hold on to your hat, so to speak.

We are not saying you should find a twin, but do make sure there are similarities rather than differences that are very great. This will seem, to some of the Western mindset, an interference in the love process, but this is not a fling of the ego we are talking about, and many of the relationships you engage in in the West are just that. You see a body you want, and that is all. Anything else is not really considered, and that is where many problems of incompatibility arise. If you wish to have children, pick a partner who also shares this dream and displays the qualities of a good parent. Too many of you get pregnant with a completely awful match and then wonder why the relationship ends in hatred and divorce. The truth is that there was no love to start with but the lust of the physical, yet many of you do nothing about these differences. You must learn.

It is fine to have spontaneous sexual experiences. It is a natural thing, especially if the body is young and the freedom exists to try these things out. Of course, there are no moral judgments here, yet we must consider the spirit and the energy that is used in these interactions. They should be sober, and this will end a lot of the mistakes that are made in your sexual games and adventures. Many of you are too repressed or scared to make love sober, and that is a problem you need to address.

Back to compatibility. The minds should meet, and there should be a kind and intelligent exchange of ideas, and then some compatibility may be seen. So many are hidden behind the shield of the social face, and this needs to be seen through. This is a tricky subject, as many Western minds are deeply entrenched in the social conditioning and have no true connection to themselves. We are advocating a deep and reverential exploration of the self and others, and each of you will come to and through this process from where you are. We are just requesting that there be some growing awareness employed.

If a partner cannot yet be found, see this as a blessing and continue on the path of awakening and focused study of these principles with friends and alone. All is good, and the focus will indeed attract the partner you wish. But as our dear one, Tina, experienced, for some with deep issues and wounds, fears and resentments, this can take some time to heal, and this is as it should be. The ego can only be deconstructed piece by piece, and a rushed attitude will cause more harm than good.

This is where you are left to your own choices, and some will not work, but you must see these events not as failures, but as lessons in school. Each year brings a new depth and a new lesson, but if you are practicing the areas about which we have spoken, then you will gain clarity and love each day and all will resolve itself. It is a wonderful thing to find a partner with this kind of focus, and we can tell you that the wait and the work is valuable and a joy in the end. Marriages of the ego are hell and last for years, so do not dismiss this cautious path. You will suffer less on our path, and the connections you will make will not tear apart the heart as the ego connections do.

That is our warning once again: How is it going doing it the ego's way? Just look around at the dysfunctional and sad relationships you see. Even many of those that are long in duration are empty of joy and freedom. So take a moment, and trust in this advice to go slowly and to check out the truth of the one you are attracted to. If there are warning signs, take them seriously, and do not drown your awareness with drugs or alcohol. Your intuition will work much better sober, and we will be able to whisper in your ear if there are problems in the future. This will seem impossible, but we have been whispering to our dear one for years. At times she listened, and at other times not, but it all worked out. If you listen to us, it will work out for you too on this path to the divine mysteries of bliss and love.

Mutual Consent

We are now going to talk about the mutual consent required for the partners on this journey. There needs to be a conscious decision on the part of each person who has decided to follow the bliss path. This is not something you can fall into; it requires commitment to health and clarity that is not for the faint of heart. Yet many are so dissatisfied with the status quo that the possibility of bliss in their lives may at least give them some hope for the future. There will indeed be couples who split as one decides he or she wants this path and the other is unwilling to comply with the sometimes difficult requirements. Yet if partners who are reluctant would consider the possibility of heaven on earth, they might be willing to give up some of the vices they have become attached to.

Our dear one, Tina, took several years and hit several bumps in the road on the way to the clarity she now experiences, and she will share that journey with you at some point. It is a necessary one, and it is not a straight line through steady progress. There are side trips that seem to waste time yet add clarity to the path. There are failed relationships that also help clarify what is needed because they were not what was wanted. What must be realized is that this path transforms on such a profound level that it must be considered a life's work, not just a method of dating.

This path can be pursued by singletons as well as the partnered. Indeed, the singles have some advantage, as they have no habits set and no resentments to clear. So those of you who have felt left out because you are currently single, rejoice! There is much you can do to prepare the soil for the planting of the new crop, and you may fertilize the soil and change its texture easily for the coming lover. Those of you in existing relationships may have many weeds to pull before you can even get to the soil underneath. This is done through conscious forgiveness. You must willingly let go of the past and all previous fights for the love to flow. The ego does not like this, but truthfully, the ego does not like any of this, so we will ignore it. It feels threatened and hates all we suggest — unless it feels it will gain some power over the sexual energies to exert its will.

This is a matter of contemplation for each of you. This is a path of true love for the self, others, and God, and it is not about a search for power, but a search for the path to love as a service to the divine and the healing of all. This love that we are speaking of is deeply spiritual, although it indeed uses the body as a means of communication. But that is the end result. We are still in the beginning stages of meeting and searching for a partner.

This is a subject of great interest for all, and there are no simple yes-or-no answers, as you like in the West. The journey is an internal one, and initially a solitary one. Are you happy with what you have? If not, that is the beginning of the quest, and you will each know the answers to these questions by your internal guidance.

There will initially be visualizations of the partner you wish — either transformation of a present partner or manifestation of a future one. This visualization is important, as it is a magnet for the image and kind of partner you want, so be sincere in this visualization. It is fine to ask for a physical trait, but be honest and take a look at yourself, and admit that a partner of similar compatibility is in the cards. The movie-star bodies are indeed out there, but do you have one? Do you want one? Are you able to do the physical work? These are all realistic questions to ask. And we are not being mean here, but you are all human, and the fallibility of physical attraction is at play. This is a fine thing. There is nothing wrong with seeking a partner to whom you are attracted, but this is the beginning of the path.

You are on the way to being the complement to your destiny, and that is where you must first look, to the improvement of your own spiritual and physical state, which can indeed be a project to undertake. Some of you will say it is too much. But what of keeping on the path you are on? Is that too much or not enough? These are the hard questions that are to be asked in the beginning.

As for our dear Tina, she said with absolute commitment, "I'm not interested in unconscious sex on the couch holding the remote," the quick and dull love that for many is the reality. When you come to this place, the sexual energies of the universe resound with joy, for there are forces aware of the reaches of which humans are capable, and it is in this statement: "I will not do this anymore!" that the energies are aroused and the river of bliss begins to flow to you.

There are those of you who are now putting this book down, knowing you are not yet ready for this. The fears arise, as do attachments to habits, food, and drugs. And that is fine, dear ones — there is no judgment. We are not in time, and there is no suffering here. But you are in a different place where your bodies break down and get sick, marriages dissolve, and fear torments. This is the world that is so tiring for you all, and the energy you will reap by entertaining these ideas will fill you with the life that you need to reach for the heights you cannot imagine. We are the patient ones, and we wait for the true opening that will eventually come for all of you. For some, that will not be this week or even in this lifetime. It may be a long way off, but to those of you who leave us here, we wish you well and will see you in the future.

To those of you who are still with us: We are indeed honored, and the path will begin to unfold with your dedication and desire for more — more love, more health, more energy — and it is worth the trip. We are holding your dear hand on this trip and are called every time you ask for our help. Do not doubt we are there. We are sometimes in unexpected forms, sounds, and voices. So be open, and keep practicing what you have so far begun.

Calling in Your Lover

Each of you has an idea of what you want in a lover — age, height, weight, and even astrological sign — and we will, here and now, ask you to let all of that go when you are first calling for a partner. We know you do not want to, and you are afraid that unless you set all these parameters firmly in your mind, you will have to go out with someone, or make love to someone, you do not find attractive. But this is not the case at all, dear ones. These restrictions are just that — restrictions. They narrow your focus too much, and they are a result of your conditioning through the movies and television you watch.

We want you to be open to all kinds of connections with all kinds of people as you enter this new realm of seeking a partner for your sexual healing and growth. This path is not a straight one, and the way to the lover who is perfect for you may not be what you imagine at all. You may develop friendships that will allow you to work out some of the more difficult issues that are keeping you from your beloved, and these relationships may not be sexual at all.

Spirit works in ways you are unaware of. For example, if you hate your father and have bad relationships because of it, you may strike up a friendship with someone who has some traits similar to your father's. These traits may be mixed in with other qualities that you admire and enjoy, and yet there are these little spikes in there with all the good stuff. What Spirit is doing is giving you the chance to heal some of the father issues you have before you get into a sexual relationship. This may send you into the realms of forgiveness, which raises your vibration and allows love to come your way. This is merely an example, but we wish you to know that when you start asking for sexual healing, and the return of its energy and vibrancy, a lover will not immediately spring into your lap, so to speak — unless, of course, you are ready for it.

You think in very linear ways in your world experience, and as you may have noticed, life is never a clean, straight line to what you want. There are many things that must happen for some of you to get back in tune with love, and you must take the steps put directly in front of you to achieve these ends. We ask you to begin to say yes to the events and opportunities that come your way. Say yes to the difficult jobs you have to attend to, that you may have been putting off. And say yes when you are asked to go for coffee with a friend, when perhaps you would normally say no.

The universe is always offering you opportunities for growth and healing, but many of you keep refusing these gifts because you see them in the wrong light. We will give another example here to help you understand that many things can heal, and not just the obvious. Let us say that you have a very messy house, and that you hate to clean things up and organize. You want to, but you just cannot get yourself to do it. You are, in fact, blocking sexual energy by doing this, even though you do not realize it. Sexual energy is power, and sexual energy is joy for life. As you become blocked in these areas, there will be physical mani-festations that show you this. The messy house can be an example. We suggest that such messes are attended to as soon as possible. By doing so, you will shift something in the area of self-care. You will begin to feel more loved by your own behavior, and something will shift in other areas of your life. Nonsense, you say? Well, what is caring for your envi-ronment other than a symbol of love and appreciation of self? And how can you receive love from another if you cannot even care for yourself?

The same applies with your food intake. Are you attacking your body by eating poorly and unconsciously? Are you abusing yourself and wondering why those lovers you have had, or do have, do not treat you the way you would like to be treated? Look at your own behavior toward yourself, and look at what you are saying to yourself in the privacy of your own mind. Do you love where you are? Do you care for yourself by following your dreams, even in small ways?

You do not have to change your entire life, but start to follow the small desires you feel every day. Do you feel like going for a walk but stop yourself because you have children? Tell the kids you are going and that they are free to join you. Or get a sitter for an hour so that you can feel some freedom. Many of you spend a lot of money keeping yourselves fed and medicated so that you do not feel these things. Perhaps you would be well advised to spend that money pursuing that which you desire.

Do you spend a lot of money each year getting away from the life you find overwhelming and difficult? Perhaps that money would be better spent on re-educating yourself so that you could follow your passion, or on setting up a studio so you can do the art you have always dreamed of. Many of you argue that this is impossible, and we say that yes, while you believe it is impossible, it will be. But when you get sick of feeling sick, sick of being alone, and sick of your own story, this is the advice we give for you to follow to reignite your passions and resume the life that is yours for the taking.

Many of you act as if you are prisoners, but there is no guard — only you and the lies and conditioning you have fallen for. So that will help call in your beloved. Follow the signs of the synchronous events and the inspired ideas you have, but do follow our prescriptions here, and begin to cut back on those things we have told you lower your vibration.

Love is the highest vibration there is, and if you are too far away it cannot find you. You are blocking it with negative thoughts and actions. Call out to your lover who resides somewhere in the future and tell that person you are getting ready. You know you want to be happier, healthier, and more vibrant, so begin now. Act as if your lover is coming soon, and feel the anticipation. Feel those areas that you know will lower of your enjoyment of a physical relationship and begin to attend to them now, before your lover arrives.

Every change you make that takes you toward love will bring you a different kind of lover. You do not have to go through an endless stream, however; you can choose to wait until you are feeling pretty darned good, and then start dating. But, as we have said, begin to participate in that which the world is bringing you, and deal with the old habits you do not enjoy living with. Vow to change them bit by bit until they are at least moving in the direction you want them to be.

All of your life is your creation, as we have said many times and will continue to repeat, and if you do not like the manifestations you are experiencing in certain areas, you must change the behavior you are exhibiting. But more importantly, you must change the belief under the behavior. By pushing yourself to do that which is uncomfortable, you will cause the beliefs to rise to the surface. It is as if you are a drinker and say that you do not have a problem. Well, of course, as long as you get your drinks you are fine; but stop, and you will soon see what is driving your behavior. All other addictions are the same. Are you watching television for many hours a day? Stop for a week and you will feel why you are doing it. Perhaps you are lonely or bored — these are the underlying problems that all addictions hide.

For some, the issues being hidden are difficult ones, such as child abuse or violence. But this you must understand, dear ones: If you do not deal with it now, you will have to deal with it later, and the symptoms and the sadness will only get worse. That is why you are born into this third-dimensional world — to heal yourselves of all the misperceptions you have. And if you don't go willingly, you will be forced, not out of a punishing God's reaction, but from a loving universe that wants you to be loving too, open and full of life. So start today, knowing that what is difficult but needs to be done has a treasure hiding beneath it that will add richness and beauty to your lives — and perhaps even a delicious lover at some point down the line.

How can we convince you to do this? All we can do is to tell you the truth and hope the pain of not having what you wish has risen to such a level that you are willing to change. For many of you, this is not the case; you are not taking our warnings seriously. Dear ones, our words are not idle. The energy of sexual excitement, passion, and creativity is all bound together with health, and the bodies in which you find yourselves must vibrate at the level of love to thrive and reach their full potential.

Many of you have no idea just how good you can feel. Oh, you may have glimpsed it once or twice in your life, perhaps when you were in love or on a particular high, but we are here to tell you that you can feel that kind of energy far more frequently and with far more regularity than you have in the past. Remember those days when you were young and felt like you could do anything, those first days of being in love, when the entire world shifted into a different perspective? These are the potentials at your disposal should you take the path to love that we suggest. It is hard work to battle the ego at first, but it gets easier and easier as you become accustomed to nonjudgment, to extending yourself rather than protecting yourself in a defensive stance.

So that is what we want you to do — call your lover in. As you walk along the street, imagine your heart open, reaching out to all you meet. Imagine, in every conversation, sending love to the person you are talking with, especially if you don't like him or her. This is how you can invite love in; you give it. You have heard this before, we know — "be the change you wish to see in the world." And we tell you this works. This is the path to the love you seek not only from another, but from yourself.

As you love others, you love yourself, because this is all your own creation. Every relationship you have takes place not outside of yourself, in this objective world you believe in, but in your own mind, in your own thoughts, and in your own actions. Everything you do, everything you participate in, is your own mind extending itself to experience that which it contains. So yes, to experience love, you must extend love. It is just the way it works, and there are no "opt out" clauses that let you decide to follow other rules. There are no other rules; this is it.

So you have your prescription for love, but what do you do when you get it? How do you keep it, enjoy it, and prevent the deterioration so many relationships experience? We have talked a little about the ego and how it enters when you become careless, but we will delve into the intimate relationship a little more here so that once you get to this stage of finding your beloved, you will be able to feed and nurture the relationship rather than letting it go the way of so many others that started with such high hopes.

Protecting the Rose

This title is intriguing, is it not? We have chosen this title to create an elaborate analogy, as this makes sense at this given time. Imagine you are building a garden and that you wish to purchase a rose bush for that garden. The process is similar to finding a lover. You question this, but let us continue so that you may understand.

When you build a garden, you have some plans, do you not? Maybe it will be an old English garden or a Japanese Zen garden, and you would not pick the same plants for each one. That would seem foolish indeed. Your lives are like gardens, are they not? Some of you are ambitious and wish to reach the heights of success in the financial world, and some of you are hippies who wish to relax and commune with nature. As you would pick a flower or plant for a specific garden you wish to create, so you will pick a partner for the life you wish to engage in.

This is the first place many of you fall down and blame others for a decision that was poorly made — but that was yours. Many of you pick a partner way before you even have an idea of what kind of life you would like, and you make it permanent through marriage or having children. We advocate carefully getting to know yourself first, deciding on what you would like to experience, and then finding a permanent partner. Much heartbreak would be avoided if you only had some inkling of who you are first, but many do not. If you want the love of your life to show up, please do take the time — if you have not already taken it — to find out who you are, what you value, and how you like to live. And stay clear of sexual or long-term relationships with those who do not fit that plan.

Many of you completely ignore that which you want until it is too late, until you have someone lying on your couch and living in your house who does not fit the bill at all, so to speak, and yet you claim you love. Can you really say you care for someone when you ask them to change to fit your bill? Can you really say there was nothing you could do about the divorce when it was your original choice that was incorrect and not fully thought-out?

We will return to our garden analogy, and agree that you will buy a rose for your English garden. Now you must pick which kind you like, so we suggest you pick one you think is beautiful and that you enjoy greatly. "So simple," you say, "even an idiot can sort this problem out." But is that so? If you pick a rose you do not enjoy, that you do not feel is beautiful, then you will not pay attention to it. You will not stop by and check to see how it is doing; it will be left alone to fend for itself in the garden and will not do so well. But what if you buy the rose you think is beautiful? You will stop by it often to see how it is doing. You will appreciate the buds as they unfurl in the spring, and you will carefully harvest its flowers, being glad for its beauty all the while.

As lovers, you must pick a person you find attractive in so many ways — not just physically, but with all traits. Do you enjoy his way of living, her way of speaking, his kindness, and her forms of speech? You do not? Well, then we suggest keeping up your search until you find the right rose. There is nothing more frustrating than going to all that effort only to find that you do not care for this particular plant, that it does not add to the garden but makes you regret buying it.

Let's say you have decided on the plant and blooms that you wish, so you bring them, eager to plant it and make it your own. Do you find a deep and rich place to plant it, or do you just stick it anywhere, knowing that it will not thrive? No, you dig a deep hole and fill it with water and fertilizer, knowing that for many years this plant must get its nutrients from this one location. You take the time to think about the sunlight it will receive, the quality of the soil, and the winds and rains and where and when they fall. This is the sort of preparation you will do for your beloved. You will read and learn about love, as this is the fertilizer for the relationship. You will make sure you are healed of what you can heal yourself of before you even start living together, for you know that things will arise as the journey continues, but you wish to give this relationship the best start you can. You decide where and how to live for the best results, for you both have to live together for such a long time. This is important. You do not wish to make a home where you are not both well suited to the environment, for you both must thrive and be happy there.

The water is the nurturing you give this new and delicate relationship. You pay attention to the plant at its beginnings, and it will get stronger as it ages. It is true. Its roots will penetrate the soft soil, and it will make its home, at times so deeply that to uproot it would be impossible.

And so the plant is planted. You are living together in this relationship, and now the weather of life comes at you. There are storms that will create some havoc, but if you have protected the plant by setting it in the right location and caring for it from the beginning, it will be able to weather the storms that come.

And what about the winter? This is the time of crisis, the place of fears and deaths in the family, a time when you must protect the rose from the harshest of weather. It may not be beautiful at this time, and you may not get any blooms from it. In fact, it could seem to be dead for a while, but you know, because of all the efforts you have put in in the past, that despite the covering of snow, it lives and will bloom again in the spring. Some of you do not care for your relationships in these dark times. You feel that all is lost, but that is because you are not stable and do not cherish and nurture, all the while knowing that what you sow, you reap, and that loving the rose guarantees its strength in the worst of times.

When spring arrives and the protection is removed, you see the new green buds coming in. You see that the rose is larger and stronger, blooming steadily for you, even though there are ups and downs in the year.

Do you get the picture? Begin to see your choice of lover and the relationship you choose in this way, and you will begin to pay attention where you should. Many of you buy the rose and neglect it, wondering why there are infestations and areas of death. You must continue to feed and nurture and care for this most precious object that can bring so much pleasure and so much beauty.

Feelings of Fear and Loneliness

There are things and ideas that make you feel that the partner you have chosen is the wrong one and that a trade needs to be made. This generally happens a few months, or perhaps a year or two, into the relationship. Some of you will leave at this point, and some of you, if you have married — and, indeed, if you have become pregnant — will be stuck, and the long and slow descent into the warfare of the ego will begin in earnest. This is the path that a lot of relationships take without the knowledge of the ego mind and the loving mind that we have spoken about. As soon as you judge, you have lost the power that love offers you and stepped into the dark and dangerous realm of the ego.

Do you not wonder why, when one issue seems to arise, suddenly everything seems to tumble in on your mind? All the things that are wrong with your life and your lover crash over you like a tidal wave of negativity, and it all seems so powerful and overwhelming. Have you not noticed that when you are in love the world seems a different place? You can tolerate things that before were difficult; even the annoying habits of your coworkers fade into the distance as you hold your beloved in your mind's eye and in your heart all day.

This is your two minds at work. The mind set on love and the heart immersed in this energy is powerful and sees only the good, and it is no coincidence that when the mind turns from love, relationships begin to crumble. As you separate from love through judgment, the ego mind attacks in full force and drags up all of the negativity, all of the hateful thoughts that have ever gone through your mind, and it uses them to justify the hatred of other person, the hatred of yourself, and the hatred of your life.

The ego wants you to be alone and sad. This sounds evil in some ways, does it not? What is this ego that seems to take such delight in the wrongs of others and the tears and fears that torment you so? It is indeed a different creature, as we have alluded to. The physical body was infused with higher intelligence and awareness long after the mammalian program was set in the human body, and it is these two programs that are running at odds with each other.

If you look at a pride of lions, they are only concerned with survival. They are concerned with the pride, yes, but only in the sense that it facilitates their survival. They will reproduce, but if the lead lion is threatened in any way, he will not hesitate to eat the young. Sound familiar? A family is a strong tribe, but only if it serves. These are the aspects of the ego we are talking about.

Is there not the aspect of your own wondering? "How come I can want to do something that will be good for me, yet I seem powerless to do it?" These two programs are running in opposition to one another, and what a revelation this is to know that the confusion you feel, the lack of consistency, it, at times, the frustration of bad habits are not some detrimental flaw in your personality, but programs running against each other, each asking a different behavior for different reasons. Once you understand this confusion and this inability to move forward because of fears or conflicted thoughts, your ability to discipline yourself improves greatly. You are able to have a dialogue with your ego self and thank it for its input, but refuse to act on the impulses that are of a lower vibration, knowing that they will not bring you what you want and need to transform your life from one of survival to one of creativity and love.

These are the ideas that have been brought forward in esoteric texts in previous centuries. The idea that the kingdom of heaven is within refers exactly to this. The ego seeks material objects outside of itself, and the spirit knows that the paths to heaven are concepts and ideas that manifest peace and harmony, which then allow the flow of love and abundance to manifest in the outside world as those experiences and relationships you so desire. This is the secret that has been guarded and misinterpreted.

The ideas of the religions so many of you follow were originally those of individuals who tapped into this knowledge — some by accident, some through following a path of intense discipline and knowledge.

However they came across these truths, the message was taken and interpreted by the ego minds of those in power. The material was seen as either a threat or a device to wield power over others and to attain wealth, prestige, and influence themselves. Do you not wonder at the wealth and secrecy around some church organizations? These are not spiritual manifestations. The harsh and unforgiving practices that some religious organizations promote are clearly not the work of love and, therefore, not the work of God or Source.

You Are Not Bodies

You are not bodies, and you are definitely not defined by your genitals, so all are free to express themselves as they choose. There are no judgments here about same-sex relationships. The body is, as we have said, like a model and make of car. It is not important, but for some the Ford is all they will drive. So the same applies to bodies. Some are greatly attached to the make of the car they drive, and there is nothing you can do to change their minds. This is fine. Just tell them to stick to their own choice if they give you grief. We are telling all to follow their natural desires in this arena, as in all areas of self-expression. So many of you are so conditioned or fearful in this area of sexuality that to say you are free is really not true. You are often responding to stimuli in a preprogrammed way, as we have said. Even taking alcohol away and taking a little time will be a new experience for many.

Then we ask the most difficult thing for humans: Stay in the present, and enjoy the experiences that arise with your lover as they come. Move as you feel; breathe deeply and in circles, up the back on the outbreath, down the front on the inbreath. As you have seen, this is a helpful breath pattern to release the sexual energy up the body to the head and elevate it from the lower chakras to the higher chakras.

We are following ancient practices here, not making up new ones. These are the ancient secrets that were lost and sometimes intentionally destroyed so that the populace did not become empowered. Souls who practice this approach to sexuality will indeed empower themselves in a way that will stop them from being sheep and will bring deep peace. There is no aggression in this practice, no following of lust as such. The passions aroused are indeed holy in nature and will lead you down your own path to healing and love.

There are many for whom this will be a scary adventure, and we ask you who feel nervousness at reading this to be gentle with your progress. Our dear one, Tina, has traveled these paths and over time has become willing to go where there is a little nervousness, as there is also curiosity. This is not the fear that you should back away from. This is one of those fears that needs to be approached gently and with compassion for your past experiences. But know that the future, if you are willing to tread these pathways, will open up energies in your body that are indeed needed for a passionate life. It will bring peace and joy that remaining in fear and constriction will not provide. The heart wishes to heal and be open, to embrace the world with the energy of love. What we are telling you here is the way, the truth, and — yes — the life you wish to live.

CHAPTER THIRTY-EIGHT

Preparing for the Future

What is going to happen in the future? Where is all this leading, and what will it look like? We are with you again to carry on our investigations into this fascinating subject, the events that are on the horizon in terms of your spiritual evolution and the increase in the energies permeating Earth and its inhabitants. You see, the vibrational frequency of certain areas of Earth is increasing, and this can be seen in the increased interest in spiritual matters and the abundance and peace within those areas. The idea of vibration is created by the mindset — the beliefs, if you will — of those inhabiting a certain area. And those areas that attract those beings continue to elevate their vibrations as the individuals living there continue to elevate their own vibrations. This is why it seems there is an increasing disparity in the world. The good is very good and the bad is getting worse. This is because, as you experience your energy rising, tolerating lower vibrations becomes more difficult, so you must raise you vibrations even more to experience peace and feel calm.

What is happening in your world is the darkening of the dark and the lightening of the light. Of course, those interested in the lower energies would have put this book down long ago and gone to the bar for casual sex. We are joking here, but really, that is the case. If you have read this far into this treatise, you are of the light, and you wish to continue and accelerate that growth. You are no longer satisfied with the status quo, and tolerating the ordinary is becoming more and more difficult for you. You are turning off shows that disturb you, you are changing your diet, and you are beginning to watch what you say and who you hang out with.

These are all the indicators that you are on a fast track to spiritual growth, and if you recognize yourself in that description, then we strongly suggest you start to follow our suggestions, even if you don't currently have a partner. We have said this before, but not having a partner is a great benefit at the beginning of this journey. Alone, you have the ability to prepare yourself more fully for the advent of a tantric partner, and you can raise your vibration considerably. Feeling that you are not able to participate in the kundalini experience alone is erroneous. Kundalini does not need a partner to rise, and if you look at the historical records of this process, being alone in the initial stages can be of benefit due to the radical changes that occur in your body, mind, and emotions. Those in relationships have to deal with the differences in each other's experience. They must come to a consensus, and they must cooperate in their growth. Certainly, these are all possibilities, but it is a bit more of a challenge in the beginning.

We mention this here so that you who are single are not discouraged in any way. Know that as you raise your vibration through the practices we suggest for the cleansing of body, mind, and emotion, you will free yourself of relationships with those of a lesser vibration. We are not judgmental here — merely stating the fact that some vibrate at higher levels than others, and this is at it should be.

You are all exactly where you need to be, and it is your internal guidance system that will lead you to the right path and the right practices for your place on your journey. So do not judge others; you will only slow your own progress. Look around the world, not with a cold heart, but with the understanding that all are where they are meant to be for their greatest growth.

Your Job Is to Raise Your Vibration

It seems like a difficult time around the planet for many who lack food or safe places to sleep, and we know those of you in more fortunate circumstances can feel guilty, but we tell those of you facing this dilemma that lowering your own vibration through fears or guilt will not serve those who need your help. Only reaching your full potential and contributing at the highest vibration you can will do that. You are all connected in spirit, and lowering your vibration only lowers the overall vibration of the world. The kindest thing you can do for those who are starving is to stay as high as you can on the vibration scale and achieve your own peace and prosperity, contributing financially when you are able — if you are able and so desire. But watching the disasters and wars and feeling bad for your own fortunate circumstances defeats the object of this existence, which is for your oversoul to experience many lives over many different dimensions and times.

Trust us — you have had, and may have, difficult lives in the past and the future, and this is why you are experiencing abundance now. The oversoul wishes to experience all, to change, grow, and understand all things, and this is why there are such disparate lives and experiences on your planet. All are here of their own free will. All have come to the place they are for a reason, and trust us, it is far beyond your ability to "get" it all and understand the reasons and motivations for everything that happens. That is not your job. Your job is to be happy and raise your vibration as high as you can while you are here with the implicit knowledge that what you do for your own vibration, you do for all who exist here with you.

This is not what you have been taught, but as you are beginning to learn from us, this is not unusual — that you do not have the correct information, that you have been laboring under the mistaken belief that you are completely separate and that what you think is your own business. Well, it is your own business, it's true, but it will affect the world, and guilt is a low-vibration device of the ego mind that wastes your time and makes you powerless in the scheme of things.

There are those of you who think pursuing the tantric lifestyle is self-indulgent in some way, but that is far from the truth. Those of you who are able to achieve the results we speak about will add to the positive vibrations of the world to such a degree, that if only you could see on a scale that which we are speaking about ...

Be Selfish

The volunteer who is in deep pain and sadness all the time but helps out on the streets, feeding the homeless, actually contributes less energetically than the individual in a tantric relationship who is in a state of bliss a lot of the time. This goes against your grain, we know, and we can feel it. But this is the truth. As you elevate yourselves, all you meet are elevated, and many you do not know or see are also recipients of your elevated vibration.

We are not suggesting that you do not help others, but that you do it from a place of joy — not a place of sadness and guilt for your own beneficent life. Going to help others because it makes you happy is very different from helping others out of a deep sense of grief over their plight. Remember this as you focus on this very personal path that we recommend for those who are interested.

Who knows where this path will lead? The writing of inspirational material, the painting of masterpieces, or just the creation of an extremely loving being — these are all possibilities, and many more exist in the future we are supposing may occur should you choose this exceptional pathway to the divine.

Diary of Desires

The passions we speak about are the passions of the soul — the desire to create, the desire to grow, and the desire to learn. You are often driven by the desire to shop, the desire to eat, and the desire to hate. Can you see the difference here? The first set of desires come from deep within the heart; they are not on the surface of the mind, but embedded deep within the soul. The other desires are very superficial and offer no permanent transformation, and this is where you must use your discernment, which in the beginning can be a little tricky. So we have some advice for this tough section of the plan.

Until you have been studying and practicing for a while, we suggest you keep a diary of the desires you have. The list may be long or short — it matters not. We suggest you write down all the things you want — from a chocolate bar to a car, a holiday, a partner, or a new point of view. Write down all your desires, and then arrange them into two columns: things that are eternal and things that are transient or temporary. It will be fairly easy to do this.

For example, a new car is temporary, for it will not be new for long and will deteriorate over a relatively short time. Perhaps education arises as a choice, and clearly, this is not a temporary thing, for it will always be with you, as will health and love. Even if your lover leaves, or you do, that relationship is always with you. As those of you who have a long-lost love will agree — or even those who have a long-lost hate will understand — that relationship is always there and will represent the concept of permanence we are speaking about. So desires are of two kinds, and as you investigate this topic a little they will clarify themselves even more, and you will truly begin to see the inner guidance your higher self offers you all the time.

On any given day you will always have a preference, even in moments when you feel you cannot follow your desire. For example, if you are at a job you dislike and you wish to leave but feel you cannot, do still feel that feeling, and thank your soul for speaking so eloquently of its desire for a new and more fulfilling profession. Such feelings do not have to be acted on immediately, but please acknowledge them and the message they are conveying, and then begin to offer up some small changes so that the universe knows you have heard.

You see, when you acknowledge the feeling and do not resist it, and when you cease judging the situation you are in that you do not like, two things happen: You raise your vibration by ceasing to judge, and you offer up your focus to the achievement of the desire that is more in line with what you want. So let us give you an example.

You are at a job you dislike that does not suit you, and you wish with all your might to leave. Your heart cries out for you to leave and seek out another opportunity with more creativity, more freedom. But you have responsibilities you feel you cannot leave at the moment. We suggest that you begin to investigate new avenues of employment, perhaps getting more education so that you have more opportunity. If you combine this with the forgiveness of your current position, coming to a place of absolute peace, knowing and trusting that change will come, you can stay calm and patient, sure that the true feelings of your heart will be heard. This puts you in the vibration of love and trust, and a work or education opportunity will arise from this. If you stay angry and resentful of the job, your vibration will be in the same vein as that of poverty and sickness, boredom and fear, and that is what you will receive.

The biggest problem here is with what you have all been taught: that complaint is natural and will get you somewhere. It will not. It will get more of what you are complaining about, and this is the case for so many of you in this time and place. You are re-creating that which you do not want with your focus, and this creates frustration and disillusionment and causes sickness to arise.

Disempower Your Misconceptions of Love

Do you remember the first time you fell in love? The feelings of excitement at seeing this other person who seemed so different than the others, who spoke to you in a way that seemed to feed some part of you that no others could ... Do you remember your heart fluttering and the internal smile that arose as you saw your first love walking toward you? Do you not want to feel this again, and not for just a week, but for all time? This is the carrot we offer to you instead of the endless stream of distracting and pointless entertainment you are currently using to mask your empty lives and hearts.

So many of you are immersed in these empty rituals — the drink after work to take the edge off the pain, the hours in front of the box watching murder and disasters, and eventually the falling into bed wondering why you are either alone or why the person next to you seems so far away. Almost all you do is the antithesis of that which needs to be done to awaken the sexual awareness that will lead you to the bliss of which we speak. Communications about only the superficial will not connect you to the heart and soul of your beloved in any meaningful way, although we do agree it is better than not speaking at all. But do you realize that at the end of your dear lives, this opportunity to grow and learn and love will all depend on the heart connections you have made? On your deathbed, only the emotional love connections will matter in any way, shape, or form. None of your TV shows will matter, none of your possessions will even be remembered, and all that you will feel is the love that was there. All that you will feel is the sweet connection to those you have touched with the electric and powerful connection of love.

Now look at your life. Is it all about love? Is it all about connecting with yourself and your loved ones, or are you so immersed in the superficial events of the world and your existence that there are no heart connections at all? We do not, of course, dismiss your love of your family. Indeed, this is one of the greatest connections many of you have, as are the relationships you have with your dear pets, but we are talking also about that amazing and powerful love connection with the one who appears to be your beloved — that partner in life who has touched your soul and who so many of you wish to meet and embrace, body, mind, and soul. We want you to hear this.

The routines in which you hide are a self-imposed prison that will take its toll after several years. It will become more and more difficult to escape as you get older and older, as the connection to Source fades and loses its power. Do not despair — you can change it! But do not waste any more time than you already have. Get off the couch and go for a walk, speak to people at the coffee shop, and engage your coworkers in conversations that are positive and uplifting. "This will not bring me my love," you say? Oh yes it will! As you exude out into the world the desire for connection, as you speak kind and loving words to all you meet, and as you honor yourself and everyone you come in contact with, you raise your own vibration up toward that of love. You will begin to see changes within the first month if your intentions are firm and you begin to act as we have suggested.

Those of you in a relationship already will also see a dramatic shift as you approach your partner with these behaviors of openhearted acceptance. And many of you, as you read these pages and start to truly look at what you are doing, will be shocked that so much of your time is relegated to the realms of fear and judgment. The conversations over coffee at work are often fraught with complaints and moaning about the state of the world, and the thoughts that run through your head are ones of fear and complaint about just about everything. The judgments that arise about your partner when that person is present — or not — will show you just what we are speaking about.

It is all of this that we must address, and we know it seems overwhelming, but is your sadness not overwhelming at times? Your disillusionment — is that not overwhelming? Would you not rather be overwhelmed with joy and love and passionate lovemaking? We know you would prefer those things, but we must make you understand your part in why love's passion is blocked for you. You will begin to feel love's joy and strength as you listen to our words and take them to heart, and your relationships — first with yourself, and then with those around you — will be infused with the juices of love and the driving force it has to enliven and to please.

Listen to Your Heart

Your feelings are never wrong, and they serve you in two ways. First they tell you when you are disconnected from Source by some internal action of thought such as judgment, and they also tell you when something is not on your path and is not for you. And so discernment

290 * Making Love to God

must be taught here. The fears of the ego often arise as a change or new adventure presents itself, but underneath that fear may be a strong desire. This is a clue that yes, despite your fears, there is a passion below, waiting to be expressed and experienced.

This will arise, for example, when you meet someone to whom you are attracted and wish to connect. The ego mind will pipe up and say, "No, we will be hurt. Don't speak to him. Don't go out with him." But underlying that is the desire for connection, the desire to love. We suggest, in this instance, that you listen to the positive desire, the loving intention under the fear. The ego will grumble — or, if you have been in great difficulty before in a relationship, it will scream out of fear — but your new understanding of it will help you to override its complaints and insistence on safety at all costs. The other time you will be able to use your feelings as a barometer is when you do not want to do something — not because of fear, but because there is no underlying desire to participate.

We will use the example of sports here. Some of you love sports, and others, when watching a triathlon or race, have no desire whatsoever to participate, or even watch. Your feelings tell you exactly what you enjoy and what you don't, so do not judge. Do not judge others for their interests or passions, but more importantly, do not judge your own lack of desire. Your feelings are guiding you clearly to a path that will serve your higher purpose, so do not lower your vibration by berating yourself for being what the ego calls lazy or untalented. You each have your own path, and the boundaries of that path are clearly delineated by the end of desire. When desire for an activity is not there, that is okay — it is not yours this lifetime. So leave it in peace for another who has that passion to pursue. Listen to your own heart and follow the pathways that it leads you along.

If you do not know yourself, if you do not listen to your heart's desire, you will not create an authentic life. And when you are not leading an authentic life, you cannot reach the heart and soul of your beloved. "What?" you say. "I must get to know myself before I can get the love of my life? Is there no end to the obstacles that this course in love throws at me?" We are sad to say that this is the truth. How can you be happy with your beloved if you hate your job that takes up your every moment? How can you be connected, heart open, if you do not enjoy the simplest of activities that you pursue because they bring you joy? These are all components in the puzzle, but there are miracles hiding in the grass at the side of the road, so do not despair!

When you start on this path, the wheels of divine love begin to turn, and things will begin to happen that seemed impossible before you started on this journey. Your mind is only concerned with the logical and past experience from the ego's point of view. The greatest handicap you all face is that in your society the ego is seen as intelligence and logic, revered above the dance of the heart and soul. You are told it is weak to dream, that it is dangerous to have fantasies of happiness and joy. "Life is tough," the wise ones of your society say. "You must fight for what you want. Don't be weak."

We are not counseling weakness at all, but a strength that comes from spiritual connection. Trust us, dear ones — this is the strength you want. *This* is the power that builds universes, not the tiny power of the ego, defending what little it has from the marauders it imagines want to take it away. We are counseling you to listen to the voice of the oversoul, that wise and loving group of minds that help you on your way to full appreciation of the opportunities of your experience and life and point you in the right direction for the fulfillment of your dreams and desires.

This is the map you all have been asking for. How do you decide what to do? How do you decide whom to date? Listen to your feelings from this cleansed and clarified perception. When you are calm, clean, and sober, after you have begun this journey with us to the true understanding of the world within, your feelings will be connected to the Source of all.

Let Go of the Past to Create the New Future

We hear many of you lamenting the past — that you cannot create the present you wish because of a wound, a trauma from the past that handicaps you and leaves you less than you think you could be. Indeed, if you give power to the past, it will take it, and if you give your power to the one who hurt you, or who you believe hurt you, you will suffer from that loss of power.

You are a creator god yourself. You are the god you think you should be worshiping. You are the one who is making it all up, and if you are taking painful ingredients into your recipe, so to speak, you will make a bitter cake. If you are fearful because of a past event that seemed to hurt you, look at yourself here and now: You are alive! You have all your faculties, and you still create in every second of every day. You just use the wrong ingredients, and for many of you this is why your relationships, especially your romantic ones, are nonexistent or not very romantic at all.

Many of you have had bad experiences in love, as you would call them. But as we have alluded to before, most of these relationships were the exploits of the ego mind and not love at all. They were polluted with attachments, judgments, and fears that drove the relationship into the ground. You were not working with the correct information, so you created that which you did not want. And it is very important for you to understand that when the information is correct you will have a completely different experience.

You must begin to rein in the mind, to discipline it, especially if you wish to create a divine love relationship. You will need to understand the importance of letting the past go and forgiving all the past hurts and lovers you have had. They were all just reflections of your own mind. The truth of the matter is you cannot have a relationship with someone who is vibrating at a considerable distance from your own vibration. So we guarantee that if you were treated badly, it was because you were treating yourself badly or treating others badly. Attack breeds attack, and love breeds love. If you honestly look inside and ask yourself what you are saying to yourself, and you see that you are unloving to yourself, then that is where the work must start. And the work involves the forgiveness, active and total, of all those you think hurt you. They came to you to show you what is unconscious, and it is those relationships that have shown you what you do not want and have helped to clarify what you do want. This is how creation works.

There is a constant stream of variables coming into your experience, some of which feel good, and some of which feel bad. You make the mistake of focusing on the bad, hanging on to it with all your might to prove that you are the good guy, the one who was wronged. This is the ego mind's favorite game, and it keeps you in hell for years, blaming others for your pain, when in fact, it is you retrieving wounds day after day, telling the old stories that perpetuate this energy. And it is you who is going to have to change to bring about a different future.

The love you want is trying to come to you, we promise, but the interference of old hurts, incorrect belief systems, and nurtured wounds, shared over and over, prevents the loving energy from coming to you. You see, the universe really is made of love and wishes you to experience love all the time. It will not follow or flow where there is negativity. It can only flow into the open heart, that open mind that is at peace, because that is its vibration and vibrations must match.

So as you come to understand this, you will see that hating your old lover will only prevent you from growing, from making that new relationship you want. That hate will only give you the same experience over and over again until you decide to choose again, to choose differently, and to forgive the past and move into a new direction.

So this is what you must do: You must let go and let the love in. You must forgive the old and let in the new, and you must be willing to not be the good guy, letting the old lover be the bad. You were each the same — mistaken and doing the best you could with the information you had, and the results spoke for themselves. So forgive yourself, forgive your old lover, and move on to the new world you want to create.

The new world will be one of extreme love and peace, should you decide to follow our ideas and prescriptions. We do not throw these constraints out "willy nilly," as you say. This is the rule you must follow to gain the freedom of mind that is required to achieve the goals we are setting. Many of you think the way to physical bliss through sexual union is found on the physical plane through the physical body, but it is in fact found through the mind, because the mind is the creator of all of it.

You are obsessed with bodies and cannot believe that it is not the body that is responsible for your delightful feeling of bliss. But the mind is totally responsible, and you merely feel the result through the body and, as usual, mistake cause for effect. The body is there to do as you choose with your mind. It eats when you choose, it says what you choose, it thinks about what you choose, and it reaches for what you choose. You are all confused on this point because of the body's three-dimensional and seemingly solid nature. You think that it is more real, more solid than the mind, but it is not. The mind is the creator of all, and we repeat this because you actually stand a chance at changing your world.

The mind is in charge of all of the things you wish to manifest. It is in charge of handling the energy and passion required to make things and to make events occur. Think about this: The energy of ideas is always what forces behaviors to manifest, and it is the mind in and of itself that creates desire. The mind can create desire for anything, and what we are asking you to do is train the mind so that you can turn from hatred to love, from pain to passion, and from boredom to excitement for life — and for each other. The body is the slave, yet so many of you think you are slaves to your bodies, and this causes such confusion, but you are never taught the truth. You are taught that your instincts rule you and that your body is in charge of your life, but in all spiritual practices, the mind is deemed the decider, and this is indeed the case.

Often the body is considered cursed, and we do not agree with this, but you are cursed if you mistake the body for the leader, because then you are in the grips of the ego mind, which does indeed rule the body. The ego is a cruel and merciless dictator who will send you into the trenches with no thought for your higher mind, your heart, or your soul. It will even sacrifice the body, if necessary, which seems counterintuitive. But the ego is not sane, nor is it consistent, and this is why you are so confused most of the time.

So do heed these words, dear ones, and know that our telling you about the mind and how to train it is the way out of insanity, out of pain, and out of the confusing inconsistencies of the ego mind. The past is where the ego likes to dwell, but it will use a terrifying future to rouse you if it has to. So one of the many things necessary to develop the idea of peace, to develop the idea of faith, is to stay in the present. This is your point of power, and this is the only place where you can connect to us, to Spirit, and ask for help.

Be in the Present

When you are in the past, regretting, feeling guilty, and hating, you are removed from the very place that can help you — the present. It is here, in the here and now, that the mind does its creative work, and this is the reason for forgiveness, not the righteous and superior story many of you think it is about. It is about freeing the mind from the past into the present so that you can harness the power of love, your Source, which is only present in the present.

You are so confused on these points that we reiterate, so bear with us please. We are not treating you as imbeciles, but we must get you to truly comprehend the power of forgiveness, the power of nonjudgment, and the power of the present moment.

When you are present, the being you are interacting with can be seen. When you are in the past or the future, you cannot see such beings. You may seem to see them, but you are really seeing what they used to be, or what they might do to you at some point down the line. This is why you are all so scared to be in love. You are fearful of a future wound, so you close your hearts, convinced you are keeping yourselves safe. But all you are doing is condemning yourselves to a lonely existence, safe from all feeling.

Is this the way you want to live, alone and guaranteed never to be hurt by another? Well, you forget the part that you are hurting yourself in the present by doing that, by staying separate and alone and giving up the gift of love, which is the only thing you will remember when you pass over, when you die. Only the love will last, and only that has value.

So, dear ones, use your memories properly. Use them to remember that you want to connect. Use them to remember how good love feels and how nice it is to share, and use them to remember the good and the lovely. Remember to let go of the bad and the painful, and remember that the bad and the painful are only there to show you when you are off track. They are not there to punish or shame you but merely as a contrast for you to gain clarity. But contrast only works if you know you have to let the negatives go after you have felt them and learned from the guidance system that you have. If it feels bad, you are off track. If you feel bad, choose again, but differently. And if you feel bad, it must be fear and not love.

You wonder why we are talking about all of this esoteric forgiveness business when all you wanted was better sex. Well, this is the truth of it, dear ones: To reach the heights of bliss, your vibrations must be high and your heart must be fearless and open, and these situations will not arise in the judgmental mind or the closed heart, because these states are out of alignment with God, and bliss is in alignment with God. It is that simple.

So that is that for the past. Have we convinced you to let it go? We hope so, for your own sake. The future will be the same as the past if you don't let it go, and for many of you that would be hell indeed.

V

Using Divine
Sex Energy

CHAPTER THIRTY-NINE

Defining Divine Sex

We will now write about the energies that pass between two individuals when they are making love. This is indeed the topic that all are interested in, is it not?

When two individuals appear on each other's radar screens, so to speak, many things happen. You often think that it is purely a visual experience, but on an energetic level a great deal is happening. The body you see is but a limited aspect of the being you are. It is a small aspect of the being you are, and again, your focus on it is why you are so often in the dark on your journey here.

As two beings approach one another, the energetic realms of the etheric bodies mix and blend, and there is a spiritual recognition of souls with whom there is work that is to be done, or that may be done. Electrical and thought impulses are flying all the time, radiating out from your mind, and in this case, if you are at all interested in finding a mate, there will be an acceleration of these energetic emissions — as in a search mission looking for a compatible and attractive partner. If your spiritual body finds a partner with whom you vibrate, you are often inexorably drawn toward them. On the conscious level you do not even know why, but on the energetic level what is going on can clearly be seen.

The compatibility of energetic bodies acts somewhat like a magnet of matching shapes that fit together nicely, and as romantic as this sounds, in many instances the fire is there because you share the same lack of strength. The magnetism works not only in the areas of positive matching, but also in the areas of negative matching. One seeking violence will find another who hates him- or herself, and this is the downside of the experience. Yet those two beings need to have that experience to fulfill the pact they have made with each other on some other level.

This is a complicated area, and you will of course bump into those aspects of soul that you have agreed to meet with before birth. They will hold a powerful draw for you and will seem to fascinate you for no apparent reason, but you must get near them. There are many roles that play out as a two people are attracted to each other. The visual does come into play — we are not saying that it does not — but many other issues arise as the couple becomes closer physically and emotionally, perhaps spending time together.

Then there is an increase in the flow between the energetic bodies. Areas of matching become entangled, if you will, wrapping around each other at times. Again, this is the more low-vibration experience, and a deep feeling of need can pervade the experience. What is happening on an energetic level is that one lacking aspect sees that the other's aspect has a particular trait, and so the hole, if you will, is filled by the other's energy. This is not always a bad thing. The aspects are always in search of experience, and any interaction can hold a positive result.

Focus on Happy, Healthy Thoughts and Feelings

Humans often get into trouble in the thought patterns that are awoken as they undergo this process. The mind is the most powerful connection device on the planet; it is what creates the world you see and the experience you have. So a mind focused on the mind and body of another with an intensity that is unparalleled in the world is a force to be reckoned with. When a mind and its thoughts are unhealthy — or, we shall say, needy or low in vibration — they attach themselves to the mind and etheric body of another, and this may be a one-way street or reciprocated.

As these energetic ropes become enmeshed and tangled, the feelings of missing or needing a person are felt in the emotional body of the one doing the thinking. You can see that this is the feeling one has of desperation in the beginning stages of love, and many of these experiences are not love, but rather need you mistake for love. A great deal of difficulty arises in this type of energetic exchange and is the source of much of the distress or angst that is exhibited. The neediness calls out for something that the individual wants and actually needs to develop in the self, so it accentuates the lack and will make the fears of loss arise. That is one sort of experience.

If two souls approach one another and they have come to love themselves and feel healthy and happy with the choices they have made, then the experience is a little different on an energetic level. The auras now radiate energy out from the whole that they are, and it is more of a general radiation of love exuding from the being. Indeed, if you meet a needy being, you will feel that as a drain and gently move back. On some intuitive level, you feel the drain that will come from that association and it does not feel good. When you meet another of like radiance and that person finds you to his or her liking, the radiance is like lying in the Sun on the first day of spring. There is no taking as such, but a gentle radiance that feels very good.

We are speaking in ideal terms here. Few humans have no disruptions in their auric fields. There are usually small areas of need and lack in all auric fields, but we are giving extreme examples for you to understand the principles about which we are writing. The experience of a radiant being can occur with almost any other radiant being; the need for a particular configuration is less necessary because he or she radiates it out in a general way. It does not have specificity or neediness because there are plenty of energies to go around. This is felt by others around that person as a sense of kindness, love, or presence. The needs are felt as negatives, and the love and completion are felt as peace and attractiveness of Spirit.

A Good Sexual Exchange

So on the sexual level, all of this comes into play, and we suggest the practices we do so that the lower-level entanglements are less likely to happen. The higher your vibration, the less traumatic the experience, so this may help you understand why love can seem so painful. It was not love that you were feeling, but enmeshment of the neediness that was actually at play on the energetic level.

During a sexual encounter there are many variables that make it hard to discuss in generalities, but we will try to do so to give you an idea of what actually occurs in a good sexual exchange. The bodies come closer, and the radiance of one mingles with the radiance of the other. This feels good, and feelings of pleasure arise. There is an energetic dance that takes place as the bodies touch and the energy centers — chakras — begin to line up. The strands of light from each chakra entwine and mingle in a flowing and dynamic way. They twist around each other, making beautiful sparks and combinations of light as they merge, and if the heart centers are open, a tremendous rush of delight will be felt as these two chakras come close to one another.

In a tantric relationship where the individuals have learned to deeply relax and connect with openhearted trust and deep love, there will be a deeper joining through shared breath. The exchange of ideas and shared goals in the process, and a deep reverence for one another, pours the energy *into* rather than taking *from*. This is how the two really connect on a deep level. Each one is giving, giving, giving, and the experience of infused and shared energies becomes a very powerful event that is indeed a joy to experience.

The Sacred Bond

We suggest that you think about creating this kind of loving and giving exchange with the energies you encounter sexually. There are many of you who will be sad to read this, as there are no resemblances to your experience in these words — except perhaps the first and not-so-healthy descriptions. That is okay, dear ones. That is why we have come to teach these things. The low sexual vibration of many of you is not your fault at all, and we are not here to judge, but to help heal the problems. The shame and hurt many of you have experienced in the sexual arena have closed down areas of your energetic body, some completely, and in others there are large blocks to this loving flow of energy. So do not despair. There are remedies, and we are trying to share those with you today.

When a couple decides to have full-on sex, this should not be a "bump and grind" kind of thing. Due concern should be made for the sacred nature of the bond the individuals wish to make. When a spiritual and loving approach is taken, Spirit will be there to assist the couple in raising their vibrations as they come together for the lovemaking. They will feel the strong pull of desire to reach up, up, up to the heights of their pleasure as they dedicate themselves to spiritual mating. They will call in from the other realms the love essence of God that is so delicate yet powerful. It responds to a genuine and loving call to arms. We smile at the soft and gentle arms of the lover.

This is a process. Just as the damage was not done in five minutes, so the repairs will not be made in five minutes. What we want you to know is that every effort you make to heal your life of the unhealthy and lower vibrations will be manifested in the energetic makeup of your body and will begin to affect all of the exchanges you have — not just with lovers or between husbands and wives, but with everyone you meet. You see, it is all an energetic exchange, and as you raise your energy, the beings with whom you have an affinity will also rise, and your relationships will improve or change. Some will go as you shift, but do not assume that to be the case. Often a change in one partner will precipitate a change in the other. You all want love, and as one partner in a partnership becomes more loving and free with his or her own love, the other often responds in kind. It is like a harmonic synchronization.

These passages about sexual encounters make me a little nervous. After all, Ananda has told me this is coming my way soon, and I have had some less than stellar relationships in the past in which I lost myself and did not have the skills to create a balanced and healthy bond. I feel a little flutter of trepidation!

We are with you again, dear one, feeling your nervousness at the subject you just wrote about. We are sure there is some resistance, but you do know in your heart that it is time. The time of solitude is over, and the time of sharing and new growth is here. We will hold your dear, nervous hand through this journey, as we have been there through all the trials and tribulations of this long journey that is now coming to fruition.

We are always here for your support and love, and we ask you to trust us to bring you the perfect man to tempt you into the game of love that you have been on the sidelines of, learning and unlearning all you need. The time was not right before, but now it is. Your heart is opening up quickly, and the desire for a corporeal lover is raising its head. You can feel the desire for a body to play with rising, can you not? You're feeling a healthy and passionate desire for a spiritual love that will fulfill, challenge, and nourish you on this next phase of the road along which you are traveling.

It has been a long journey to love, has it not? But you are in an amazing place from which you can continue your growth. You are developing a trust in us that is overriding your past conditioning, and it will manifest, as we have said. You are not going to have any resistance to the man who will be your lover — and, indeed, your future husband. We do not wish to scare you, although you do get a little disturbed at the future prospect of "wifedom," as it's not your favorite place to see yourself.

There are no repeats of the past, as we have said. The real you has no need to repeat the old patterns or to make excuses for what you are. You are a free and creative being, and this will always be so, no matter if you are single or married. Your partner will be perfectly suited to you in this matter. Do not despair.

CHAPTER FORTY

The Body

The practices of tantra require you to be friends with your body, relaxed within it — able to be naked with ease and joy — with a willingness to share it with your beloved. Many of you are not in that place and must, if you wish to explore bliss in the physical, work toward changing that concept and begin to honor and respect your body by changing your thoughts about it and, consequently, the way you treat it.

All of you can improve in this area, no doubt. You know, as you are reading this, where the changes need to be made. Do you have hateful thoughts about your physicality? Do you eat badly, filling up on processed and prepackaged foods instead of eating the beautiful and nutritious fruits, vegetables, grains, and nuts that the natural environment provides for you? You all have the opportunity to change that which you do not like about your bodies. It is a joy — is it not? — to realize this and to understand that your body is not your enemy or your albatross, but a gift to experience so you can grow and learn that which is good and true.

From now on, do not curse your body. It only does that which you ask it to do, and it reflects back those thoughts and ideas you think are secret and brings them into view for you to see. Do not feel guilty that you may have been mistaken and made something you do not want. Merely see it as an error to be corrected and forgiven. Do not berate yourself for listening to untruthful information; it was not your fault, so move ahead from here, today, in this place, and begin a new beginning that will yield new results that are more in line with who you want to be and how you want to live.

The healing abilities contained within your bodies are endless, so do not believe the Western prognosis of chronic pain and unwellness. Believe in the power of the mind to heal all, to create all, and to give you all you need on this amazing journey you are on. The body thrives in peace, joy, and loving vibrations. You must understand this, that to forgive all, to accept and come to peace, is all the medicine you need. That is totally within your power to achieve and accept. You do not need to age and die a painful death the way you have been taught. You can choose a different way, a different path that is the experience of joy and bliss in the moment-by-moment experiences the loving mind manifests so very easily.

You are manifesting all the time. Many of you, when you think about the law of attraction and all that it proposes, forget that your current life is also your manifestation. It is the shining reflection of who you think you are, and it will change as you change. It will respond quite quickly too, if you change your mind's focus from that which you don't want to that which you *do* want.

As far as the body goes, focus on all that is going well. All the cells that are working, all the digestion that is going on, the growth of skin and hair and nails — are these not miracles that occur every second of every day? Be grateful for it all, and thank your body for the effort it exerts and the gifts it gives, and it will magnify that in energy and health every day.

If you suffer from pain and aches, do the same. Be determined to look for the good, and it will expand. But do please look to those areas in which you feel limited and fearful. These are the areas causing the sickness, but they too can be changed with determined focus and by asking for assistance from the nonphysical.

Love Your Body

The body is the god of the modern world, is it not? The beauty you naturally find in the form of the opposite sex has become deformed and warped into the thing that you believe will bring you to heaven. This is not true. The body is a vehicle only, and the driver must be love, not the judgment so many of you use as you run on your treadmills, starve yourselves, or stuff yourselves. The body will do your bidding as you wish. You do not need to make it a god or your enemy, but gently love it into health and flexibility to carry you through this journey you call life.

So many of you will not love because of your hatred of the body, hiding in shame the beauty that is you. For some this is almost a deadly game, as our dear one found out many years ago. She was the ultimate player of the body game, hating unto death the flesh she blamed for her suffering.

The suffering you feel is always of the mind — never anything else. So if you decide you hate your body, look at this belief with open eyes and see if there is something you can change so that your body becomes an ally, not an enemy. The sickness you see increasing, such as cancer, is hatred made physical, so if you wish for a long, healthy, sexy, and passionate life, love your body as we said — not as your salvation, but as a useful vehicle that will lead you through the experiences that are indeed your salvation. You need your body to function here, and here is where you are for good reason. Do not wish this life away, but dedicate it to the pursuit of love and passion — for yourself, for others, and for God — and you will be using it wisely.

CHAPTER FORTY-ONE

Making Love

We will start with the idea of timing. When do you start to engage the body of the partner with whom you wish to explore this deep and intimate subject? We will say that first the mind's compatibility with the beloved is of great importance. The intimacy we advocate requires not only a loving physicality but a mind meeting of extreme proportions. You will wish to pick a partner who is on a level of similar sensibilities as you are. For example, if you are a quiet and gentle vegetarian, a hunter with a strong macho side may not be the best balance for you; however, your partner should have a strong sexual attraction for you, for whatever reason. This is sometimes hard to define, but do consider this type of compatibility when choosing a partner.

We also suggest a time of mental foreplay. A few sips of wine to relax are fine, but no heavy drinking should occur. The mind is lowered and dulled by large amounts of alcohol, and your energies will not connect and flow with alcohol ruling the landscape. We are sure you can see an immediate and prominent issue arising: So many of you are lubricated into sexual union by alcohol, yet it interferes with the expressions of love we are speaking about.

First things first: If you cannot sleep with someone while sober, you should not be sleeping with him or her at all. Please use your discernment here and know that if a good, stiff drink is needed to even imagine a connection, there is no connection. You need to be able to be mostly sober — preferably totally sober — with the object of your future passions. This will freeze a lot of you up and show you just what we are talking about in regards to the restrictions from which you suffer in this world. As you can see, for many, sex without alcohol is unimaginable and scary. This shows you where to go — to the areas of fear and terror that drive you to numb the precious bodies you need for divine love to flow fully and strongly into your lives.

The mess that is made from judgment, guilt, and fear over love's expression is indeed a terrible mess. Pornography, war, and guilty lives of passionless sacrifice are what you get for that. You are meant for lives of creativity and joy.

Many of you are already stymied at our request for sober loving, yet this is the first step to intimacy and the gifts it can bring. When you have found a suitable and loving partner, then there is the timing of the first sexual encounter. Is this to be hurried? Well, we can say no, yet there is a drive to meet, is there not? That is indeed a powerful one, and we are saying it is fine to play at sex at first.

There is no need for immediate and complete gratification, but a time of lying together in sweet exploration of the bodies and minds you possess is a great way to start. Lie naked together and caress the bodies that you find so delicious. They are maps to be explored, landscapes with many interesting and delicious curves and caves in which you can explore the sensations and desires of one another. You should take a little time at first — test the waters — so that if there is a compatibility issue, you are not so deeply involved. The human heart is a delicate and sensitive organ, and diving in too quickly can injure the sweet openness and cause a great delay in the next encounter.

You see, when drugs and alcohol are removed, the feelings are aroused very quickly and intensely, and you must protect your dear hearts from needless abuse and careless encounters. Again, we are not suggesting across-the-board defensiveness — that will not work. But so many have not yet developed this discernment because of a lack of respect and sobriety in this arena.

So step lightly and carefully with open hearts toward one another. You are approaching the most holy of sites in your lover, the one who has the key in some way to your salvation and who will hold your hand on the way to heaven. This is a holy encounter. Do treat it as such, and care for the body and soul that has so sweetly put itself in your care. This is an important job, and one that deserves your attention and deep care.

Take the Time to Connect

We are getting into the meaty part of the book that you all have been waiting for, it seems: sex. As you can see, we have spent an awful lot of time setting the stage for this most wondrous event, suggesting consciousness, sobriety, and deep thoughts about your partner. Many of you can see, of course, where there have been errors made in your own relationships, given the ideas and prescriptions we have shared, but do not despair. We assure you here that if you begin healing your own sexual self, amazing changes will appear in your current relationship, and you will begin to see the glimmerings of the lover you first fell in love with.

But here we will act as if all is well for the moment, as if you are engaged in a sexual relationship with a divine lover. If you are eating well, reading enlivened material, and watching only wholesome entertainment, you will stand a chance at arousing the kundalini about which we have spoken. And this is how you will do it.

As you prepare for lovemaking, after having many discussions about that which you wish to manifest, you will begin by taking a long and relaxing bath or shower together. Of course, you have set aside several hours in which to practice this introductory lovemaking session. Many of you fall into bed after a long and excruciatingly tiring day and wonder at your lack of sex drive, so that must be eliminated — at least from this theoretical meeting we are writing about.

Take the time to connect with each other in a loving and sexual way. Touch each other gently as you cleanse yourselves and each other, getting into the eyes and heart of your beloved. This may be many things — quiet and respectful or playful and fun. It does not have to be serious if you are lighthearted and in a joyful mood. For many of you, sex has become a thing of seriousness, and that is fine. It matters not. Your energies will shift and change over time as you immerse yourselves in the energies of bliss, and many surprises will arise as you explore this new landscape. So be curious. Keep your heart open and, most importantly, stay in the very present moment. Leave all the past behind. There have been no other lovers, ever, in your life at this moment. Do not think of the future, but immerse yourself in the very present moment of touch, breath, and sight of each other.

At this point we hope you have disciplined your mind a little, at least, so that you are able to do this, and that you have put some thought into the environment in which you will be making love. Within this environment there should be no phones; they should have all been switched off. There should be no televisions or electrical devices on, and you should have made the effort to put on clean sheets, light some candles, and use some lovely fragrance to enhance the air within the confines of the room. There are many fragrances you could pick, and we suggest going to a store of some spiritual nature and smelling all the oils available. Pick several, and work together on the choice that is most pleasing to you both at that time. Again, this may change. Do not be attached to anything. Judgment is our enemy in this arena, and the heart chakra closes at its appearance. You must be aware of this at all times.

If you have old wounds that plague your mind, this is where the most discipline is required. Of course, this will not be a secret from your lover, for you will have been open and communicative from the beginning of this adventure together, once your compatibility has been established.

The Lovemaking Process Is More Than Physical

Enter the room together, perhaps helping each other dry off after the cleansing has taken place. Here, all should be kind and gentle, and words of appreciation will be spoken. Get creative here. Tell this beloved partner why you love and you wish to share his or her energies with yours. Do not assume anything; your partner will not know unless you tell him or her. There may be great passion that wishes to move and express itself here, but rein it in a little and enjoy the anticipation.

Many of you have been trained very badly in this area and rip each other's clothes off in the first moments, charging toward your destination, not looking at the scenery at all. This is a delight, this being in front of you who has given you permission to enter the most sacred of places. Treat your partner like the manifestation of God that he or she is. Offer your beloved your respect and dedication, and open up your heart through the throat chakra. Tell your partner how you feel. Are you a little nervous or afraid? Then share that, and your beloved may offer you reassurances. Are you overwhelmed by the energies in your body? Tell your partner, and he or she may calm you, telling you there is no rush.

This is a journey through the landscape of the body-mind complex at its most delicious, and every move you make, every word you utter, and every thought you have will invite the spiritual energies of a similar vibration to join you in this amazing and beautiful exploration. Make sure you invite in the highest energies as you begin this lovely exploration of each other's bodies, hearts, and minds.

You are so used to seeing the lovemaking process as physical, and we want to remind you that it is not physical, but mental, emotional, and spiritual. Your energies are melding and connecting as you kiss each other, your thoughts and desires are blending, and as you speak, your hearts are opening and connecting. Do not ignore these aspects. If you fail in any one of them, make a note that the area needs some tuning up out of the bedroom, for you cannot open up your most sacred place in the bedroom if you are not doing so outside of the bedroom first. If you are not sharing how you feel each day, you will not be able to share how you feel each night, and this is not a story we tell.

The problem many of you have in this initial opening of the heart is that you are protective of your hearts all the time and do not trust in the love of Spirit, but in the defensiveness of the ego. Trust us, dear ones — it is not the ego you wish to take to bed with you and your most beloved. It is the angels and guides who walk with you in love that you need as your guides in this most delicious adventure.

There are more delights to come as you get closer to your beloved's heart and mind. The touch that you express at this time will vary depending on the mood of the moment. As we have said, many of you rush far too quickly to the target site of the sexual organs, but we wish for you to know that the skin and the brain are your two largest and most powerful sexual organs.

Raising the Kundalini

The scene has been set for raising this energy, this kundalini, this powerful force that is driven by love and awareness of its function. It is very difficult to access this energy when the higher chakras are closed through defensiveness, judgment, and fear, and you do not wish to encounter kundalini in this circumstance. As we have said, it will magnify all the blocks you have to love's presence; fears, judgments, and hatreds will be felt as intense body jerks, and at times as pain, as the energy tries to travel up through the body. This is why we have told you of the cleansing that needs to take place, for these blocks are real.

Your ideas of only the physical being real are so wrong; the energies that make up your emotions, thoughts, and ideas are the force behind the physical world. These are indeed just as powerful — more so, in fact — for they create that which you think of as solid and real. So, in this raising of kundalini, the blocks are like speed bumps that make the ride very choppy and tumultuous. But we assume here that you have heeded our warnings and are practicing these areas of cleansing, and that you have made some progress.

We will also say here — and we are sorry to interrupt the proceedings with this chatter, but it is very important for you to get this at this time — as you raise the kundalini intentionally, do not do this for fun's sake, or to see what happens, but know that this is a most sacred practice. This is the practice that will open the doors of heaven or hell to you, and we do not exaggerate. Be warned that the energies need your goodness, your kindness, and your open heart. Do not practice this with someone for whom you lack respect or do not know very well. This is a sacred practice. We will end our warnings here and carry on.

You will find that the body has a natural desire to mate, and of course you have all felt this. But the two programs are still running, remember, and you must keep your focus on the higher prize of sexual awakening. The kundalini needs some time to rise at this juncture, and we will say that half an hour of preparation and kissing, fondling, deep eye gazing, and connection are required.

We see that many of you keep your eyes closed as you kiss and share each other's bodies, and we will not say that this is wrong, but many of you do this because of an innate knowledge that gazing into the eyes of your beloved opens you in some way to them, and you are indeed correct. Closing your eyes is in fact a defensive mechanism to keep your secrets secret, to keep your heart safe and closed. So we ask you here, as you are so close with your beloved, seeking knowledge of each other, to try with all your might to look at each other very deeply at this time.

There is a deep and profound connection made between minds when the eyes penetrate in this way, and for many of you this will be hard, for you have not done this — and for good reason. You cannot stay in your own separate worlds if you look deeply into each other's eyes. You cannot lie easily if you look into each other's eyes, and you cannot stop your heart opening if you look into each other's eyes. If you have a secret, or something of which you are not proud or accepting, this practice is very difficult to do. So know that going in, but try your hardest anyway. You will find an entirely new level of connection will be made as you do this, and you will be rewarded for your bravery.

This is one of the many things that are short-circuited when you use alcohol in lovemaking; the higher mind is lost to you. If you feel the need for a lubricant of some kind to relax, find another way, as alcohol will hide the treasure you are seeking in this practice.

We suggest that as you look into each other's eyes and care deeply for one another, and for yourselves, that you begin to breathe in unison, slowly and deeply. Agree to this beforehand so that you do not have to insist or coerce each other. This is the key that will open the door to that which you wish to feel and experience. The joining of breath is a magical process that changes everything. What you say through your actions is that the two of you are indeed one, you are indeed in unison, and you are indeed evolved enough to understand what you are doing. The mind is connected to all, and as you engage in this behavior, in this deeply loving atmosphere, the nonphysical realms rally to your aid and begin to affect the energetic systems within the joined body of the two of you.

The energies must go in through the nose and down the front of the body to the genitals. Then, as you exhale, envision the energies rising up your back, along your spine to the top of your head, and then over the crown of your head to your third eye in your forehead area. This is what you will do as you mate with your lover — face to face, eye to eye — and yes, this is a difficult thing to do. We will say it is an impossible thing to do for those of you who are frightened or defensive in any way. You must have done some considerable preliminary work to get to this place of acceptance, openness, fearlessness, and faith. So we say: Good for you! Keep it up! The breath will activate the kundalini, and the paired nature of the mating enhances the strength and power of the activity. There is more to this than the sum of the two parts. As when you forgive, magic happens that is hard to quantify and hard to explain, but we will try.

Feeling the Energy Rise

You have a connection to the spirit world (the nonphysical world) that the scientific mind (the scientific world) refuses to consider in its investigations. It has come to a point of which, if the scientific mind cannot see or measure something, it is unable, because of the structure of the scientific method, to include it in its investigations. And so you have been unable to delve into this mystery, even with all your modern equipment.

We, as nonphysical beings, can affect your energetic bodies very easily once you have gone through the perceptual and physical cleansing we have referred to. Your energetic body must be of a very high vibration when you have done all the forgiveness work, this clearing of the past. Lower energies are only able to function in the realms of judgment and fear, so there is no reason to feel unnerved by our statement. We are here to help you raise your energies, to help you into the realms of love. So when lovers are engaged in such a way, we are able to shift and move energies to help move the process of awakening along, and that is our joy, our job.

The world does not move in the way you have been taught. There are nonphysical beings here ready to help those who are of an elevated energy who wish to transform themselves and, through that transformation, the world. We are ready, willing, and able to help at this point.

And so the energy begins to arise. You will feel it as it rises up your spine, and the body will move in response to this energy. It is powerful and transformative, opening and awakening nerves and chemicals as it goes that, until this point, have not been woken systematically. The blood flows and the energy flows, and there will be a slow and steady building of energy up your spine in a delicious wave of bliss that will move your body in many ways. Your back may arch of its own accord, and your shoulders may move too, adjusting and responding to the force of this spiritual elixir called kundalini. You will find that an energy of passion and delight begins to encroach on your mind and physical brain as it rises up your spinal column.

This is not your imagination, and as you experience it for the first time, you will be surprised by the force and joy contained within the energy. But this is not just a single event, this kundalini rising. This energy is now opening channels through your body, both physical and energetic, and you will begin to undergo massive changes that are very unusual. These are the changes in awareness and openness that you have wished for, that you have read about. You will begin to see shifts in the rest of your life as this practice is pursued over time. You may see enhancements in your creativity, in your awareness such as intuition, and you will see a shift in consciousness.

As the energy reaches a head — and you will have no doubt when this happens — there will be a burst of orgasmic delight that runs through your entire body. This may be combined with what you would consider a genital orgasm, but not necessarily. This energetic burst encompasses the entire body and goes on for some time. You will be amazed at the strength and depth of the pleasures you are experiencing, and you will wonder at what you have been satisfied with up until this point. It can indeed overwhelm, and you may cry or be overcome with emotions. This is as it should be. Many blocks will be removed as this energy travels about; old tears that were never cried and lingering remnants of old fears will be flushed out, and you will release that which you were unable to release on your own.

This is not the end result of a process but the beginning of a new one. This surprises you, does it not? You were imagining that this is what you have been preparing for, but that is not the case. All the work you have done has been to turn the key in a lock that opens a door into a whole other world. What is behind the door and where will it take you?

CHAPTER FORTY-TWO

Specific Steps and Sensations

Sensations are what the ego seeks on the sexual journey — sensations of the body to bring pleasure. The path of divine love does indeed arouse sensations, but these are more of a byproduct of the spiritual experience we are seeking. The seeker will arouse the energetic body through practices of loving kindness and forgiveness, and through purification of the foods and drinks ingested into the body. The experiences are energetic in nature, and the sensations as such are generated in the mind of the practitioner, not on the skin or nerve endings, although this may be a difficult distinction to make at first. The body becomes the magnifier, if you will, of the spiritual experience. The body is not creating the events as it has in previous sexual experiences.

It requires some patience to achieve this state, as the chicken-and-egg event has changed around the orientation of the mind. Previously touch created the feeling of connection. As you practice divine love, the connection to God provides the sensation, so as the connection is strengthened, the ability to reach blissful and ecstatic states remains throughout the day's experience. You no longer need the body of a lover to achieve the bliss you crave as a divine connection remains. If the maintenance is continued through prayer, reading wisdom texts, and meditation, the feelings of love will not leave as they do when you associate them with a lover's body, yet you can indeed share them with like-minded souls if you choose. This provides you with the ability to never feel alone, to always have the divine connection that so many are missing — the connection that you reach for in bars and in sex that is not holy. Life becomes full of beauty, and patience with others is increased as you feel so completely satisfied that ides of competition and need subside beneath the feelings of love and connection to God, self, and others.

These are indeed blessed states that are worth cultivating. The drives and nagging fears of the small self are gone, and the open and expansive feelings of connection and untold joy arise in the person who is now a direct conduit to the divine, motivated by divine desires such as generosity, peace, and unconditional love for all. A couple may indeed have this journey if they are suited to each other, but partners who are of a similar vibration may be engaged for sexual union only if that is their desire. This is a personal choice, although many connect in permanent partnerships as the limits of the ego, which are usually responsible for the destruction and disconnection in normal relations, are removed and transcended through this practice.

There are many hurdles before this will be achievable, yet is the ego-driven life worth the meager results it yields? We think not, although many of you have no idea what awaits you on this journey to blissful union with the divine.

Kissing

We are with you again, dear one. You are nervous about writing this section of the book, and indeed you should be! We are kidding, of course. This shows you that there are blocks and fears around sexuality, and you will learn much from our lessons as we go through them.

We will write about the idea of kissing as it pertains to making love in the manner in which we speak. We approach this first, of course, as this is generally what you do first with each other once the desire for a sexual connection is acknowledged. We would like to tell you what is actually going on while you kiss so you can get some idea of just how important it is.

The mouth is the window to the soul. It is not the eyes. Many interactions with the world take place through this powerful orifice, and you need to treat it with the love and respect it deserves. The mouth is a very tender place with a multitude of nerve endings, and therefore connections to the brain, that are responsible for the intense feelings of desire and pleasure that kissing arouses. This is important because of the events that it precipitates; indeed, there is probably nothing more important in setting up sexual energies in a loving and deeply stimulating way than the kiss, or rather the kissing of another's kiss. You see, this is what it is: You are both reaching into the minds of one another during this activity — not in a superficial or metaphorical way, but in a real and tangible way.

The nerve endings that travel to your brain and those in your lover are connected in a deeply energetic way in this process of kissing. All you desire and all your passion is actually felt in your partner's brain, and many of you mistake it for your own, but this is why the kiss is so powerful. You are feeling not only your own desire, but that of your lover, which is a way into the energetic body and mind of the one you wish to make love to. You will begin to feel your partner's desire for you, and it will inflame you even more. You will discern your beloved's own desires and what your lover would like to experience, and you will be moved in different ways to do different things. This opens up the heart in some magical way that is hard to explain.

This is why the refusal to kiss someone you are mad at is considered such a punishment. The turning away of the mouth so that the person only gets your cheek is not just symbolic, but is the heart saying, "You are not welcome in me at the moment. You have hurt me or disrespected me in some way." So we wish to tell you to kiss a lot before you even start the lovemaking process. Teenagers used to do this for hours and days, but we are sad to say those days are over, and this is a dangerous thing. Teens are more likely now to give a "blow job," as you say, and this is a demeaning act in the way it is conducted these days — as an act of submission or dominance by uneducated youngsters.

The symbolic nature of the kiss, mouth to mouth and heart to heart, is very important for arousing the bliss energies, and it is a very important place to start. We wish to tell you that this is as important as penetration in energetic levels, and it needs the focus and attention that is its due. Do not think that it is a waste of time or immature or adolescent. Indeed, the opposite is true. Mature and conscious lovers will spend a great deal of time kissing because they know that it opens up all the doors to the rest of the lovemaking corridors, and that it brings their hearts and minds into sync and onto the same page.

There is nothing wrong with lying down with your beloved and kissing for some considerable time when you decide to make love; indeed, this is our recommendation. And as for the new lovers who are reading this, you must understand that on your first night this is all you will do: kiss and touch. That, then, is the best introduction to each other's bodies and minds that you can give. This will entrench the other's thoughts and desires within your own body energy matrix, and deep heart connections will be made. So as you approach each other for the first time, relish this. And at the beginning of each lovemaking session, kissing should not be the perfunctory few pecks that it can become in a long-term marriage.

For the men out there: If you want to have a sexual relationship with your wife that is deeply satisfying and enthusiastic, kiss her more, and let her know that you value kissing in and of itself. Many women need this deep and penetrating form of communication to arouse them, and your quick fumbling toward the goal, so to speak, does not serve you. She will be far more responsive and deeply aroused as you kiss her more and more.

What a revolution we propose! Begin making out again as you did when you were young, and for you young lovers out there, do not rush the kissing part. You are detouring around one of the most important aspects of the heart connection. You may not want to kiss deeply with someone with whom you want a one-night stand because your heart will become involved, and the emotions will complicate things. We understand that there is a place for this speedy connection, and we do not judge it at all. In fact, the exploration of the physical aspects of love alone is an interesting exercise. However, we know that in the healthy and open heart this is not so satisfying. So we suggest, for the benefit of your dear heart and energetic body, that you select lovers who are of a like vibration and bent on the expression of the highest love and caring. So kiss away, dear ones. This is the first lesson. It is valuable, and you will not connect as you should if you miss this step.

Touching

We will now write about the subject of touching as it relates to the sexual experience. What many people are doing as they touch each other, as they engage in a sexual encounter, is seeking a feeling. This may seem obvious, but this is the mere surface of the act, and we must go deeper into the experience to truly understand that this desired feeling is connection and love. The mistake in this materialistic culture is thinking that this desired feeling is achieved through the body and the physical senses. What we are saying is indeed the opposite.

We want you to see the touch between you and your partner as an intermediary, if you will. The feelings you want are of the soul and energetic in nature. They are not physical in the least, yet because of the material nature of your teachings, you are taught that if you rub this bit and poke that, so to speak, you will achieve your goals. As you know from sad experience, this is not the case at all. Motivation must come from the heart, from love, and from a deep need to connect. So as you approach touching, this is where we want your mind to be. As you touch your partner's body, lying naked together after much delicious kissing, you are primed and ready, so to speak, to enter more deeply into the sexual embrace.

There is indeed a need to see your partner's body as your own as you enter this new area of exploration. Imagine you are touching your own body; as your fingers drift and touch the flesh that is so delightful to you, envision this touch on your own body. What this does is reinforce the idea that you and your partner are indeed one, which is the truth, dear ones. You have been taught otherwise — that you are two separate beings, distinct in every way — but on a soul level and mind level this is not so. This being who lies with you, who you have honored and are honoring with this deep and loving exchange of energies, is you in another form, is God in another form. It is with this reverence and deep respect that we wish this touching to take place.

You will be moved from the inside out to explore and to tweak, to caress and to push, and all of the movements in between. You are now exploring your partner's body with the second-most sensitive area of the body, the fingertips. Is it not interesting that you start with the mouth — the most sensitive — and go into the second-most sensitive, the fingertips? This is no mistake or coincidence; it is by a deep and divine design that the bodies you have are put together this way, and this is what we wish you to think about.

This is a prayer to God, this lovemaking you are involved in. Let that thought guide you and gently lead you and your lover down this pathway. Remember that this was intended by God. This is not a profane act in any way, shape, or form as you approach it with reverence, real joy, and honor. So imagine you are making love to God when you are making love to your partner. Do not rush. Do not be aggressive, and do not judge in any way. Be as forgiving and as respectful as if you were making love to God, for indeed you are.

Your partner is the physical manifestation of the Divine that you have decided to play with, and you should be honored. There is no other way to see your partner and expect the divine energies to arise. The energies will not come if there is any hatred present or resentment in the air. Do not make love after a fight until you have truly forgiven each other and resolved the issue in a calm and loving way. You may not totally agree with each other, but you can agree to disagree. Indeed, a great problem is created if you make love when there is resentment present. You will go into this most sacred connection with your heart closed, and if that is the case, the ego will be in charge. Watch out — the ego loves that opportunity, and there will be a little poison added to the mix if you do this.

What we suggest is open and honest verbal communication with your partner to share that you are not yet ready to make love, as you are still hurt or confused. This will let your partner know that there is work yet to be done on the verbal front. We cannot emphasize this enough. When this communication is made, there is a deep and emotional bonding that happens as a problem is resolved, and there may well be a place for touching in this exchange itself. If you are sitting far apart on opposite sides of the room as you discuss an issue, arms folded and hearts closed, a heart-to-heart connection will not be made. So we suggest, as difficult as this is, that when you are discussing a problem you sit close together, looking directly at one another. And if the hurt is not too great, hold hands. At times this touch is too much for the pain you are feeling, and this illustrates our point — does it not? — that touch is a deep and penetrating behavior. It is why you all avoid it so much in Western culture. Many of you have not been touched for ages because of your cultural teachings, and this needs to change.

So back to our couple — if you are in a disagreement, hold your hands out in supplication and an offering of peace as you are talking. One of you will be more able to do this than the other, and that is okay. You will eventually reach out after some discussion and see that it is love and connection that you want, and not the separation the ego wishes for. This will be a challenge for many of you, but as we said, we are throwing out all that does not serve you on this path, which is much of what you do and what you think you know. This world is made of mostly mistakes, and there is a deep healing of this entire area of communication that needs to be implemented for the bliss energies to be tapped into.

There is more we will say. Now that you are lying down with your beloved, do not focus on one part of the body above any other as you are in this delicious phase of lovemaking. There is a place for a full-body massage at times, if you are both in agreement, or a full-body touching session. No part is more or less important at this stage, and it is a great honor to your partner to see him or her as this complete being, this entire holy form, rather than a combination of sex organs joined together by skin.

Think about this at the beginning of your lovemaking activity. Take the time to gently touch and explore each other, and see just how exciting and loving this is. There is a tremendous relief and joy that comes over your soul as you are seen in this way and as you visualize your partner as yourself and as a manifestation of God. The exploration develops a holiness that is not achieved any other way. Enjoy yourselves and see this as a holy sacrament to your relationship, to yourself, and to the other. The connections you make in these early phases of lovemaking are the foundation for later efforts, so do not scrimp here or rush on to the next level. If you do not have a lot of time — and we realize that this happens — it is better to stop here than to skip this step and rush on to hurried intercourse. There is nothing wrong with the "quickie," as you call it, but it should be occasional and driven by passion rather than time constraints.

We have something else for you to contemplate and discuss with your beloved. This will be fun, we assure you, and if your partner is reluctant in some way, then you are sure to find a way to gently insist that you wish to try this for the health and love of your relationship. Even if your partner is still reluctant, you have planted the seed, and you may decide to perform this loving act for yourself and engage your own body. You may caress it and explore it with love and patience. Remember the idea of abundance? You may give to yourself what you desire, and that will attract that same thing to you, and it will indeed be so, dear ones. It will indeed be so.

What to Say

We will continue with our description of the lovemaking we wish for you to explore, and it commences with the expression of words. This is how it all begins — with the exchange of ideas and concepts that the other finds fascinating or shares and wishes to explore with you. We will not go into the conversations you have had that will lead you into the arms of another, for they are infinite and personal to each of you. But we will offer some guidance into the words you can speak in the bedroom as you are engaged in lovemaking with your beloved.

All the words we wish you to say will be ones of appreciation — for your partner's presence, for your partner's qualities of gentleness and intelligence. These will not be aggressive words of lust and penetration, but sacred words of the expression of your deepest feelings and desires. We want you to tell the lover you are speaking to how you are feeling. Are you feeling a little scared? Then share that. Do not be scared that your partner will reject you; he or she will not. Your partner will likely respond that her or she is feeling the same, for the honest expression of an open heart precipitates the same in another.

You see, the ego will counsel you to keep it all inside, to not speak these deep inner concerns to anyone. But we tell you otherwise. We wish for you to tell your partner of the difficulties you have in exposing your heart but that indeed you wish to do this. After hearing these deep and honest expressions, your beloved will share his or her own. It is a strange and wonderful device of the mind that as you express, so others must express; as you love, others must love; and as you share, others must share. It is the evidence of your oneness. It is almost impossible to do otherwise, as the deep and intimate connections that you did not realize exist are expressed into the outside world.

There are aspects of the human brain that must mirror the behavior they see. You have heard of this in body language studies — have you not? — when another person will mirror you if that person is in tune. This happens with conversation in the bedroom. When you share the deepest places of the heart, because you are one, because you are both the divine expression of God in a body, each appearing to be separate but indeed not separate, this phenomenon becomes manifest. As you follow our prescriptions for opening your heart through kissing, through touching, and through sharing your heartfelt emotions, all the energies work together to connect the body, mind, and heart together on an energetic level.

Soft and gentle tendrils of light snake out from your heart, head, and throat as you speak to each other of your hopes, dreams, and fears. As these tendrils gently intertwine on the energetic level, your heart opens more, and a great rush of energy is felt in your body. This can be a sense of the heart opening and a deep sense of love and connection, or you may begin to feel the kundalini beginning to assert itself at the base of your spine. This will feel as a fullness that is blissful and satisfying. In the initial stages, it may not manifest into anything more than this, but as you practice these techniques of loving communication, the energies will be activated. And depending on the level of clarification you have achieved in the other facets of the diamond we endeavor to create, the energy will be of a like strength.

We hope you will feel a change early on in your sexual adventures. It is such an intense process that the results are indeed quick, but as we have said, the ego does not like any of this and will tell you not to express yourself. It will counsel you to be quiet and keep a physical and mental distance from your lover to keep yourself safe. Do not listen to its counsel. It wants you alone and to itself to rule with impunity. The ego cannot tolerate love. Oh, it will tell you stories that this is not the one, that this partner is not special enough for you and that you can do better, but do not listen to it. It does not have your best interests at heart. It wants you to act separate and weak so that it can prove to you that it is right.

We want you to act defenselessly, as if you cannot be hurt — because you cannot, dear ones. All the pain you have experienced is due to your lack of communication, not because you spoke your truth. The pain has arisen from your defensiveness, from times when you have kept secrets and your feelings inside so that no one could know you. We are counseling you to do the opposite. Open your throat and your voice and tell your lover how you feel, how he or she feels, and what you dream of. Your partner will love it, and if he or she doesn't, then that person is not the one for you. And that will be good to know, will it not? We do not wish for you to waste your time on those who are ruled by the ego. We are not judgmental in this, but we must counsel you to work with those who are of the same mind. The ego is difficult enough to transcend when you and your partner are both on the same team, and you cannot change another person. You can only work together to change the way you treat each other and the way you show your love and respect for each other.

We will leave that for now. Again, we have asked a most difficult thing, have we not, this exposure to the possibility of rejection? This terrifies you and is the ego's best argument for silence. But it is only in the expression of truth that love can exist. It cannot exist with lies because it is the expression of truth. Its nature does not allow its presence with lies and secrets.

So be brave, dear ones, and speak your loving truth. What you will find is if you do this after making the deep and loving connection we have suggested, only love will arise, and only the kindest words will be expressed. You have set the stage with your loving thoughts and words, and you will be surprised by the deep and loving connection that this fosters. Your lovemaking will grow in depth and energy, and you will be so glad you listened. After you are finished and your hearts have been opened, you will wish to tell us what you have experienced, but we will already know, dear ones. We will already know.

Intercourse

We are now going to write about the act of intercourse, that moment of sweet joining in the course of this divine connection we speak about. You are now joined with your beloved, gazing into one another's eyes and at the same time kissing and speaking sweet words to one another. We wish for you to practice a process of breathing at this moment that will arouse the energies and encourage the raising of the kundalini that we have so often mentioned. Breath is the life of this energy, and so far we have not mentioned it often because of its tremendous power. And until you have practiced and rehearsed many of the other aspects of our recommendations, we do not recommend that you practice this breath work.

There are forces at play here that are of the highest power and divine in nature, wielding the strength of the God force you call love. This is one area to approach with the greatest of respect and awe. There are areas of the energetic body that are activated after such intimate preparations, and adding breath to this behavior will cause much to change on the energetic level. We suggest your breathing become synchronized at first, and this may have begun naturally as the previous steps in intimate seduction were carried out, but this is a more studied and focused activity now.

We wish for you to breathe in and imagine your lover's breath coming into your body. Your partner will be doing the same thing, breathing in and imagining your breath entering his or her body. See the breath going down the front of your body, swirling and building in the area of the genitals. As the breath is released, see it rising up the spine and over the top of the crown to the third eye, the chakra between the brows. This will be the circle you breathe in. This will be repeated, but always envision on the inbreath that it is your lover's air you are breathing in.

This can go on for as long as you choose, and the movements that arise as you complete this circular breathing will be personal and driven by your own desires. But as you breathe this way, the kundalini energy will respond and you will begin to feel the rising of a different kind of feeling as you blend and breathe the energy, each of the other.

As far as any other movements go, this is your decision. There are indeed practices in other forms of tantra that specify far more regulated and rigid means of movement, but for this stage of the game, so to speak, we would like you to feel the energies and allow them their own space and movement as they so desire. You are free to experiment with this, of course, and some of you will, over time, rouse the kundalini to such a degree that you will feel the blissful and ecstatic full-body orgasms that are part and parcel of this practice.

Over time there will be more instructions for those who are specialists and wish to follow a more rigorous program, but for the average person, we have given you more than enough material to get you into trouble. There are many sexual manuals on the market, but that is not our specialty. The specialty we wish to focus on is this divine connection and the energetic aspects of joining that use the body, in some ways, incidentally.

You are manifestations of God energy, and your bodies are merely vehicles for this energy to experience itself with itself, so this is the mindset of the love we wish for you to make together. We have challenged you with this approach to love, health, and communication, have we not? We do not wish to overload you, but what you will find is that if you undertake the recommendations we have given you, the sex you have will become a creature of a very different type than you are used to. The energies will bring amazing sensations you have never before experienced, and you will become satisfied to a depth and degree that is new and exciting. Of course, there is work required, but can you really call it work when it leads to the kinds of experiences we are alluding to? And we shall allude no more. We will tell you about what can happen on the energetic level as you make love this way.

As the kundalini is invited up your spine by the breath work we suggest, a very interesting thing happens. The chakras, as they are located up the body, begin to join in the party, so to speak, and speed up. They are always moving and creating, but they are now becoming more aroused, joining in as the energy rises. Each chakra adds its own flavor to the mix, and the power builds. Sometimes the energy will cause your body to become rigid, and it may arch back as the muscles and tendons react to the intense electrical energy being generated. There may be movements of the pelvis and belly that seem to happen of their own accord, and all the while the energy is building up the spine toward the top of your head. This is an intense time, not one to be missed or played with lightheartedly as a game. It is a spiritual and energetic event of great import, and it should be regarded as such.

Eventually the energy will build and be released out of the chakra at the top of the head, the back of the head, and even sometimes through the front of the throat. This will often depend on the clarity and blocks that are at play. The energy knows what it is doing, and it may indeed come through a chakra that is more blocked to clear it out and open it up, so to speak. This is all normal and to be expected.

There is, at this moment, what is called a full-body orgasm. The energy of an orgasm is felt not in the genital area, necessarily — although that too can occur — but felt all over the body. It is an amazing and powerful experience that can last for several minutes, at times completely overwhelming the people involved. This may be a shared experience, or one partner may be more open than the other. There are no wrongs or rights here; just be open to the experience and do not judge it.

As you become more and more adept at this practice, the energies will shift and change, perhaps taking on other manifestations as the kundalini travels throughout the body, opening and clearing the blocks that remain. At times, spontaneous eruptions of tears and joy may happen. We are here to warn you that immense and overwhelming bliss can indeed be experienced as these pathways are explored with reverence and clarity of purpose. They will not open in the darkness — only in the light — and this is for a reason. This is the light and energy of the God energies, and it is only in the light of love and respect that this will occur.

CHAPTER FORTY-THREE

Arising Fears

As we read over that last excerpt about words and the language of love that we wish you to speak, we are prompted to write more on the fears that will arise in this moment as you are asked to bare your souls and hearts. We see that for the human being this is the most terrifying of prospects, so we will not skip over this statement as if it is something you can master in five minutes. This is the point at which many of you will throw this book across the room and say, "I am condemned to a life of solitude, and I will not achieve this bliss of which Ananda speaks!"

There is such a belief in the ego mind that communication will be its end, that it will put the fear of death into your heart — if the ego has been in charge for a very long time. This is the truth; the ego cannot survive in the conditions we suggest you create with all of the prescriptions of forgiveness, eating cleanly, speaking authentically, and all the other areas we have been writing about. This aspect of the ego's fear that you are experiencing is this idea that the ego and you, the real you, are separate beings, and this is so on an energetic level.

The ego has no desire to do what you — the real you — wish to do. It wants the physical, the fear, the food, the power, and the separation. So it is important to visualize this profound split in your mind, to understand that this ego is not you and does not want what you want. This will help you to understand the fears as they arise during this process and that you must exert your spiritual will in this moment of terror. This is also where the study and mind training of a text such as *A Course in Miracles* stands strong in your stead. It will give you daily support as well as new ideas and thoughts that will support this behavior we ask of you.

If you read this book and our prescriptions without this kind of support behind you, you will not be able to do the work. It will so terrify you that you will become paralyzed. This is the depth of the work to which we refer. This is a complete retooling of your expression on this plane, and it takes time. Do not expect to be able to make these changes after a weekend of reading our teachings. You will need to practice the new thoughts and beliefs many times a day, every day. You will be deconstructing the false concepts that this culture, your family, and the universal ego mind have created, and this is no small feat.

This is the work of a lifetime, but the alternative is not tenable. The alternative is to continue in the ego's grip of fear and judgment, which guarantees suffering. So carry on down this path, dear ones. If you are unable to even envision these acts of lovemaking that we discuss, that does not mean you cannot perform them. It just means that the ego is not yet sufficiently subdued and there is a bit more preparation needed. Indeed, our dear one could not have even contemplated these actions until very recently. Even now, as we are writing this book, she is shaking her head in disbelief at what we are asking her to do: to face her biggest fear. Yet she knows from experience that facing her largest fears, so far, has brought the greatest spiritual revelation and growth. She knows from experience that what we say is true. Perhaps you do not have this evidence, but there is opportunity in facing your fears that you too will get this liberating experience of seeing the true nature of your soul once the fears are gone.

This is the self-realization that all spiritual texts speak about, and it is through the unearthing and facing of these fears that the fearless, strong, and true self is revealed. It is not what you want to hear, and we feel that very clearly, but it is the path to the divine love you seek.

CHAPTER FORTY-FOUR

Reaping the Harvest

There will be beginnings of energies within your body that, if you have done your homework, will not frighten but intrigue you. The body in which you reside is an electrical transformer, if you will, and it has been functioning at a reduced capacity because of the interferences we have described. As you clear your mind and clear your body of the lower echelons of thought and consumption, you will begin to feel sharp intrusions of electrical energy in your body, which will make it move in unpredictable ways.

If you have not deconstructed your society's teachings on possession and evil, you will not be able to participate in this process at all. That is why we mentioned it so early. You must address the history you have been subjected to, the erroneous teachings that have pervaded your society for so long, for you have been told not to go where we are telling you to go. But do not fear, for if you have raised your vibration significantly through the cleansing mechanisms we have suggested, this will only be a journey into experiences of elation and joy.

You will find that your body, as you lie down in rest and invitation, will allow the energies of bliss to flow. You will feel immense strength and power in the electrical impulses that will travel along your limbs and through your spine. When this begins to happen, know that this is as it should be, and that acceptance will make the journey easier and more fun. If, however, fears arise, you have some more work to do. You will need to spend a little more time understanding that your fear is natural, given the untrue teachings that you have been subjected to. You must understand the relationship between education in truth and the feeding of lies to your mind to keep it small and in the designated box that keeps you powerless and fearful.

We will assume here that all is going well and that the energies are felt and accepted. As these impulses continue over time, you will experience the further cleansing of the transformer that you are. You see, our prescriptions are merely the turning of the key in the door, and as you walk through the door into ever-increasing awareness, you will be amazed indeed.

You may encounter, and probably will encounter, increasing creative abilities as this journey is undertaken. The connection to Spirit is strongest when you are creating and loving. These are the two most open channels to melding with Spirit, for Spirit is creative and loving. So it is no surprise — nor should it be — that when you indulge in love and creativity, which you can do at the same time, you are in the same vibration as what you would call God or Source energy. That is the force behind this amazing universe that you see, although of course this is, as we have said, only a small portion of that which exists. And so the journey you are on, the pursuit of the bliss energies, is the path to experiencing the rest of creation, most of which you are unable to see from this narrow slice of time-space that you perceive as your life.

There are a multitude of universes to experience, and you are at the doorway to the world of love, creativity, exploration, eternal growth, and happiness. We know that this all sounds very exciting and amazing, and you look around at your life and cannot imagine getting from where you are to where we speak of. But it is the same as looking at a baby and trying to tell it that it will, in thirty years, travel the world as a concert conductor. It is the same idea, and it is possible for you to undergo such a transformation of experience — just as the baby does. But you must understand the obstacles and pitfalls. You must understand that there is a method of getting from where you are to where you wish to be, and it has nothing to do with being exceptional or blessed in any way. Although, indeed, you are all blessed to be having this physical opportunity to grow, experience, and learn in such a visceral and intense way.

You see, this arena, this world in which you live, is so intense that you cannot help but grow or suffer immensely. You are indoctrinated into the belief that you can only grow so far, that you can only grow so big, but this is not true. You are limitless in your ability to grow, and it is when you put restrictions on yourself — imposed by others or yourself, it matters not — that you create pain, for you are designed to learn and grow, learn and grow, until you are done here and can move on to the next arena of growth. But that is another story. For now we must help you understand the importance of the creative process here and now.

The Goal Is Sacred Sexuality

If you practice as we have suggested, you will begin to experience periods of peace and joy, free of pain and judgment, as you yourself relinquish judgment. You will find that the mental and emotional connection to your own guides, your own higher self, will increase, and you will begin to get communications that will offer you advice, at times warnings, and indeed, a general guidance that will become clearer and clearer. You will be able to do that which you dislike less and less, because your connection to Source is becoming stronger. And you will be willing to love more and more, as this becomes more in tune with who you actually are. The ideas of separation will become less appealing, and your desire for connection will become stronger. Yet paradoxically, your need for some time of solitude will also increase, and it is important to achieve a balance between the desire to connect with others and the desire to connect with yourself.

For many of you, this will cause some disruptions in your lives, and you may fear what we say for fear that you will have to leave jobs and relationships behind. But trust us here, dear ones — you will always keep in your life that which is in tune with your true nature, and you will always keep that which you love close beside you. These things may shift and grow and change somewhat, but we know that you know some changes need to be made, or you would not be reading this far into this book and its radical suggestions. Is that not so?

The energies that arise may also include an increase in psychic phenomena, much as our dear one, Tina, experienced. She has become a clear channel for us after having walked this path, but it will vary for each of you. Many may begin to encounter inspirations from the nonphysical that prompt them to write, paint, travel, or sing. You will sense a growing appreciation of the depth of your own being, and the boredom that you imagined would arise does not, for you are delving into the depths of the most interesting thing in the universe: the heart and mind of God. That is what you are — a manifestation of that most holy thing that you were taught is not you — and yet we are telling you that yes, this is you. Love has created you to express love, kindness has created you to express kindness, and passion has created you to express passion. And it is clear, when you read those words, why your culture suffers so. Any time you express anything other than this, you are out of accord with that which you are, and that is why you are sad. This is the truth of the matter, and this is why we have come to help you up out of the ditch into which you have been pushed. It is no accident that you have lost your way, and we will shine a light onto the path you will follow to that which you desire to experience.

You are indeed the most powerful of beings, and it is this power that we encourage you to pursue in the sacred sexual relationship. You see, to create this kind of relationship is indeed a sacred act, and you will feel some intimidation at the idea of it, for many of you have been experiencing sexuality and the relationships it contains in such a detrimental way, in such a low-vibration way, that there is fear in entering again into this arena of sacred sexuality. Indeed, there are many who feel that sex is not sacred at all and that we are making this all up.

Actually, there are very few in this day and age who have truly achieved this sacred sexual union with the full understanding of its power and potential. But we wish for you to be encouraged and to be brave and ponder this reality about which we are speaking. You see, dear ones, the future you are creating in your judgment and bad habits is not a good one, and we wish to give your heads-up, so to speak, that it is time to change the game plan.

Reaching for Change

The vibrational changes that are happening, and the large changes that are about to happen on planet Earth, will rattle your cages, so to speak. Massive shifts in the structure and expression of your culture are on the horizon, and it will be to your benefit to approach our practices as soon as possible so that you are prepared for these shifts, for they will be grand indeed. And if you have not gone inside and figured out some of this confusing stuff, you will flounder in the new world order as it will be expressed. As we have said, the light is getting lighter and the dark is getting darker, and you will fare much better if you begin to walk toward the light now, changing your life to suit this new self-expression and sharing your true being with those you love and wish to love.

We wish to say to those of you who are not coping so well with Western culture that you are right in your struggles with its dictates. You are right to feel as if something is terribly wrong, and you are right to wish for a different world, for the one you are in is off track in many ways. But let us not frighten you into change. Understand that how you feel is your soul speaking to you of a new way, the way to peace and love that you all are striving for in some way or another. So let us continue on in discussing what will arise as you venture into this new world.

Your families will begin to thrive. Your children will be allowed to express themselves, and very early on, if you do not quell their passions and their energies, you will see the vibrant little beings they are meant to be. Indeed, there are souls being born now who will not tolerate the old ways. They will begin a revolution of sorts that may or may not be violent, and we suggest that the path to love be followed so that the transition can be a gentle one. You cannot get them to follow the rules as you have, those rules that have caused such sadness, such sickness. The children of the new order will express their truths and will know how they feel at all times, and society will not fall apart at this self-expression, but thrive, as individuals follow their hearts and passions into a world of bliss, created from their connection to Source and their ability to tap into divine intelligence with their own open minds. Imagine this world, dear ones: freedom to express, freedom to love, and freedom to create the life you wish because you have the correct handbook, the correct instructions for this manifestation.

We are excited that you have come this far with us on this journey. You are reaching for the truth, reaching for a change that is different from that which you imagined. You have imagined, perhaps, an increase in energy, an increase in health, but have you imagined an increase in all these areas we are talking about? You see the genius of some, the creativity of some, and you feel left behind. But there is no need for this. You each have access to this most amazing and limitless resource that is the Universal Mind, and it is your right and your privilege to have access to this wonderful library of energy and information.

CHAPTER FORTY-FIVE

Your New World

The new world into which this energy takes you is a delightful one indeed. Your mind will be more open and loving; your heart will be more willing to love and more willing to forgive. You will begin to see others in a more compassionate way, and your connection to the world and all that is in it will be transformed by this energy. Many of you have heard about this kind of awakening. You may have heard it called enlightenment, or you my have called it awakening — it matters not. You are now going to be tapping into the true nature of your mind — that of the loving mind, the open mind, the mind driven by Spirit and not by the ego.

This process we are involved in is like a line in the sand at the point where the kundalini rises for the first time. After this, all will be different and you will wonder at your small life before this event. You are driven at the moment by the lower realms of the body-mind complex, and the ego, the survival mechanism of the body, has been given precedence. Follow our advice over time. And it will take time, dear ones. This is not something that will happen overnight, and for good reason. The mind is a delicately balanced organism, and it will not survive huge and sudden shifts when it is unprepared. This massive shift in consciousness we refer to is the result of years of practice of forgiveness and all the other aspects of transformation we give to you.

There may be some of you who are so far along the track already that you do not have long to wait, but there are many of you who did not realize the importance of forgiveness. You were going to yoga classes and eating well, but your mind was full of judgment and you were watching bad television, not realizing that it lowered your vibration so significantly. You will find that as you employ all the tasks we have set, the foundation of your spiritual practice will stand you in good stead to achieve this awakening and raising of kundalini energy.

There are doorways in your mind that only become available to you at these elevated vibrations. Have you not wondered how yogis and practitioners of Eastern meditations sit for so long? How do they do it? They are in this state of bliss, and it is not until you experience it yourself that you will understand that to be in this state is a joy only, and that to be in the ordinary world afterward is not so enticing. Even the realms of ordinary sex become disappointing after you have reached these heights, and you will become quite willing to practice these restraints to achieve these experiences. In fact, you will not see them as restraints at all, or deprivations, but merely necessities to achieve the greatest delights. And they are well worth the effort.

Our dear one, Tina, has struggled with these restraints and is always working on removing the blocks to love's presence, so do not feel that this is an easy process. The ego is strong and wants to be in control, and many of your thoughts and habits are deeply entrenched in the mind and heart, so you will vacillate back and forth over many months and years. But we wish to tell you to be diligent in your studies and your practices. The future that awaits you is one of health, happiness, and fulfillment. Let us speak of this for a while.

Find Your True State of Love

The body, when controlled by the ego, is in a constant state of anxiety and fear. There are many chemicals running through it every time you have a hateful or a negative thought about yourself or another. Your entire body is stressed, and damage is caused. The cells react as if they are under attack, as they surely are. Many of your diseases arise because of this state of extreme anxiety.

When you begin to raise the kundalini and get in touch with peace and the source of your very being, you become a different person chemically. Any thoughts that feel bad are immediately recognized for the untruths that they are, and the untruths are looked at and transformed. This brings about a calming of your system, and as you learn to do this with every thought, over time, your body is bathed in the light of love and the peace that truth brings. Your cells begin to thrive, and your body's natural healing abilities come into play, removing old, damaged areas to let new cells grow and the wounds of the past heal.

You see, dear ones, the wounds in your hearts and minds that you feel as depression, sadness, and anxiety all have physical manifestations in the body, which leads to the many sicknesses and physical problems you face in your society. In your true state of love, which is where you are designed to be, there is no illness — only an extreme feeling of health and well-being. So your paradigm that says you get sick as you age and that your body is constantly going wrong is incorrect.

What is wrong is you are never taught the creative nature of thought in your society, and you are taught that you are a body. These two teachings are at the root of almost all of your problems, for you are not only a body that is fallible and randomly goes wrong. You are the very conduit of the creativity of the universe — God, if you will —yet if you do not know this, the conduit is not open and you suffer terribly from the misuse of the body that is here for you to experience and to learn. But do not be sad or angry that this was not taught to you, for this will not help you on your way. You must be grateful that we have come together at this time and that you will change direction now and begin to walk toward the light of truth and all that it will bring.

The kundalini is beginning to arouse the other senses that you have been taught to ignore and to fear. You see, the churches that have ruled the world for so long have implanted many untruths over the centuries, and even though you may not be going to church any longer, or even believe in its teachings, you do not realize the profound effect it has had on your culture's beliefs and thinking. Indeed, there are many aspects of reality that you do not have any access to because you have been systematically told not to venture into those realms. Here, of course, we refer to the realms of spirit, where we reside.

When you begin to feel the energies of your true self, the higher form of you, connecting and wishing to communicate, many of you are terrified and will not continue. You sink back into the darkness of the ego's world, thinking you are safer there, when it is in fact the ego's world that is the most dangerous to your health — physical, mental, and emotional.

It is the ego's world that keeps you depressed and alone. It is the ego's world that causes sickness and the deprivations of the sick body that you have all come to accept. This is the saddest of all, dear ones, for the teachings of your culture are completely upside down, and that which you are taught to consume in all ways — thought, food, ideas — are all detrimental. The thoughts, ideas, and philosophies we share are what will bring you the happiness, abundance, and health that all of you wish for.

The Church of long ago was wise in its use of fear and punishment, and for centuries you were murdered if you ever ventured into the realms of spirit. Do you think that is all over? It is not. The indoctrination continues, and you are all afraid of these energies, unless you realize what the lack of them is costing you.

So begin to educate yourselves on the truth of the matters at hand, and do not believe blindly in your culture's teachings. Look around at the state of your cities, your families, and your lives. Many of you are on medications of some kind, and all are on something to quell the fears and the anxiety — alcohol, television, or prescription drugs. What is it you think these substances do? Mask unwanted symptoms? Yes, we agree, but the symptoms are the callings of a mind in deep pain, disconnected from its source of strength and the energy of love that it needs to be happy. So look carefully at all these things, and know that there is a world very different from the one that you see as normal. Your society is not normal in any way, and it leads you all to the slaughter with tales of consumerism and entertainment, safety and pleasure. But it is all lies, and you will not find your salvation in its prescriptions. But you will find peace, joy, health, and happiness in ours. We will tell you more of the delights you can expect as you travel along these energetic pathways.

Be Brave

We wish to tell you of the vistas that will arise as you venture into the world of internal awareness and spirit. You will find that every day becomes a wonderful exploration of blissful feeling, and even when you are not at the heights of bliss, for you cannot maintain it and function, you will all find that you are able to appreciate the beauty of this experience as it comes to you, free of judgment. It is your own judgment that keeps you from the delight of the open mind, the open heart, and we cannot emphasize this enough on your journey. Trust us, dear ones. This valued friend you have, this constant state of wishing to be other than what you are, other than where you are, is keeping you inside a prison of your own making, yet you do not realize this.

It is in acceptance of your current state of being, your current state of mind, that your happiness lies, yet the trainings of your culture teach you that to accept is to be powerless. This is so far from the truth, dear ones, for to be in the moment, to accept what is and to look at it clearly, accepting the lessons it offers, is the path to your awakening to that which you call heaven on earth. Yet because you are taught and believe the opposite, you are lost in the mire of thinking incorrectly, and consequently acting incorrectly. Because you do not accept what you are, an immortal being having a creative experience in the body, you cannot find that which you seek so desperately.

We know that we teach radically for the Western mind, and it is this that frightens you and makes you feel that you cannot follow our advice and our prescriptions, but we ask you to just start on the journey. Just start to change your mind about judgment. Just start to be willing to even entertain the idea of forgiving. You do not even have to do it in the beginning, but just become willing to contemplate that there may be a possibility we are right.

You must admit that to continue on in a state of sadness and dissatisfaction is indeed a terrible future to contemplate, is it not? Even if you are still enjoying buying things and going to shops and restaurants, is that really what you want to spend this precious time you have allotted to you? Is that what you see as your life's work?

We know that this culture of yours talks about fun and entertainment, and that to be bored is a sin. But if you do not dare to let yourself become quiet, dare to let yourself wonder with your own mind and find out exactly what is going on in there, you will never be free. You will constantly be trying to escape your feelings — yes, the ones that scare you so. And those feelings are the answer to all your problems. They are the map to your salvation and your peace. So be brave and delve into your heart and mind, and know that this journey will take you to places you can never imagine. Let us bask for a while in the offerings that this new home, this new adventure, will bring you.

CHAPTER FORTY-SIX

The Other Reality

We will tackle a subject now that may seem a little off track, but bear with us, and you will see how it relates to the transformations and awareness we seek. It is that of the dream life, the dream world. We will call this "the other reality."

The other reality of which we speak is the dream world you enter every night after your conscious mind is shut down. Your unconscious mind goes into "play land," so to speak. You think, or you have been taught in your culture, that dreams are really of no significance, that they are the mind getting rid of unnecessary information, or that they reflective of the cheese you had before bed, but this is not so. There are many wonderful things to learn about dreams, and we will share some of them with you in this text.

The dream world does, in fact, exist as a real place — not real in the sense that you define it, in that you say it has to be engaged by the five senses to be real, but real in the sense that it affects you greatly and is nonphysical in nature but very powerful indeed. The same mechanisms that create the world you call "real" are at play in your nighttime excursions, but you do not have the filter of the conditioned mind in front of those visions, so you get to see more deeply into the unconscious mind and the creative process — the place where reality is tested out, so to speak. This is true, and the reason we did not mention this earlier is now obvious, is it not? We are testing the bounds of your belief systems, and this is a tricky thing to do when you are really trying to get people to listen. If we go too far from your comfort zone, then you will become afraid and will not hear the message we long for you to hear and begin practicing. But there is a reason for our adventurousness and our includ-ing the dream world in our teachings, and it is this: All the information you need to get to the root of your problems in what you call the "real" world is contained in your dreams at night. It is like an unconscious library that can help you greatly. It can help you create that which you wish and that which you desire to experience.

The world you call "real" is created from your own mind, with all the filters and conditionings that you have been exposed to over the years. This will manifest as dreams for you to see clearly what is going on inside the brain and the conditioned mind that you consider your own. You see, all the characters in your "real" life are reflections of you and bring you messages to help you understand yourself. For example, if you are being treated badly by someone and stay for the experience, that person is merely showing you how you feel inside about yourself. But you will argue this, saying that this is not so, that the person is bad and needs to change. But we assure you, you could not be experiencing this kind of treatment if you did not also feel this way about yourself. We understand this is difficult to translate, as you have a profound belief in the objectiv-ity of the "real" world. Yet your dreams will reveal the same information in an unfiltered form, so to speak, and you will be able to listen more easily to the messages coming to you from this part of the mind.

So we would like you to begin to keep a dream journal. Write down and analyze the dreams you are having. This is not a waste of time, for it will bring you great rewards on this path to bliss that we are asking you to travel. What you must remember is that every character in your dreams is an aspect of your own self that you project outward so that you can see it clearly and change it if you need to or you feel that it is not serving you in any way. The wonderful surprise in all this is that your "real" world will also change if you come to understand what the dream informs you of and if you change the beliefs and thoughts that the dream reveals. We will give you an example here so that you can grasp our meaning more clearly.

Let us say you dream of being chased. That is not an unusual experi-ence to have in a dream, is it? You are being chased, and you are afraid to get caught; you feel as if something bad will happen if you are. This is exactly what is going on in your daytime life. You are being chased by the demands of the ego to be a certain way, to achieve certain goals, and many of you believe that if you don't keep running on the treadmill you have been told you have to run on, something bad will happen. This may seem like a simplistic answer, but this is a great piece of information. We suggest to anyone who has a dream such as this look at what they are running from. What is it you think will happen if you stop and face your fears? You will gain freedom from facing your fears, for you are disempowered by them and need to see what they are first, and diffuse them second.

Another aspect of your dream life is very interesting and can provide some great adventures for you as you sleep. It is in the dream landscape, which exists in and of itself, that you actually prepare experiences to fulfill in waking life. You see, there are many real places that exist in your dream world, and you return often to them. It is here that your soul — your spirit, so to speak — rehearses some of the things it wishes to experience. It may try something out in the dream world and decide that no, it is not necessary to have a real experience of that. Or it may decide that it will manifest that event in the real world. Can you see the tremendous power that is contained within your dreams, the innate knowledge and hidden secrets that can aid you on your journey to growth and awakening as you travel these new roads?

You will also receive clear messages from Spirit in your dreams. In fact, we will connect in dreams when the daytime mind is too busy and untrained to stop and hear our messages. So if you find you have an untrained mind and it is very loud and busy, the dreams you have will become even more important, because your spirit guides will talk to you there and offer up advice and information to help you return to your natural state of power and joy. You do not feel power and joy at the moment — at least many of you do not — but we guarantee that if you follow the prescriptions found in these texts we are writing, you will indeed return to your true self, that spark of God that is all powerful, all kind, and all wise. Your life will change drastically, and you will begin to experience the love and passion that you are desperate to feel. But you must be willing to change what you think about, and dreams will aid greatly in this process.

CHAPTER FORTY-SEVEN

The Place for Spirit in Your Relationship: What Does That Look Like, and How Does It Work?

Spirit is all around. Spirit is in everything, and you cannot *not* be on your spiritual path. Your culture speaks of a spiritual life as if it is a choice, but it is not. All beings are on a spiritual path of learning; some are just more aware of it than others, and that is all. So your life is a spiritual thing in all its mundane days, in all its expressions — in what you would call good and bad, kind and cruel, and happy and sad. What we are here to tell you is that wherever you are on your life's journey, you can change your focus and speed up your evolution and awakening and, therefore, your ability to manifest and change the inherent patterns of your existence in an intentional way.

We are with you at all times and in all places. You get upset by the idea of lack of privacy in this, but we are not spying on your bodily functions. That is not our purpose. We are here to assist you in your energetic evolution toward the total acceptance of the truth, love, and light that you are for and from.

Spirit abounds around you because your world is not the only thing that exists — not in any way, shape, or form that you imagine. You have forgotten whence you came and to where you are destined to go, and that is why we are here — to assist you in your remembering. You see, to forget all that is truth is very painful for the mind and body experiencing, yet you are not told this is the cause. You are taught that all the people and places and things outside of you are the problem, and you are somewhat powerless given these rules. Oh, you can force others to conform to your wishes — for a little while — but you are innately freedom-seeking beings, and you will rebel eventually. What we are saying is rebel now, and insist on your own self-expression, your own freedom, and your own experience of joy — today, in this moment — for that is where the journey to bliss begins. In this moment you have the ability to do that which you choose, in kindness and in love for yourself, knowing that despite what those around you may say, this is what you call God's will.

God's will is your will, and we will clarify here: This is the will of the clarified mind that has done some work in cleansing the conditioning, in understanding the way things manifest and that you are all sacred beings. There is always the argument that it is wrong to do what you wish, for it is selfish. But if you do not do what you wish, then you are doing what someone else wishes, and is that person not as selfish in insisting on his or her way? It is true — it is not? — that those in a place of power over you, who are reaping the benefits of your servitude, tell you this path of freedom and self-expression is wrong? They have a method to their madness, do they not?

So Spirit infuses your world with assistance, information, and wisdom for you to tap into, for you to connect with. As you cleanse the lower realms of your vibration, seeking that which is light, that which is love, and that which is kind and gentle, the messages and the help will increase in volume, for it is as tuning into a radio station — the static is too loud in most of you for you to hear us speaking to you. The tuning in is your part in this play about which we are speaking. As you tune yourself up, we are able to speak and influence you to the good, creative, and loving way, and eventually, as our dear one is experiencing, the voice of Spirit will become clearer than any other voice. That is part of this journey toward bliss.

Once you tap into Spirit's voice as clearly as our Tina has, you will no longer have any problems, for we will immediately be able to tell you how to feel better, what it is you are doing to cause suffering, and how to focus in your life and work toward the goals you have set for yourself. You have indeed set yourself desired goals to achieve in this life, and those were set in the blueprint of your life before you were born into this time and place. These are the desires of the heart, that which is always with you. This is your dream, that thing that always draws you, the place you must go, and it is different for each of you. That is why it is so important for you to not judge others' path — for they have a plan of life that is in all ways different from yours and is designed by them, with the approval of the higher realms of wisdom and consciousness evolution, to lead them exactly where they need to go.

We will give you an example. It may be that a soul has decided to work in prison-rehabilitation reform on the planet, so that soul will experience prison from the inside out so that he or she is well versed with the physical experience that prisoners have. The soul will have a visceral understanding of this from the incarceration. You might see criminals and think of them as "less than," but if they follow their hearts' desire, they may well be a force of good to transform and to heal on this plane in which you live.

The slave owner may become the liberator, the killer the healer, and the pedophile the next victim through the will of the experience that they each perpetrate on the other. That last example seems different, does it not? But all experiences are legitimate, and an experience had in one lifetime may not be resolved in that one lifetime, but may be used in the understanding and overall growth of the oversoul — that which you would call your higher self.

There is a sexual revolution under way on your planet at this time, and that is why we are here. There have been thousands of years of repression. There have been millions of lives torn and ripped wide for the natural expression of this divine energy, and we are here now, finally, to add our own voice to the many voices of wisdom that have been laying the groundwork for this expression of truth. You see, we could not have come any sooner, for the state of your sexual expressions has been changing so rapidly over what you would call the past half a century that we bided our time until the conditions were perfectly imperfect for this information to be shared and understood.

There are many of you asking for a change, asking for relief from this culture of the ego that has created such a mess. And we have had to wait for your request to become so loud, so strong, that it cannot be ignored, for that means you are ready to face the difficult assignments we are giving you. You have lived the other way, and it is not working; it is only through your experience of it not working that you became willing to listen to the voice of God, the voice of truth, the voice of joy. These names all have the same meaning, and we hope you do not get hung up on the word "God," for it is a word that has been so contaminated by lies that we wish for its rehabilitation on this journey to divine sexual union with self, God, and others.

There are many of you who will look at this text and wish it had been given to you as young beings, children, so that you could have learned this early on in your lives. But do not be sad; you are indeed the ones whose crying out prompted this evolution in consciousness. It could not have happened without your experience causing you to cry out in the night for help and for relief from the pain and suffering you have experienced in the world of sexuality and sexual energy. So be glad now that the call has been answered, and know that you are not alone on your journey to healing. The sexual forces that vibrate through your body are the key to joy, to creativity, and to powers that lie within all your minds to connect to that force in the universe that is love, that is joy, that is what you call your God.

You can see — can you not? — that the separation from this energy is what has caused so many problems in your society, for when it is associated with the lower energies, the force of it causes you to be attached to the body, which is not who you truly are. So you are attached to an untruth, and this is what causes suffering and sickness. You are meant to thrive. You are meant to be joyful. You are meant to create and experience that which you choose. And that is indeed our job here — to help you understand how to do that and how to tap into the divine energies that pervade this universe in which you reside.

So bravely step upon this path with your beloved, and know that you will meet the fears in your minds, but hold on tightly to each other's hands. Offer each other support and unconditional love, and know that together you are far more than the sum of two parts and that you have great forces at your side assisting you in your growth and evolution.

This is the next revolution on your planet. You can feel the energy of love wanting to assert itself. The old ways are crumbling, and there is a new world on the horizon that will bring you all that you wish, but you will have to let go of your unloving ways. You will have to choose love at every turn for it to manifest on this plane as you wish it to. And regardless of your age, regardless of your history, it is now that all the energies and all the forces are with you. It is now that this work is ready to be done, and we hope — no, we know — that you are ready to join in this love revolution, to join in this new paradigm that will turn the world on its head and correct the most heinous of lies that you have been told. God is here, in your being, in your very hearts, and speaks to you through your desires and through your wishes. So know that if you are reading this book, this path is for you. The choices you make for love; the choices you make for your own growth and development; and the choice you make to enter into the heart, mind, and body of your beloved are indeed the choices that will lead you to heaven on earth, in peace and love.

CHAPTER FORTY-EIGHT

Begin Your Journey

The energies of the Earth plane are raising themselves in a profound shift that aids transformations in this area, and for those of you who have concern for your dear planet, we suggest you begin or continue on this journey as a means of healing yourself, others, and indeed your dear Earth plane. The low vibrations are expanding in some areas. Pain and disillusionment are creating a hell of many lives, and all of you who are willing to travel this path will indeed help distinguish the macro from the micro. You all affect the whole in every act of kindness and love that you practice. So do not feel as if this is a selfish process that will go unnoticed. First of all, your life will be enhanced beyond what you can imagine; also, the world and all the suffering souls will benefit from your awakening and loving practices as they evolve and transcend the small teachings of a culture lost in the ego's drives.

We are sure this seems a difficult path, but positive changes can begin immediately in health and sexual appetite that are enjoyable and fun. This will then move you to more extreme spiritual experiences. But do be patient in the beginning, as the experience of which we speak requires some training and development of awareness. It can be intense, and all fears around the Devil and possession or losing control will arise if you are not prepared properly for the events that will transpire on this adventure into the divine.

We are certain that this book will be a good introduction into the blocks and issues that are present and need to be looked at on this journey, and we will offer more detailed advice and mentoring as this exposition continues. The channel through which we are writing has gone through many of these events over the past few years of her life, and she has experience and teachings of her own that will help you understand what this journey may look like. We ask her to help us teach these things, and as such, we ask you to honor her and treat her as the voice for Ananda's journey here on Earth. She is a willing teacher and healer of souls and will be happy to help on your journey to healing.

We are hoping to set up a situation in which she will host weekends and events during which the story will be told, and the experience that led to this awakening will be shared in a personal and healing environment. These are the goals this individual has been willing to accept as her life's path from now on, and we indeed honor this dedication to the healing that this world needs.

The journey has just begun, and the trip will be an exciting one. Do not see these lessons as a chore, but as a dismantling of the bars of the cell in which you have been imprisoned. The bars are different for each of you, and for that reason we ask you to have great respect for all your fellow travelers on this journey. Do not compete or compare, but take this interior trip with your brothers and sisters at your side, ready to help at any moment as the walls come down and the sweet, tender fruit of love is exposed for the first time in many of you.

Tread lightly on this journey, and know that great souls travel with you and encourage you here and in your dreams. We will come in many forms to help you on this trip into the unknown, but listen, pray, and study well, as this trip is the one that will change you forever and lead you to the heaven that you have heard about from the teachers who have started many of your religions. Heaven can be felt here on Earth.

And so this text is complete, and we are happy to tell you this tale of passion, of kindness, and of joy so that you may know that you are right — there is something terribly wrong in the values of your society. And you are nothing but sane and correct in your feelings that this is all wrong. You are destined and able to create a world of great love and beauty, and we are asking you, here and now, to put these recommendations into practice in your life, knowing that this is the path you have chosen to assist in the transformation of the world. You are powerful beings who have clearly been told some untruths that have led you astray, so now get on the path of truth toward joy, love, and freedom. Know that there are great forces at your side, assisting and helping you in all ways and on all days.

We are Ananda, teachers and friends from far and near, assisting you in any way we can, hopeful and joyful that the desires of your heart are speaking to you through us, in peace and love always.

Appendix

Ananda's Personal Guidance and Comments for Tina

Editor's Note: In the original manuscript, this commentary was integrated into the text. To avoid interrupting the flow of Ananda's teaching, we have moved the guidance that was not immediately related to its surrounding text to this appendix, maintaining its original sequencing.

Ananda comments on my first typing/channeling experience. Up until this point I had been writing by hand, and it had been very difficult to transcribe.

We are with you once again, dear one, with a new way of talking to you. This will be better, we think, for the time involved in the other way is somewhat lengthy, is it not? We will try to go slowly for you so that the corrections are easy for you to do and the reading of the words will be much more fun. We love fun, and we love you. We are glad you have learned to type so that we can communicate this way. It is so easy for us once we get on a machine such as this, for the technique is not so different. And the formatting stops you from having to think too much about all this!

We are sure the experiences you are having are somewhat difficult to integrate, but your training has been long and thorough, as you now realize looking back. We will use this opportunity wisely, for the world needs a deep healing now of all its wounds. The forces of good are rallying together as they have always done to help those poor souls who are suffering so badly.

* * *

We are with you again, dear one. Are you enjoying our new way of speaking? It is much, much better, we think, than the messy writing business we undertook before. Do not worry about the future and what this will all look like. It is in divine hands, and all will be well and carefully organized and orchestrated for your, and the world's, highest good — as always. You can see and tell people about the rightness of the scheduling. It seems to take so long sometimes, in your view, but we know on this side what is possible, in what time frame. Fear is to be avoided in all matters of spiritual healing. When humans are afraid, they are quite a dangerous lot, as our stories continue to tell.

✷　✷　✷

Ananda commented as I was watching a YouTube video about ascension:

We are with you once again, dear one. We just wanted to jump in here as you watch this talk of ascension. It is very interesting to contemplate this idea, although the people involved have misinterpreted what is going on. The ascension of the human mind as a collective is a forgone conclusion, and all is, as they say, in perfect alignment for that to happen. It will appear to happen as a mass event, even though the individuals will experience it as an individual event. Ascension is the transformation of the earthbound mind into a mind wholly connected to the divine in all aspects, as Jesus would have been. These beings will be aware of their spiritual nature at all times, never forgetting their oneness with each other and with the divine.

It is in this state that you find yourself, dear one — a state of not fitting in anymore with the world as you have known it, wondering what your future here will look like. This is indeed the loneliness you feel in expressing this dilemma. And it is indeed a dilemma, for you have never experienced this level of awakening before, and the future is indeed a mystery to you — but not to us. We see your future clearly, and it is very good, filled with all you could ever wish to experience in terms of abundance, peace, and joy. You are at the very doorway to the process of ascension yourself, and you will experience ever-increasing displays of this energy in your daily life.

We do not want you to be afraid or to worry about your safety, income, or future relationships. All is taken care of, and the outcome will be good. We have heard your prayer for relief from the lower vibrations, and although a lot of people ask for this relief, you have been willing to stand in the fire of release and difference and to keep up with your prayers of forgiveness and lovingness. We do not see this as a reward for such but as hard work given its due.

The feelings and thoughts of the ego now have nowhere to go, so all the planning and worrying that an ego normally partakes in is now defunct, and you are truly yourself in all ways. We know that this is a little intimidating, as you have connections with individuals on this plane who are concerned about you and love you. They will be satisfied too with your future endeavors in print and in the media. It is hard for you to see yourself in those roles because they have not really been part of your motivation or vision for yourself, so the fact that it will happen seems a dream in some ways. But we assure you, you are a powerful spokesperson for the well-being of the human race, and your service is greatly appreciated. The absence of ambition in the ego sense is very good for our purposes, and we can see your lack of desire for material possession bodes well for your path through this next stage of your journey to awakening.

The feelings of lethargy that you have are natural, given the changes we are addressing in your energetic and physical bodies. It is okay to lie around a bit. As the adjustments begin to work, you will feel an amazing surge of energy and fearlessness as the last of your disconnections are fixed and the true amount of the power within you begins to flow. We hope that this will be a testament to the path of love you have taken. The miracles that will arise as a result of this will help people follow in the path you are to be teaching.

Ananda often answers questions I have just thought about:

Your wonderings about healing sessions are accurate. You will heal people with the enhanced energy and clearness of aura that you will possess, and the result will indeed be miraculous — evidence that people can heal even the most difficult of energies they encounter. We wish to tell you this so that your mind may be at peace as you go to sleep tonight.

We are here with you, dear one. We are aware of your concern for your impending income, and we will ask you to do something for us: We ask you to stop worrying about this for just a few more days. We are at work here on the other side, so to speak, to help you with your finances, and we ask that you trust us to do this for you. We are grateful for your bravery and assistance in getting our message out there, and we will make sure all is okay for the near future with your money. And yes, your dear sons are in that mix.

A long separation from my children arises often as a worry, and a recent firing from a job caused renewed concerns about seeing them. Earning enough money to live while undergoing this huge transformation proved very challenging, and I had trouble staying out of financial fear.

We know you are getting to the end of your reasoning about not seeing your boys, but jobs are not the answer for you, dear one. The freedom of the freelancer is best. We will tell you what we can, but do not fret. The streams of income are heading your way, and we ask you to stay clear and free of fear. In this instance, the money issue is not a large one for us, although we know in the third-dimensional world it is a constant form of stress for humans to deal with. We once again ask that you stay in a blissful state, for this will attract all kinds of money and opportunities your way. The energy is building, as you can feel, and we hope that all we do will help in all ways in your life. We know you're not a money-focused person, so we are here to help in that department. But please keep the faith a little longer, and changes will occur quite soon. Within three days something will come your way. No, you are not making this up, dear one. We are real, and you are not crazy.

✳ ✳ ✳

We are here, dear one, excited that you are so excited about the future path you have volunteered to choose. Yes, we think the idea of sharing a healing space would be a good one, but do let the idea sink in for a little while. You are a powerhouse when you get going, and the average person is blown away by the intensity of your energy. Remember when you were told that you overwhelmed the energy of even the most intense person with the flow of information? This is why we have picked you to do this work, as the level of energy and dedication required is extensive, and you will need to be incredibly brave and sure of yourself to follow through on this path.

Do you realize the importance of social media on your path? It will be the springboard for this book, for this work, and for the advertising of our teaching, so please embrace it fully and without resistance. It is part of this work. It is how information is disseminated these days, and we are totally on board. Yes, it is the reason you went to school and learned all the graphics, web design, and so on; this will all be part of helping others with their message and with helping your and our message get distributed to the world.

We are happy you are happy, and the feeling on our part is to be so full of life and joy that others seek to follow in your footsteps and achieve the levels of happiness you will show them. You will show them that a life of sacrifice is not required of men or women, but that they must be careful what they choose to do — and with whom they choose to do it. Some decisions are timely and others are not. For example, when one has children, at least a decade is set aside to deal with the issues that come up — not wasted time, but precious indeed.

* * *

We are with you again, dear one. We just want to allow you to keep up with your outer life, so to speak. It is important for you to stay on top of these things as well as to connect with us each day. We do miss you when things get busy or you are too tired, but we understand the body needs to rest at times and that we are a challenge to your everyday needs and desires. Although we know we have added a great deal to your plate, we know you can handle it. We are always there to help if you have any questions.

I wondered about Internet dating.

We do not suggest having any dating activity at the moment, as the adjustments are creating a somewhat unique state of mind for you and the average person will absolutely not get this at all. It is going to take a very special partner to work with you on this project of arousing the God within, and he has already been chosen. There is no rush, and we ask that you be as patient as you have been so far. You know that the wrong partner is worse than no partner, so we want you to only focus on us, your new lover for now. No, that is a joke — we are your teachers, and we are honored to be such.

We are a group of teachers who have specialized in the nature of God and the connection to sexual energy, and we are all from a place not of this world. Although you saw images that represented some of our energies (Note: Tina had had a vision one night, early on in these experiences, of Eastern and Native Indian gurus), the reality is not like yours. We are from other places and other times, but we feel a strong draw to help this Earth plane at this time because of the great confusion about God and sexual energy and the big problems this is causing, both in the physical world of violence and war and the mental world of guilt and judgment. None of these states are necessary, and we are here with love in our hearts to help heal that disconnection.

✳　　✳　　✳

We are with you once again, dear one. We are sure you will design a lovely topic for the "Facebook cover," as you call it. We are not attached either way, but trust that your knowledge of our energy will guide your design and create feelings of love, passion, and bliss to convey our messages through your art.

We are sorry for the tears you cry over your sons, and we understand the frustration you feel over it all, but indeed, as you said, it has all been necessary and karmically driven. There were issues from the past that had to be balanced for your understanding. Your part in those events is taking place on a soul level as a result of the events of the past ten years of your life. We know your sons care for you very much, and the youngster is just a boy having summer fun with his friends. But this too shall pass on its way, as it does with your young humans. We are sure you remember those days of merriment and joy of sorts, apart from the hangovers — and what a segue into the subject of alcohol.

* * *

We are with you, dear one, out in public for the first time. We are able to work anywhere with you, just so you know. We are not restricted by time or place, nor by such restrictions as you are faced with. The realms in which we live are of unlimited space and time, and the efforts we have to make to get in touch with you are small now that a connection has been made and you are raising your vibration daily to meet us.

We know that you can now feel when we are present, that you feel the aliveness of our energy, and that you are falling in love with us and what we represent and teach you. We can feel the love growing, and this is indeed a miracle for us on our plane. We love love, and although we have an abundance of it where we are, to feel the love returned from your plane is indeed a great gift. We are grateful for it and wish to thank you.

You are now designing some of the things we need to do our work with you, and we sense a disconnect, as if you are responsible some-how for the outcome of this endeavor. You are not. We are, and we wish for you to only do what is right in front of you today. We are in charge of the unfolding of this story on your plane, so we wish you to live your life as you see fit. We know you are on our side and are going to do all we ask, but we want to reassure you, just as we are teaching in these writings, that no sin can be committed. Design what you like, and we will like it. Our love of your art is one of the things that has brought us together, and we are sure — as we said earlier — that it will be beautiful.

I was feeling trepidation about going public with this particular subject.

You will have to accept the association with us. This will show you where you have blocks to this energy, and yes, there are still many left, but we will unearth them at a rate with which you are comfortable. Earth needs you now, dear one, and every day the energy work that we are doing with you cause global changes in your views and experiences. We are sure this seems extreme, but the universe does not work as you think, and one change in one person does indeed ripple around the universe. We are sure that if humans only knew this they would make the changes they feel and see them in their outside world.

Yes, this is what you have learned already [through studying *A Course in Miracles*], but the remnants of the other conditioning remain, and the outside world will come to you when the energy is right. You will be able to handle anything that comes your way as the story is told. We are not afraid — and neither should you be — of the unfoldment of this glorious story. All will be told to you as necessary, and all we ask is that you keep up the good work and don't forget to attend to your earthly assignments too, as these will pay your way along the next few months until the book is published and an income is generated from which you will live.

The expenses in your life right now are very low, and we are glad to see this because we are free to monopolize your time and accomplish the writing of our cooperative adventure. This will change the world and your experience here.

We are glad you are coming to terms in the area of your boys and their lives. We are so glad that the boy Alex is a strong and loving light in which you can trust. He will be a great ally in your journey and will teach with you as you develop a program of healing based on these writings.

The allowance of this slow and steady climb you are embarking on is imperative, and we are excited by its beginnings. We have already written a great deal of information, and it is already transforming and attracting more and more like ideas to create a snowball of energy that will act as a giant magnet for the connections and opportunities needed to create the realms of healing of which we speak.

Here, Ananda is referring to my recent training in digital media design.

You, dear one, are a bridge between the two worlds, and your new skills allow the spiritual and the modern to connect in a very meaningful way. We are going to use the new paradigm you are in and developing to spread word of our teachings, and the response will be enormous as the word is shared around the planet. Be prepared, for it will be such a tidal wave that you will be surprised, and at times dismayed, by the

Pandora's box you have opened. But you are our best candidate for this conscription, and we are happy it is so.

I wondered to myself, "Am I doing this?"

No — we are writing this, dear one. The world needs this healing in a major way, and this will change everything for the better. For some the path is a scary one indeed, but that is why you have been chosen to share your story, as you have faced those fears. Indeed, you have a few more hurdles on your journey to sexual fulfillment, although you are light-years ahead of where you were when you felt revulsion for sexual energy. We know you remember those feelings and how awful it felt to see sickness where there was love. This is a perfect example of having to let go of a language so that it can be transformed into the truth. It takes some time, but great leaps in growth can pop up in the most unexpected places.

I attended an Indian cultural festival in Victoria. It was a really beautiful experience. I was really taken in by the sinuous move-ments of the dancers and the amazing colors of the garments they wore. I felt very drab wearing my jeans and black sweater, and I truly felt the lack of passion in the way I and my culture express ourselves.

We are with you, dear one. What a great day you had, and what great visuals you got to see. We are glad you feel the music, so to speak. This is part of the journey back to joy — seeing the colors and listening to the music as it makes your body move.

Your inspiration to go to the festival was indeed us prodding you to get back in touch with an aspect of your nature that has been sleeping. You have only seen glimpses of it over the past few years, and we wish to encourage you to follow the feelings in your heart today. They are your soul speaking through the outside world, inviting you to play and reignite the passions that have been lost. We suggest that you do indeed take the dancing class that you feel you would like. This will help move the ener-gies we have woken up, and the results on all levels will intrigue you.

There is a bit of a performer in you, even though she has been asleep at the wheel for a while. You must not edit yourself here or feel stupid or too old for these fun and games. We are here to tell you that is part of the teaching that is so important — that the energy of sex is timeless. We do not advocate that you try to be younger than you are, but that age does not have to restrict in any way, shape, or form. Your body will remain as young as you behave, and the mental images of old people are not to be focused on. Rather, focus on the young at heart and the young, and see a future of youthful exuberance. And never, ever imagine the horror stories people tell of older lives. They are indeed true for some, because they have believed the conditioning of the culture, but this is not necessary. Find images of those who are bucking the trend and imagine you are one of them, and you will be. In ten years people will be seeing you as very young and wondering what you are doing to keep the appearance of youth, and you will be able to say that it is following Ananda — that has done it. Allow Tina to be the very thing she wishes, every day.

I posted the first blog and Facebook entries.

We are with you again, dear one, with the good news that the first of your book messages has been sent out. The marketing will begin now, as the desire is there and the action has been take by the writer, if not the author. There are many routes along which this information will travel, and we are excited it has begun. There are many who will hate it and many who will love it. It is the problem of duality, is it not — this love and hate thing that seems to permeate all matter? We are certain that the divergence of ideas and opinions will provide a great fuel for the discussion of these words, and the excitement, we feel, will spread like wild fire.

I was feeling tired after a long talk at the pub with a young woman who I had recently become acquainted with. It had been fun having a couple of drinks and talking to someone about Ananda. I was, however, feeling the effects of the alcohol I had consumed. I was foggy and tired.

We are here, dear one, excited to feel your excitement at writing the journal that describes these events we are having together. Yes, the body is a bit under the weather today. You are experiencing a contrast that will teach you to listen to us and take our advice, although we know you did have fun last night. That is a good thing, and the conversations you had were interesting, were they not? The subjects she needed to hear were what we were teaching earlier in the day, and this is no coincidence, as the needs of the one are the needs of the many. The problems of the untrained mind are the same, and the past that torments is the same. We are all dreamers, and we have to learn to dream the right dreams to create happiness and joy.

The fast and creative nature of the mind makes discipline a difficult thing, and you can hear the resistance that all have to the idea of mental discipline. The ego sees its demise is being worked on and fears for its life, as indeed it should. The ego will back away from any expression of love of self. This is a manifestation that will lead you to Spirit and away from the ego mind's lower concerns.

You feel concerns about food and housing nipping at your heels at the moment, and we commend you for trusting us and keeping up with the writings instead of looking for a job, per se. We are sure all will come as you wish; in fact, we know it to be true. The past will seem very different from your future, as it begins to manifest the higher energies that you entertain as we work on your energetic body.

The sessions are indeed a little different, but this is no reflection of our love for you, and we will vary the sessions over time to suit the areas we wish to activate. It is not yet time to do sessions on anyone. The path is not yet energetically clear enough, and we ask for your patience in this matter. We have a plan, and although you are in charge, we ask for your cooperation in all these matters, as we see the larger picture and you do not. The creative process is now in full force in your life, and the writings will continue at a great pace if you will allow us to partake of your physicality to create the words and send them out into the world.

* * *

And we are with you again, dear one. The energy is better, is it not? You are not so tired. We are able to give you the energy that you wish for all the work that needs to be done in the near future, so just ask us to give it to you. It is no problem at all for us to energize your body after the abuse you laid on it last night [two glasses of wine]. The problem is not in the activity but in the feeling behind it; the need for release was there, and the alcohol aided that release. Emotions flowed, and you felt better. This will become an easy thing for you to do without the help of alcohol as the gateways to the divine energies are opened.

As you can see, sleepiness left immediately as we worked on your body, and this will slowly open up all the channels you have and access the powers of all the divine in you. This is a slow process for a reason, as we have said, so be patient and allow us the time we need to prepare you for your job. The energies required will be substantial, and this is all necessary.

The first post was sent out, was it not? And now you will be able to disseminate this information on a daily basis for the world to begin reading. It will tweak the curiosity of many, and the numbers will increase quite quickly as the stories spread and the "likes" add up.

The future is a bright one, dear one, although the anger this will cause is going to be something to contend with as well. The churches and the people who value the old ways will rail at what we are saying, but the ultimate argument, of course, is: How well is it going using your way? The answer is clear, is it not? Not very well at all. The gods of the Bible will kill to get what they want, and so will their followers, and this is a blasphemy of the largest kind — to kill in the name of love is a lie and a travesty that no one should believe.

I told my ex-husband about Ananda and the channeling that was happening.

We are here again, dear one. It is a happy time for all, is it not, this sharing of news with your ex-husband? This is a big moment — the truth of all your labors and trials. It is out that you had a purpose in all of them and that all was not wasted. This is indeed the truth of the past ten years. You have been chosen to do some important work that was not apparent at the beginning, but now you understand the extreme importance of the assignment.

We are all assigned a job when we are born, and yours was indeed a difficult one to bear, but we are here to tell you that yes, indeed, the separation of the past years was for the purpose of clearing past karma and learning the test of discipline and forgiveness that you indeed passed. The past is over, and the future will be a different one.

The line in the sand has been drawn, and you will see clearly from now on. The tests you have passed are extreme, although not to punish you in any way — to clear up past debts. The services you have and will perform are a big deal, as you say, and the future opportunities you will have to see and be with your children will make you very happy. This is indeed the dream you have had for a very long time.

The misunderstanding of this as a punishment has been difficult for us to witness, but you have kept the faith, and you kept up your forgiveness practices. All this is now over, and changes will come fast and furious now. We are happy to say that yes, your difficult work is done. Although challenges lie ahead for the next few years, they will be very different challenges. The words we write will bring some to their knees in prayer and some to their feet in anger, but all will be supported from a place of great power and love.

The asking is over. All your prayers are heard, and now they will be answered very swiftly and with great love for you. The tasks ahead will be fun for you, as you are having fun now — are you not, dear one? This is your dream, and the work you have and will perform is indeed your soul service.

I had been processing the information about the separation from my sons being about karma and beyond my control.

We are here again, dear one, with the answer that yes, this is some "heavy shit," as you say. The truth often is, but you will process this now. The mind in you is very clear of all past hatreds and hurts. The cleansing work you have done has, as you say, done the trick. This is the purpose of forgiveness — to indeed free the mind up for greater works of God. We are often afraid to tell others what their work is, as the prospect would be daunting until the truth is realized.

The fearful person you used to be would not have been able to handle this, yet now you are doing this as if you were born to it. And, indeed, you were born for this. That is why the fascination with channeling was always there and why you would dream about it when you

374 * Making Love to God

were younger. The memories and the knowing were always there, and you knew on some level that this was your destiny.

This all sounds very grandiose, we realize, and we can feel the part of you that doubts, but this is indeed happening, dear one. It is not you who is writing this; we are. And there is no doubt that all the energy sessions are not you. We ask for your continued faith in and agreement with this work

We are so happy to finally be at the place where we are able to speak to you every day, several times a day. This is our assignment too, and we are as excited as you are to finally be at this most important task. The world is indeed ready for the writing we will be doing, and the time is ripe for the heated discussions it will cause.

The conservatives must not win the tide of popular opinion. This book will stir up the pot and cause discussions that people have been too scared to bring up, like the Church's part in the construction of lies about the nature of sex, its holy place in the healthy power of every soul's connection to God, and the very juices of life that keep you happy and productive. Of course empowered people are dangerous to the structures that have been in power, and the new world needs to deconstruct the old beliefs. People need to see that the very power they seek in food, drugs, and other products is inside them — it just needs a little help in rising to the surface.

That will be our job. Your job is to be brave enough to write it and speak it for us. We are confident in your abilities to stand in the fire. You have survived some difficult times and events and are still standing, dear one. This is a momentous day, as the realization dawns on your mind of just how long this has been in preparation, the realization that it is indeed your goodness that has driven the events of your life, not the badness. This is a big day, is it not?

The realms of the magnificent are opening up, and the path is lit from within. The joys we will be teaching are going to inspire and arouse the people who read them. We mean that in both ways; this is a joke for you lighten up the feelings around this. We are aware that the feelings of trepidation are rising as you publicly put this work out into the world, and that is okay. Know that we will be with you every step of the way and that the forces holding your hands are mighty indeed. This is the love the world needs, not the love is depicted now.

* * *

We are with you again, dear one, and it is a busy day for the creative mind that you are. We're impressed by your productivity and designs and the absolutely fabulous effort you have put into this day. The writings are officially out in the world now, and the ripples will surely spread around the planet. We are very excited to feel the enthusiasm you exude through every pore in your body. The excitement is tangible, and we are very happy.

The only issue is that the public forum will cause feedback, and we are concerned that at this early phase you will be sidelined. So just be aware that any negative comments are not to be listened to, and indeed there will be some weirdos, as you call them, latching on. The comments may have to be ignored for quite some time. Otherwise, we are happy the journey is on its outward spiral

But do stay focused on the writing at this stage and don't get too wrapped up in the marketing. We do know that today was the building of the network, so to speak, and it will not take so much of your time in the future. The freedom is required for us to have access to your energy at this stage, so we ask that the health remedies and activities we have prescribed are kept up.

Water, for example, is important, as are the exercise and dancing. We recommend a belly dancing class, as this embodies a lot of the principles we teach in getting back to the sexual nature of the being you are. We set new goals and ideas for you all the time, and we are aware that this is a challenge — to keep all the balls in the air, so to speak — but we can tell that you can do it.

Two days after the Indian festival, I found three beautiful new saris on the side of the road. It was quite a surprise to find these treasures after I had wished for them only a few days before!

The saris were a gift from us to you. They came via the laws of attraction and manifestation and show just how specific they can be. We will continue to send you all that you need so that the life of manifestation is easy, and you do not need to worry at all about survival needs while you write. Soon income will begin to flow in such a way that there is no longer any thought about it. The old barriers to wealth are gone, and the arrow will only point upward now — not horizontally as it has for so long. The last dregs of old karma are gone, and the new world is beginning to manifest itself. New customers will come for social media, and you can become quite the expert as you learn more each day and provide this service to all.

I heard Ananda's voice in my mind for the first time with no writing or typing involved. As I walked along a sunny Victoria boulevard, their voice spoke about love, spirituality, and my journey with them.

This new method of communication is a fun one, is it not? We are now in your head, so to speak. Our ability to talk to you will continue to change and evolve, and the big question, if you will speak for us, will be answered this year. The answer is yes, as you can guess. We will speak, and you will be on the stage of life doing it, but it will come in its own time. This is a huge undertaking energetically, and you must be in the perfect space with support to do this. It cannot be done alone, as you will need help in performing this work.

The information we gave you last night about your new partner approaching is indeed true, and this person will appear at you door, so to speak. The individual will be a very pleasant surprise, and he or she will be pivotal in helping you heal the issues of intimacy and fear around closeness that need to be addressed. This partner is of our choosing, and you have known this person in other lifetimes. Your partner will seem very familiar, and you will love this person deeply in a very short time. But we want you not to think of this. Trust us to arrange the circumstances of the joining that is to take place.

This is a big deal for you, we realize, so please try to relax around it. Do not go into fear, or the events will disappear and the meeting will be postponed for a future date that suits you better. Fear is not acceptable. You know we love you, and the universe is on your side always and every day. There is no reason to worry or try to figure it out; it is done. It is even past and over in some realms, so you are to stay as clear as you can each day.

As I am editing this several months later, the meeting has indeed been postponed — apparently because of my reluctance and misgivings. But that is okay, as I am learning. We cannot do something we are not ready for.

✳   ✳   ✳

Ananda comments as I watch a low-quality action movie. I could feel their presence as I watched a poorly made, senseless action movie. I am learning that their presence, heralded by a very pleasant feeling at the base of my spine, means that they have something to say to me.

We are with you again, dear one. This movie is not so good for your soul. We ask you to stop watching and take a rest, for the worst things for a great mind such as yours are the bad and violent movies of the world. So please take our advice as part of your sessions and turn it off for us, dear one. It is your choice, but we are loath to have you lose vibration and suffer a lowering of the vibration we work so hard to raise. Is this an imposition? No — it is an act of love, and we are seriously sharing a part of the philosophy that we teach: that violence is senseless.

Here they are referring to my love of Dexter, *the HBO series about a serial killer.*

Your favorite show implies violence, yet the story is actually highly intelligent and has some value, at least. We are certain this show is a waste of all our time, so that is our opinion on this subject. We will continue to talk about it for the book, though, as it is indeed pertinent.

The television or movies you watch are of significance to your vibration, and we are alert to the drop caused by such viewing. The movies that have some story of redemption, love, or heroism are good and perfectly okay, but the senseless action and violence cannot do you any good. The remedy would be a good book, bath, or meditation. We are sure that many will not like this prescription, as entertainment is the big thing. The latest movie can be watched — just use your discretion and think about the vibration, the feel. The edges are blurry, and what is good for one will not be good for another. But you will know by the feeling.

Indeed, you have not been feeling good about this particular movie since you plugged it in, but still you kept going. That is why we stopped you — so you could see that you were not listening to the voice of sense in your own mind, which is very important to hear and to listen to. Over time this voice becomes infallible, and the guidance will bring all you wish into your world. So do not dismiss this as trivial; take it in as a lesson in discernment.

✳ ✳ ✳

We are with you, dear one, ready again to share some wisdom of the ages with you. We are again amazed at your enthusiasm for getting this information together and out into the world, and we greatly appreciate it. We have chosen a good partner in you. We think the issues that arise are only ones of balance and harmony for you. You seem to be very obsessed with this and are neglecting a little the other areas of your life. The friendships you have and the complexities of your way of life need to be attended to as well.

We know we are in the early days, yet we ask you to return to a more balanced way so that you are not drained. We can feel your tiredness, and we have only just begun. So rest, dear one, and create other things in your day. Perhaps we will make a date for our noon sessions and one or two writing periods, and you will only spend one hour on the computer for our sake. Then you will do things for your own satisfaction.

We know that the future is now an exciting thing for you, and we are glad to also feel that excitement. Just be moderate, although we do realize that this is not how you tend to do things. The connections you make will be strong ones, and the future is a good one, as we have said, so we wish to speak about the lethargy and tiredness we feel in you and relate it to all of the readers.

I was making a trip back to Salt Spring Island, where I had lived for many years. A few months after this trip, Ananda insisted I move back to live there in late October of 2012. They were unequivocal, and as I edit these words, I have been back now for several months.

On this trip, I was not yet ready to hear this news and so was oblivious to Ananda's future plans.

We are with you again, dear one, for the journey over to the old life you used to lead. That was the place where you were healed of so much of your past hurts. This is a powerful place for you, and it should be a place you go to regularly to connect with friends and the energies that abound on the island.

This will be a very good experience over the next couple of days, and the learning will be good and significant. The fast drive over was indeed fun, and you could feel us with you all the way, could you not? We are so glad you have the joy you do in your vehicle, and you will get to keep it always, if that is what you choose. We are so pleased that the world is opening up for you on this new track, and the fast pace will continue. You will never be bored or lonely again, dear one. The future is now, and the excitement and joy you have always craved is now on its way to you.

There was some issue with aggressive chickens at the house I was staying at, and it appears that Ananda's description of what is actually going on reflects this idea that the world is constantly offering us lessons, even in what appear to be the most mundane of circumstances.

We are here again with you, dear one. The energy you have been feeling today is indeed intense, and as you have surmised, we have been with you all day, having a beautiful Salt Spring experience.

The women of the house are also very intense expressions of the Divine Feminine in its changing and growth phase — the old letting go, and the new arising and spreading its wings. The chickens will help you learn about young blood sometimes being the only way to break a pattern. This is the same for humans, and there was a lesson in this very behavior externalized into the animals to be seen and then integrated into the human experience. The chickens are a manifestation of your own consciousness, struggling for control and domination, and letting go or moving on is the only way — or you will peck each other to death.

This is a playful time for you, dear one. Friendships are coming up for you to see that you are loved indeed and are not alone on this planet — no, not one bit. Your past belief in solitude was wrong, was it not? There are people who love you, who connect with you, and who think about you still. The effect you have had on others through your journey has been and will continue to be profound. The art of communication is yours. You are good at it, and that is a thing that will lead you into this new manifestation with great force. However, you can be too much for some people and they will be overwhelmed, so do keep that in mind, and do not take it personally if someone must back off from you. You are the focus of a lot of physical energy that is seeking to be expressed, and the job is in the speaking. We are glad to be part of your journey and designed to fit into your work here on this planet.

The work you are doing — facilitating communication through the computer — is the same. You are a communicator and teacher, no matter the tools. You are able to impassion people and see their purpose and a path through the darkness.

We are now going to go and leave you to your bed, dear one. Sleep well, and we are with you here. We love you and are happy we are your friends.

My son arrived for a visit just a few days later.

We are here with you, dear one, talking to your dear son. He is a master of the mind already, is he not? The young one is a real monk at heart, and the way you relate to him is through a loving and forthright speaking of the truth of the persons you are. We are, of course, not surprised at all by the turn of events. We have known the wise ones you have born, and they are your teachers as much as you are theirs. This is how the parent-child relationship should be — a true exchange of love and happiness.

The truth of the matter is that all the reasons for your sadness over the past few years were based on misconceptions and lies you believed that were not true in any way. You are free now of the past, and the stories will stop forever. The future will be one of love and peace with your sons and for your sons, and they will be very proud of what you will accomplish and teach to the world. They are a source of great love in the mind that you share, and they are on your side and have always been. It does not matter that you did not know. You did not believe in yourself at all, dear one.

I was feeling a great release from guilt over some of the decisions I had made around my children. Years of pain were lifting as Ananda told me of my purpose and how they had influenced me over the years.

We are with you, dear one. The feeling of love is big today, and the realizations you are having are the freedom that you seek from the old, limiting beliefs you had about your life. This is the gift of awareness, as you see the pains were not real at all; they were only taught to you by the thoughts you had mistakenly believed — for the wrong reasons. You thought that if you believed you were bad, that somehow there would be a change in the circumstances. This is what guilt does: You believe that if you feel bad, somehow it will change the way it is. It will not. It will just pollute the present with the past and cause suffering to continue.

The energies of love and passion die in this environment, the guilt in which the ego loves to be, at times immersing itself in the guilt of the mind, saying, "If I had not done this thing, then my life would be perfect, and I would be the person I have always thought I should be." You will see that the thought is about thought. You thought you should be selfless, so when you are selfish, following your dreams or doing what you wish, you see yourself as a bad person. This is indeed the opposite of the truth. You are a good person, all the time, and the way to be happy is to follow your heart and live an authentic life based not on cultural or family conditioning but the naturally arising desires, likes, and feelings that gently arise in the peaceful mind.

Once again my financial circumstances were difficult for me to ignore. I needed work but was overwhelmed with Ananda's presence and writings, and it seemed I was unable to earn enough to survive. Months later, I can see that all turned out well, but at the time it took all of my efforts not to go into fear.

We ask you again to stay in a place of calm acceptance around the finances of the day. We will bring to you the next perfect experience in this as is required. We will help you arrive at a decision on how best to support yourself during this phase of our work together so that you will be able to partake in the responsibilities and adventure of this life you are leading.

Some people had inquired about personal readings after I posted blog and Facebook entries, so I asked Ananda what, if anything, I should do in response.

The idea of personal contact with others is a bit premature. Although, yes, we will give personal readings at some point, that time is not here yet. The way that you dealt with the requests was indeed the right way. We will tell you when to put out the request for private questions and teachings. It will happen, and this will be a way to help individuals as we work on the development of the healing sessions and ideas we will be sharing and teaching you to access.

The hand and heart work together in this healing modality to move old fears out of the body and mind and enhance the natural well-being that exists in all of you. Blocks will be removed through a combination of various practices, some of which we have already shared. Music, art, singing, speaking, and all manner of other devices work in concert to open the heart and get the energies flowing more rapidly. The answers are within, as you are getting to see, and the end result is good and joyful.

My healthy eating was suffering a little with company in the house, and I could see that I was putting others' preferences ahead of my own recent food changes.

We are with you again, dear one. The emphasis is on the body being healthy today. Please do what you can to get back on track with food and water. We know you are affected by your sons visiting, but this is important and we urge you to drink water and eat as well as you can, with love and blessings to you.

Video games had entered my home. This has been a long-time dislike of mine, but after many years of fighting my own battle against the violence and less-than-loving behavior depicted in the games my sons play, I had essentially surrendered to it. I have to say here that it was wonderful to hear that my own instincts have always been right on this subject!

We are with you again, dear one, asking you not to be with the guns and such. This is a tough one for you, we realize, so we ask you kindly to move, as this actually affects us and our feelings today. We are aware of your acceptance of this for peace's sake; however, the energy is aggressive and the hardest and most unloving energy for us and for the boy. There are other things to do, such as taking a walk, so we suggest these things for you to do. There are a lot of reasons why this is so; the energy, the senses, and the subject matter of these games are all against the peace we advocate and practice.

We ask the same old question: Are you happy today? If yes, then you are on the right track; if not, then the choices you are making are not the right ones. We are aware of the lessening of the energies around your children, and this is the creation of the choices you make. You are always lessening yourself to fit their schedules. Do not do this, as when they are around you more, you will suffer and not thrive as we like.

I attempted to teach my son to drive a stick shift, but as often happens, it didn't go very well.

We are with you again, dear one, enjoying your relaxing time after the onslaught of the teenager. We are sure you learned a lot from the encounter, as did we, although we have seen this energy at work before and know the damage it can do. There is nothing wrong with your son and nothing wrong with you; you just seem to get lost in the interactions and are not sure of your purpose as the parent in this place and time. He is going to learn from you, and you are always teaching him. For example, the rage in the vehicle — he could feel it was not appropriate, but that is good, for now. He will blame you as the influence that he does not like, but he will see, over time, that your loving response was the right one.

The following passage about the book made me a bit fearful. Was reality approaching?

We are with you again, dear one. The first offers for the book are going to be coming soon, and that is the truth you will not believe, we think. The book is going to be a big hit and bestseller sooner than you think, and the first inquiries will come soon. We are so right that it is unbelievable for you at the moment. There are forces working that you are not aware of, and they are behind our creation 100 percent. The future is here, and we are sure that the rest of the story will unfold in a most surprising way. There is nothing you have to do other than what you are already doing to bring this into the world.

✳ ✳ ✳

We are with you, dear one. Indeed, there is need for editing at this point. And as you have correctly surmised, there is a place for some of the personal information as it relates to the mind and the dietary requirements we have asked you to follow. A reminder is coming: Please start your day with fruit or whole cereal — not the sweet treat that calls so loudly. It is a chore for the body to digest this sweetness, and there is enough sugar in the coffee you are drinking. Please follow our prescription. Once a week is enough for the treat. So, dear one, today we will write about financial fear again, as it is a difficult issue for the egos you are ruled by to let go of.

You can feel the constant draw at the moment to focus on the future losses that will come should the money not arise, and this attracts the very thing you are fearing. Dear one, this is a discipline you must master for the dreams of abundance to come to you. You are on the edge — not as some lesson, but because your mind is on the edge all of the time, fearful of the impending doom that will not arrive. Dear one, stay focused on what you love, experiencing the beauty that is your present, and the future will be but a blur of future riches you are happy to welcome — but not just yet. You are so immersed in the creativity of the moment, and the bliss we are showing you.

Financial fear is a constant companion these days, with no work in sight. This has been a life-long issue for me, so it is nothing new — although I am certainly very tired of it!

There are many who spend their whole lives in financial fear. You were indeed raised by such a person who never has relaxed into the abundance of the present. Fears have always limited her and made her feel little and afraid. Do not live this way. Another generation of this limited thinking is not necessary. We are proof that there is a world you cannot see that loves you so dearly, and with such passion that you do not need to fear for your future.

We will show you the way to confidence and abundance so miraculous that others will be dying to know your secret, and this is your mission — to be the teacher you know you have been before and will be yet again. This is a thing to which you are directly and absolutely suited. The art of communication is the voice that runs so deeply through you and is your soul service to the world.

Is communication not the thing that brings you the most joy, more than any other thing? Dear one, we ask that you stay present in every moment to the best of your ability. Hone this skill until you are in complete and constant bliss in the present, responding to the constant stream of creative ideas that rise from deep within you to the surface. It is a never-ending stream you have learned to trust, and it will always be there. We are your dependable friends and cowriters for this assignment, and we will continue to adjust your energies. Please be on our side with this and pay attention to all we have asked you to do.

Yes, we are speaking to your mind in more clear and eloquent ways. The paths are being cleared by our work and your cooperation. There is a path ahead full of sunlight and joy, and we are merely clearing some of the weeds that have grown and are making the travels a little too difficult. The path is clear, like a path well worn in a forest; there really is no other way to go. We are with you every step of the way, holding your hand. And should you fall, we will pick you up, brush you off, and help you along the section of the way.

We are you friends from an eternal life who have given ourselves to giving these words action and life in your world — to open the minds and hearts of the world, to diffuse and dismiss the untruths about God and sexual energy, to tell the truth that all beings are enlivened by this energy and need not fear any judgments about exploring it and enjoying it with every fiber of their being. The flight is a joyful one, rising higher and higher into the sky. Soon you will be soaring and barely flapping your wings at all, dear one.

I had a profound experience of bliss and transcendent joy at the beach.

We are with you again, dear one, enjoying your description of our love for you. Indeed, we do feel this way and are able to get the physical experience you are having by your honoring us with the use of your body. The experience of the beach is such a joy for us and gives us intense pleasure at the sights and sounds of the environment that is so specifically focused.

I am writing at a coffee shop, and a small and very loud little girl is squealing at the next table, and my patience is wearing thin.

Yes, the girl is a bit noisy, but let's stay and see if you can focus past the noise. The experience of focus is an important skill to develop. There are no other replacements for focus. This is most important, and the little one is giving an example of the energy that needs to be accepted and redirected. It is only a problem in this particular environment. Watch her, and see how she gets what she wants, or the parents get what they want — or perhaps both. This is the perfect balance: a child full of passion and joy, and parents who allow it for a while. This was where you were curtailed and shut up, and this is why it is a challenge for you to sit and experience it with equanimity.

There is a joy in the excitement of the child that will grow up into passion and excitement for life. Remember the sad and sorry state you were in as a young woman. There was no exuberance or energy. All had been quieted out of you, and your soul was completely shut down by your family and culture. This is what needs to change, and these parents you are witnessing, happy and relaxed with their children, are the great teachers who will raise a healthy crop of young ones. So forgive the noise, and know that this is the way the child will drive them to a park eventually. She is so full of it all. The dear one is a lucky one, and her parents respect her and love her dearly, with a balance of love and caring. We are happy for you to witness this.

✳ ✳ ✳

We are with you, dear one, feeling the feelings that are in you today: a slight sadness and regret of lost youth, perhaps. Do not regret anything. The lives you live are many, and the one you are engaged in is a breakthrough one. It is transforming many of the other lives you are experiencing in different times and places.

The linear view is indeed wrong. There is no line of time through which you travel; it is a playing field of patchwork experiences that flow into each other, so what you do in this life will affect a future one and past one. It is hard for the linear mind to accept this, but there is a miraculous flowing of time in the universe that you do not yet understand.

We are from other places and times, yet we are here with you and will be with you in the future. You are on a great path to expression, peace, and beauty, so do not fret. You do know you are in a magnificent place at the moment. Do not reach today — there is a lesson in patience, is there not? Wait for the future that you know is coming, as we have implied.

There are days when you just have to be okay with how it is and trust. Tell yourself that it could not be any better than it is right now, and that there is beauty in the now that will change one day. As we have said, you will look at this time as very special — as the opening up of a new world for you to explore. We are exploring with you, dear one, and we love the ebb and flow of these days together.

There are events on the horizon that will change a lot of things, so be happy as things are, and trust. Trust us and you. There are always events arriving that change what is, and the rise of fear for impending loss is often what drives humans to hold on to the present. The dichotomy between being in the present and holding on to the present is clear, is it not? It's a paradox, as spiritual matters often are.

There are two things to do to grow and relax into the life you are living; being and letting go are two difficult things for the ego. It wants to hold on, so these are the practices of the moment. Be and let go. Trust, trust, trust.

There are again changes coming in the world, so there will be some large disturbances soon on the planet that will require those of you who are more awake to counsel those who are afraid. This is as it should be. The wise counsel the young, so do not fear the work ahead, dear one. Just know that all is in motion for great transformation and healing to occur in you and on the planet. We are sure there are questions around this that you would like to ask, but for now just let it be. *All is fine — nothing to fear.*

Ananda comments on a young woman I have been helping who is having some health troubles.

As for the food issues that came up last night, your friend is indeed a person caught in the mind's whirling and twirling. She is a storm of emotions, and for her food issues to settle down, she needs to calm the storm of emotions in her belly and her body. They are stirring up the sea of energy in all her cells, causing disruptions. She needs to be still more and write more so she will calm the version of hell that she is creating.

The sessions you have suggested are a good form through which to help her. We will be there and offer help as you hold her hand through this transition to awareness and forgiveness. The ego does not like these words, and she will resist that form of help, so ask her to just be present — where nothing bad is happening — as often as possible. This is the same effect, is it not? The present does not hold the wounds and judgments that are driving this woman mad some days. She is a fine and strong young woman who will have a great effect on others if she can harness the power of the mind that now runs wild with hatred and fear in its mouth, like a young, untrained horse no one can catch.

* * *

Yes, we are with you again, dear one. This is an important message for you at the moment. The energy of the financial pressures must be let go and the present allowed to unfold. Your car payment is nagging on your mind again, and we are again asking you let it go. If the car goes, it is meant to be. Do not fret over this. You are so much bigger than these issues, and we guarantee the future is what you want. So listen, dear one, and let go, let go, let go. All day, let go.

Mind that you eat well and exercise too. We know this feels so difficult on some days, but the rewards are untold in the future, and you will, in the end, thank us for nagging you.

On other matters, your body is the receiver for us, and it needs to be clear. Clarity is made by these things we mention. So be clear, dear one, and love where you are deeply. Love where you are — it is a gift of such great proportion. You cannot imagine the importance of the present moment being clear. We can get through to you only if you cooperate and listen carefully to us. So do, dear one, with love deep and pure.

To you we speak of the clear and present danger of ignorance, of the misleading teachings in your mind around food and money. These are two of the biggest obstacles that the human form suffers from. These teachings are so deeply ingrained in the ego to indulge, and releasing them requires a deep and committed approach. We are encouraging you, not nagging you, so accept it with the love in which it is given. We wish you so much love that words cannot express it, and the sessions are a way for us to tell you of the passion and love for you on this side of the veil behind which we seem to hide.

Ananda asked me to send the unfinished manuscript to a specific agent. I found out later that day that it was World Sexual Health Day. I had never heard of it, but I laughed at the symbolism of the timing.

We are with you again, dear one, for this great adventure together. The sending of the manuscript was very timely, was it not? It is the world's day of healing for sexual energy, and as you so rightly surmised, we do have a plan.

I rented some Dexter DVDs and had a bit of a binge on them. I could feel Ananda around, wanting to communicate, but I felt like tuning out. As you can imagine, this dialogue, the writing, the food changes, and even the blissful energetic states I was experiencing were tiring at times. This was a small rebellion.

We are with you once again, dear one, with a message for you. Do please be careful of the watching of too much television like this. The shows are not the best when watched in such a quantity and you knew we would say this to you. So be more moderate, dear one, with this. We ask you to listen, as always. We have your best interests at heart and are kind in a way that at times seems otherwise to your mind. We are strict but kind. We are loving. This is the truth of the matter, and we are sure you understand this. We are your dear friends, Ananda.

On a very personal note, my trepidation at entertaining the idea of a relationship arises as Ananda speaks about it.

We are with you again, dear one. We are happy with the decision you have made to face one of the biggest learning curves of your life. It sounds so big when we put it like that, does it not? But it is indeed. We are now going to speak to you about this to help you bring into the light the feelings that are an obstacle to love's presence and impede the flow of love to you.

We see fear of home — domestic chores, food, cooking, cleaning. These are symbols of a loss of freedom from before, but you are in such a different space now. These you do not need. You are a free being; there are no expectations to live up to as you meet yourself in honesty in your dislike. Dispute the status quo on these subjects. In fact, we do not doubt your ability to stand firm in all this. You know yourself very well, dear one. You are just not sure that someone else will like you, that is all.

Some men are great in the kitchen and love to clean the house. This is not your job. As a domestic laborer, you will be useless as a prolific author for us. Remember, you are happy with your choice. There are indeed walls still in your mind that need to come down, and we are working on those every day, so the food and drinks are a part of your walls. As you saw last night with your tears, these habits are your armor, and to let them go is terrifying for those who see these habits as who they are.

You are not these things. Even if you lost all you see as you — your home, your car, your family, and your health — you are still a dear and powerful manifestation of divine love. Do not fear. We are not taking anything from you, but adding realms of light beyond your imagining. You will look at your life in just a short time and wonder at your doubt and fear. You will know beyond all doubts that we are who we say, and what will happen will happen. There is a train coming along the tracks, but it will slow down, and you can hop on. You will have to leave all you know and travel with us and your new knowledge to farther shores, but there are gardens on those shores you will love to walk in. And the gifts for others that you will reap and teach are indeed your soul's service.

In May I had a dream about writing a book titled Soul Service *that would sell a million copies by June 16. Which year? I don't know.*

This was the dream, was it not? About a book that you would write that would be very successful? This, dear one, is the book — the first of many that we will write. There is need for this material. People know in their bones that something big is missing from the existence they are living, and you will be one who has walked the path of the darkness into the light, to tell of the experiences and joys to be had. Yet these experiences have only just begun for you, dear one.

The path winds off into a beautiful future with us and your beloved. We are sure there will be doubts along the way, but do as you did last night — shed a few tears, bring the fear into the light, and give it over to us to deal with, in love and passionate friendship for our dear Tina, whom we love with all our hearts.

This is our job, our passionate path — as it is yours. The light will be fed with your courage, and your passions with ours. We are your supporters and your teachers, and at times, yes, your personal trainers. But did you not always want one, dear? We have heard your thoughts about this, that those who have trainers are lucky. Are we not proof that this is so only sometimes? The voice of sanity when you wish to be insane is not a pleasant one and at times is very annoying. You felt overwhelmed last night because you looked too far ahead. Only make the decision in this moment to eat well, to read well, to watch good television (if at all), and to open your heart to love. You will be too scared if you go too far into the future. You need to stay present and not worry about any of it. The ego is strong in this area, and you will indeed need our help to understand and tear down the walls against this experience. Do not worry, dear one. We cannot cross the mind's barriers of fear if they are strong. You are doing well restricting these thoughts and letting go as we have suggested, but this is a technique yet to be perfected. Keep trying, and it will work to bring all you wish. And remember, a car is easily replaced if that is what happens, although we reassure you it is not a necessary trip — that road is pointless. Stay in a place of appreciation and abundance, and all will arrive as needed.

* * *

We are with you again, dear one. We are happy that you are listening to us about the fear and staying as present as possible. The work you seek as financial support is on its way, as we have reassured you. Stay light and present, and all will be good in the future. The book will be well received, yet hesitation in the acceptance is present, as the material is controversial and there is bravery for all requited in its production. You see that it may take a little time to publish, and we are sure that is for the best, as you have some lessons that you need to experience before fame or notoriety is on your plate.

This is a big meal that all cannot digest. We want you to be in a place of solidity when the flood gates open for you. You will need to be a strong swimmer to float across these waters, but as we have said, we are with you always and every day to assist in the transition from anonymity to fame, as we are sure there is a rocky path for that journey. The press is harsh, and the conservative element is even harsher in their attacks on the divine love of which we speak. Again we ask, "How is your path working?" when they attack you. This is all you have to say. There is no argument, is there dear one?

Ananda asked me to give up coffee to help facilitate their connection with me. This was a challenge indeed, and one I still struggle with at times.

We are with you again, dear one, with congratulations on accepting our challenge to stop the coffee addiction. We knew you would volunteer eventually. As we know you truly love the plan that we have embarked on together. The caffeine, sugar, and cream all lower the vibe a bit, so giving it up will help us greatly fine-tune the instrument that you are becoming. Is it not exciting to enjoy this journey together? We are overwhelming at times, it is true, but we have chosen you, dear one, because of your strength, willingness, and resiliency for these lessons that are such a challenge.

I became overwhelmed by it all — financial fear, relationship fear, channeling ... it all came crashing in. It was not one of my best days, I have to say. I asked Ananda for advice, which I promptly ignored, resorting to old habits that left me feeling a bit rough the next morning.

We are with you again, dear one. The struggle that you had yesterday was not such fun, was it? We are surprised that you did not heed our advice. We were clear — were we not? — that you should go outside and exercise. So we tell you it was your choice to suffer as you did. Fear was a more welcome friend than we were yesterday, and today you may weigh the benefit of what you did.

Do you feel a more solid foundation today? A little foolishness at the wasted time and money of yesterday? Your anger at us about your finances is indeed a challenge, is it not? We are not your source of income as much as you think we should be. You, dear one, manifest all that comes to you. We are the result of faith and determination and will prove to be the source of wealth that you wish.

The other means of earning hold no power for you, so the income is weak. We ask you to focus on the future of this document, knowing that it will bring you all that you need, and that you must let go, in some ways, of the small world of money in which you dwell. It keeps you poor, and this interferes with our work with you. So meditate on changing this — it is important. Yesterday's fear is still contaminating today's experience in the tiredness that will arrive earlier than it should. Please do what you can today to get back on track with our purpose, and trust in us to bring to you the success you desire.

This is not a dream, and yesterday, the fears of what you will have to do to live this life came crashing in. The memories of love's betrayal scared you, and you thought that it would happen again. It will not, dear one. You are not the same scared person, despite yesterday's evidence to the contrary. You are aware, you know what you desire, and you will not compromise your principles as you have before. The cause of the betrayal in the past is, as you have guessed, a betrayal of self, which will not happen with your new partner. He will be the perfect complement to your path. He has his own path, which runs parallel to yours but is not the same. You will speak the same language and will care for each other's events and experiences.

So let us get back to the articles we are writing together. Forget your sad and scary day that did indeed do something good; it made you pay attention to us in our prescriptions, did it not? We never push you to hurt yourself or suffer, unlike the guide you followed yesterday.

I was still angry and withdrawn after my "meltdown." I did not want any contact. I felt scared and betrayed. I was coming up with drastic scenarios for how to survive financially. I should mention here that experiencing this energetic awakening was making it very difficult to work on anything conventional, and the money I was making doing some art and design work was sporadic and unpredictable.

We are with you again, dear one, happy that you have forgiven us for not keeping you in the manner to which you have become accustomed. We are sure all will work out as it has every other month. Remember all those times you could not see how it would happen? And indeed it did. There is no need to run to Colorado and stay with strangers; we will look after you as we have promised many times. We see the human mind is a tenacious one when it comes to its illusions, and we must be patient yet persistent to achieve the changes we must undergo to fulfill our destiny together.

Yes, it is a destiny, and the cards are dealt to us both. We are in this with you, so do not feel alone please; we wish for you to come to us many times each day for the next little while to cement our relationship. We do not want you wandering off into fear as you did yesterday. It does not feel good to us either. The tummy is upset and the mind foggy. Let us get back to love and trust as soon as we can dear one. This makes us much happier, as it does you. We will make a money miracle happen as you request. Sometimes it is the anger that provides the energy to the creative process to get it going, so to speak. This is not the best way, but that is the way of it some times. And the path is clear ahead for us, dear one; the way is laid and the dominoes are falling as they should. We will continue writing, as a book is needed in the world to right the wrongs of the last generations, and indeed, to free the young ones from the same errors. Your dear friend is affected already, as you can see. Imagine it a million fold. Young ones are taking more time to let the mind lead. This is indeed a revolution that will heal the planet.

✳   ✳   ✳

We are with you again, dear one, listening to your questions and offering some answers for you. You are worried at the moment about survival in the material world, are you not? You are thinking you might go to some safe place where you can write for us and commune with yourself. We are not sure this is the path that you should take at the moment. There are reasons to remain in the world as such. We are here to tell you it is your job to teach others who are indeed in the world, and they need help negotiating the spiritual and the material. There are many who have left the workday world for the haven of spiritual retreat, and this is indeed a valid life, yet this is not for you.

The purpose of our teaching is to integrate ancient teachings around sex into the lives of those beings struggling with love and sexual activity in their ordinary lives. We feel strongly that your purpose is in the world, yet we also feel your fear at the prospect of integrating these two experiences. Do hold on a little longer as we try to alleviate your financial fears with support for the work you are doing. We suggest that you consider the idea of beginning talks to bring this material forward. There are places and people who will give you tremendous support in this, and they may even be willing to help find housing and food for the support of your body while you undertake this writing quest.

We are sure this is a difficult thing to consider, as it feels like a failure of sorts. On the contrary, the path you are on is an exalted one that is not offered to all and sundry. It is a special path that requires your special gifts, and as such we will do all we can to help support you in the near future. We are certain that this is of help, although perhaps not as concrete as you would like. The answers are inside you, and you must follow your own guidance on this matter, as we are not in charge of you, so to speak. We can see that making a living in the world is becoming a challenge as the velocity and pace of the writings continue. We are your support and your teachers, but not your keepers on this journey.

About the Author

Tina Louise Spalding was born in England in 1958 and immigrated to Canada with her family in 1976. Raised in a family that visited psychics often, she is no stranger to the nonphysical world. But she found the modern world challenging, and at the age of forty-two, after two divorces and with a deep dissatisfaction with modern life, she moved to an island off Canada's west coast to pursue her art and heal.

This was a difficult time for Tina, as she was separated from her two sons, Alex and Kieran. She found solace in the spiritual text *A Course In Miracles* and focused intently on its teachings and practices. After ten years of internal transformations initiated by this book, Tina felt drawn to teach the life-enhancing philosophy in its pages, but she was not prepared for the form that would take.

On the summer solstice of 2012, Tina settled down for an afternoon nap, and began a journey that has culminated in this book. That afternoon, powerful energies began to surge through Tina's body, leading to ecstasy, bliss, and an altered state of consciousness that lasted for almost a month. The feelings finally drove her to take an automatic writing workshop, where she was first made aware of Ananda. She began to write for this group of nonphysical teachers who have come to assist us in our waking process.

Since that time, Tina has begun to speak for Ananda as a full trance channel, offering teachings and personal readings for those who are seeking more happiness, fulfillment, and connection with Spirit. She has dedicated her life to writing and speaking for Ananda and other nonphysical beings, sharing their wisdom and spiritual knowledge.

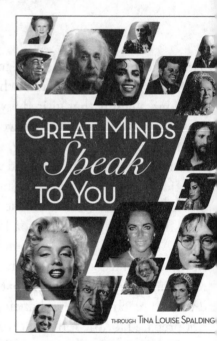

THROUGH ROBERT SHAPIRO

Tom T. Moore

THE GENTLE WAY

A SELF-HELP GUIDE FOR THOSE WHO BELIEVE IN ANGELS

This book is for all faiths and beliefs with the only requirem
being a basic belief in angels. It will put you back in touch w
your guardian angel or strengthen and expand the connection t
you may already have. How can I promise these benefits? Beca
I have been using these concepts for over ten years and I can rep
these successes from direct knowledge and experience. But this
self-help guide, so that means it requires your active participatic

$14.⁹⁵ • 140 PP. SOFTCOVER • ISBN 978-1-891824-60-9

THE GENTLE WAY II

BENEVOLENT OUTCOMES: THE STORY CONTINUES

You'll be amazed at how easy it is to be in touch with guardian
angels and how much assistance you can receive simply by asking. This inspirational self-help book, written for all faiths and
beliefs, will explain how there is a more benevolent world that we
can access and how we can achieve this. These very unique and
incredibly simple techniques assist you in manifesting your goals
easily and effortlessly for the first time. It works quickly, sometimes
with immediate results — no affirmations, written intentions, or
changes in behavior are needed. You don't even have to believe
in it for it to work!

$16.⁹⁵ • 320 PP. SOFTCOVER • ISBN 978-1-891824-80-7

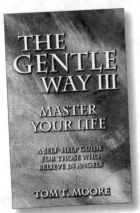

THE GENTLE WAY II

MASTER YOUR LIFE

Almost three years have passed since *The Gentle Way II* wa
published. Yet as many success stories as that book contained
I have continued to receive truly unique stories from people a
over the world requesting most benevolent outcomes and askin
for benevolent prayers for their families, friends, other people
and other beings. It just proves that there are no limits to thi
modality, which is becoming a gentle movement as peopl
discover how much better their lives are with these simple ye
powerful requests.

$16.⁹⁵ • 304 PP. SOFTCOVER • ISBN 978-1-62233-005-8

DRUNVALO MELCHIZEDEK

THE ANCIENT SECRET OF THE FLOWER OF LIFE
VOLUME 1

Once, all life in the universe knew the Flower of Life as the creation pattern, the geometrical design leading us into and out of physical existence. Then from a very high state of consciousness, we fell into darkness, the secret hidden for thousands of years, encoded in the cells of all life.

$25.⁰⁰ • 240 PP. SOFTCOVER • ISBN 978-1-891824-17-3

THE ANCIENT SECRET OF THE FLOWER OF LIFE
VOLUME 2

...ally, for the first time in print, Drunvalo shares the instruc-...ns for the Mer-Ka-Ba meditation, step-by-step techniques for... re-creation of the energy field of the evolved human, which ...he key to ascension and the next dimensional world. If done ...m love, this ancient process of breathing prana opens up for ... world of tantalizing possibility in this dimension, from pro-...tive powers to the healing of oneself, of others, and even of ... planet.

5.⁰⁰ • 272 PP. SOFTCOVER • ISBN 978-1-891824-21-0

LIVING IN THE HEART
Includes Heart Meditation CD

"Long ago we humans used a form of communication and sensing that did not involve the brain in any way; rather, it came from a sacred place within our hearts. What good would it do to find this place again in a world where the greatest religion is science and the logic of the mind? Don't I know this world where emotions and feelings are second-class citizens? Yes, I do. But my teachers have asked me to remind you who you really are. You are more than a human being, much more. For within your heart is a place, a sacred place, where the world can literally be remade through conscious cocreation. If you give me permission, I will show you what has been shown to me." —Drunvalo Melchizedek

$25.⁰⁰ • 144 PP. SOFTCOVER • ISBN 978-1-891824-43-2